DISPUTED QUESTIONS
IN THEOLOGY AND THE PHILOSOPHY
OF RELIGION

D0789974

142

Disputed Questions
in Theology and the
Philosophy of Religion

John Hick

Yale University Press
New Haven

Published 1993 in the United States by Yale University Press and in the
United Kingdom by Macmillan Press Ltd

Library of Congress Cataloging-in-Publication Data
Hick, John.
Disputed questions in theology & the philosophy of religion / John
Hick.
p.   cm.
Includes bibliographical references and index.
ISBN 0–300–05354–1 (cloth)
ISBN 0–300–06505–1 (pbk)
1. Religion—Philosophy.   2. Religions—Relations.
3. Christianity and other religions.   4. Theology, Doctrinal.
5. Jesus Christ—Person and offices.   I. Title.   II. Title:
Disputed questions in theology and the philosophy of religion.
BL51.H488   1993
200—dc20   92-19344
                                                            CIP

10 9 8 7 6 5 4 3 2

Printed in Hong Kong

Contents

v

101814

Contents

PART V LIFE AND DEATH

PJ8101

Preface

When medieval theologians wrote their *Quaestiones Disputatae* the disputed questions concerned relatively secondary and peripheral topics; for all of the most basic and important matters were agreed within Christendom. Today, however, even the most central issues are disputed; every theological topic of more than antiquarian interest has become controversial. Further, Christian discourse itself is now part of the wider universe of discourse that includes all the great religious and philosophical traditions of the world. Christianity has to be seen as one among several great world faiths. And because we are today irreversibly aware of this, we have to do our theological thinking consciously in the presence of our Jewish and Muslim, Hindu, Sikh and Buddhist, Taoist and Confucian, and also our immediate post-Christian and humanist neighbours. This means that instead of taking for granted inherited beliefs that strike those neighbours as groundless, arbitrary or arrogant (or indeed all three at once!), we have to ask ourselves if we have good grounds on which to hold them; and if so, whether the ways in which they were formulated centuries ago in a very different intellectual world are still appropriate today.

This book deals, then, with some of the living and disputed questions of today. It begins in Chapter 1 with the fundamental issue of a religious, versus a non-religious or naturalistic, response to the mystery of the universe and of our existence within it. Is religion a wish-fulfilling projection of our own ideals and hopes upon the fabric of the universe; or does it, although undoubtedly culturally and psychologically conditioned, constitute at the same time the range of our human responses to the Transcendent? My answer to these questions is based upon the fact of religious experience, in the broadest sense of that term. Chapter 2 accordingly inquires into the nature of religious experience, its relationship to other modes of experience, and the rationality or otherwise of basing beliefs upon it.

We then turn to specifically Christian beliefs. Their traditional structure hinges upon the dogma that Jesus of Nazareth was God the Son, the second Person of a divine Trinity, living a human life; and that as such he is the one and only source of salvation for human beings. It follows from this that Christianity, alone among the reli-

gions of the world, was founded by God in person and accordingly
has a uniquely superior role on earth. But this conviction, with its
baleful historical influence in validating centuries of anti-Semitism,
the colonial exploitation by Christian Europe of what today we call
the third world, and the subordination of women within a strongly
patriarchal religious system, not only causes misgivings among
many Christians but also alarms many of our non-Christian neighbours, creating invisible but powerful barriers within the human
community. There are of course other religions that make their own
equivalent claims to superiority, with equally alarming historical
consequences. Thus the whole question of religious absolutism is
due for critical re-examination. As a Christian theologian, however,
I see it as my primary responsibility to contribute to the rethinking of
absolutism within my own tradition.

The Church's belief in the deity of Jesus has come under criticism,
in our own day, on both historical and logical grounds. Historically,
the recent intensive study of Christian origins by a multitude of
scholars has made it clear that, so far as historical evidence can tell,
Jesus himself never claimed to be God, or the unique Son of God, or
God the Son, or the Second Person of a divine Trinity, incarnate. It is
much more credible, in the light of modern New Testament scholarship, that he saw himself as the eschatological prophet within Israel,
proclaiming the imminent coming of God's kingdom. The Church
thus finds itself today in the new situation, precipitated by the work
of its own biblical scholars, of officially proclaiming a momentous
proposition about Jesus which Jesus himself did not believe and
which he would indeed probably have regarded as blasphemous.
And so Chapter 3 discusses these historical questions and then out-
lines the kind of understanding of Jesus, as a divinely inspired
human being who has made God real to millions, to which many
Christians are today moving, or have indeed already moved.

Chapter 4 turns to the logical problem created by the traditional
Christology. This is the problem of squaring the theological circle of
the official dogma that Jesus was both fully God and yet also fully a
man: how could Jesus have both divine omnipotence and genuine
human weakness, divine omniscience and genuine human ignorance, divine goodness and genuine human temptability, divine omnipresence in a finite human body, and the divine status of uncreated
self-existence and yet be a genuine human being? In this chapter I
examine the most recent major attempt (and it is a philosophically
highly sophisticated and impressive attempt) to square the circle,

that of Thomas Morris in *The Logic of God Incarnate*, and seek to show that it does not succeed. And in Chapter 5 I look further at some of the historical outworkings of the traditional dogma, mentioned above, and argue for the emerging new self-understanding of Christianity as one among the great religious traditions of the world, but no longer claiming a unique superiority.

Among the other religious traditions we perhaps have most to learn today from that which is in many ways most unlike Christianity, namely Buddhism. Having been involved for some years in Buddhist–Christian dialogue I seek in Chapters 6 and 7 to benefit from this at two points. One is the Buddha's teaching about the 'undetermined questions'. Here I distinguish between (contingently) unanswered questions, and questions that are not only unanswered but unanswerable because posed in human terms about that which transcends the network of human concepts, and suggest that most of the conflicting truth-claims of the different religions are about one or other of these types of issue, and that it is reasonable for different human groups to live with different answers to such questions. The other is the notion of religious teachings as 'skilful means' to lead us towards the transformation from self-centredness to Reality-centredness that is the essence of salvation/liberation. This opens up the possibility that different sets of teachings may serve this same spiritual function within different traditions.

The way is now open to the pluralistic view of the great world faiths as different but, so far as we can tell, equally valid ways of conceiving, experiencing and responding in life to the ultimate Reality that we all affirm in one or other of its differing manifestations to mentalities formed within the varying cultural ways of being human. This is the subject of the next three chapters. Chapter 8 is a brief personal note about the way in which I have myself come to accept religious pluralism, namely through extended experience of encounter with people of other faiths and of interaction with them, both in Britain and in India, Sri Lanka, Japan and the United States. Chapter 9 comes out of the ongoing three-cornered dialogue between Jews, Christians and Muslims. And Chapter 10 offers the outline of a philosophy of religions – a conception of the relationship between the religions of the world and between them and the ultimately Real.

Finally, we return to our immediate situation as mortals facing the ultimate mystery of the universe and the personal mystery of death. Here, too, we can, I think, learn from the other religious traditions; and I try to do so in outlining in Chapter 11 a possible conception of life after death. I believe that any serious religious understanding of the universe has to include this dimension of our existence.

Thus this book, whilst written from within Christianity and addressed primarily to fellow Christians and to the semi- and post-Christian majority of our humanistic western culture, is also addressed within the new global dialogue to neighbours within the other great world religions, particularly within the other two Abrahamic traditions of Judaism and Islam and within the profound eastern tradition of Buddhism.

In this book I have omitted the diacritical marks from Sanscrit words. For I think the time has come for our Western discourse to expand to include key Buddhist and Hindu terms; and this becomes a little easier when we do not insist upon the diacriticals. And so such words as *nirvāna*, *śūñyatā*, appear on these pages as *nirvana*, *sunyata*, etc.

Some of these papers originally appeared in various places during the last five years, though all were written within the overall plan of this book. I am grateful to the editors and publishers listed in the Acknowledgements for their permission to use the material again in this way, usually in a slightly revised form.

JOHN HICK

Acknowledgements

I am grateful to the following for permission to reprint material which originally appeared in their books or journals:

Macmillan, London, for 'The Real and its Personae and Impersonae', from *Concepts of the Ultimate*, edited by Linda Tessier, 1989; 'A Possible View of Life after Death', from *Death and Afterlife*, edited by Stephen Davis, 1989; and 'Religious Language: the Realist/ Nonrealist Debate', from *Is God Real?*, edited by Joseph Runzo, 1992.

Westminster/John Knox Press, Louisville, Kentucky, for 'An Inspiration Christology', from *Encountering Jesus*, edited by Stephen Davis, 1988.

Orbis, Maryknoll, New York, for 'The Nonabsoluteness of Christian ity', from *The Myth of Christian Uniqueness*, edited by John Hick and Paul Knitter, 1987.

Cambridge University Press, for 'The Logic of God Incarnate', from *Religious Studies*, edited by Peter Byrne, 1989.

Wake Forest University, for 'The Buddha's Doctrine of the "Undetermined Questions"', from *Hermeneutics, Religious Pluralism, and Truth*, edited by Gregory D. Pritchard, 1989.

Kluwer Academic Publishers, Dordrecht, Holland, for 'Religion as "Skilful Means"', from the *International Journal for Philosophy of Religion*, edited by Eugene Thomas Long, 1991.

Edwin Mellon Press, Lewiston, New York, for 'A Personal Note', from *Odysseys to Dialogue*, edited by Leonard Swidler, 1992.

Part I
Epistemological

1

Religious Realism and Non-realism

I

The debate between realist and non-realist understandings of religious language exposes the most fundamental of all issues in the philosophy of religion today. I say 'today' because, although logically this is basic in a timeless sense, it has only come to be generally seen as an issue at all during the last 150 or so years – roughly, since the pioneering work of Ludwig Feuerbach – and has become sharply focused within the western religious consciousness only during recent decades. Throughout the previous centuries, and indeed millennia, religious self-understanding has been implicitly or explicitly realist – perhaps the only significant exception being within one strand of what we now see to be the highly variegated Buddhist tradition. But today there are confident non-realist interpretations of Christianity and Judaism as well as Buddhism which make a wide appeal within our contemporary industrialised, science-oriented, de-supernaturalised western societies.

Philosophical discussion cannot, in my view, settle the debate between religious realists and non-realists. It can, however, help to make clear what the issue is; and this is the limited task to which I am now setting myself.

I shall proceed for the most part in terms of the Judeo-Christian-Islamic monotheism which has provided the framework of the western debate thus far; but with reminders from time to time that the same basic issue arises for the eastern traditions.

II

The first point to be made is that it would be inappropriate to speak of realism, or non-realism, across the board, as though one is obliged

to be consistently realist or consistently non-realist, in the interpretation of all types of language – perceptual, ethical, aesthetic, poetic,
scientific, religious. There are in fact probably no pan-realists, believing in the reality of fairies and snarks as well as of tables and
electrons; and likewise few if any omni-non-realists, denying the
objective reality of a material world and of other people as well as
of gravity and God. Thus we are not confronted by two logically in-
dissoluble packages – or even by invariable correlations.

We would therefore do well not to get our contemporary realist/
non-realist debate concerning religion confused with other realist-
non-realist discussions. It is quite distinct, for example, from the
medieval dispute between realists and nominalists. This concerned
the status of universals – goodness, redness, roundness and so on –
the realists holding that these exist independently of our conceiving
them, as transcendent Platonic Forms, and the nominalists the contrary. This is a quite distinct issue from the one with which contemporary religious realists and non-realists are concerned. The latter
are free to take either or no side in the medieval debate. Some
religious non-realists will also be non-realist about universals and
logical and mathematical entities and truths. But others will be non-
realist only about the objects of religious discourse. Likewise, religious realists can equally well be either realists or nominalists in the
medieval sense. Some (such as Richard Swinburne, for example) are
inclined to be realists in relation to at least some universals and to
logical truths, whilst others (such as myself, for example) are inclined to be non-realists at that point.

Our current religious debate has borrowed its terms from western
epistemological discussions that were at their height in the first half
of the present century. The general realist view was that in sense
perception we are in touch with an environing world that exists
independently of all perceivers. The polar opposite was the idealist
view that the perceived world exists only as a series of modifications
of our own consciousnesses: to be is to be perceived. Realism then
divided into naïve realism, holding that the world is just as we
perceive it to be, and critical realism, holding that there is an important subjective contribution to our perceiving, so that the world
as we experience it is a distinctively human construction arising
from the impacts of a real environment upon our sense organs, but
conceptualised in consciousness and language in culturally developed forms.

III

Although the issues in the philosophy of religion and of sense perception are logically independent, the distinction between naïve and
critical realism in relation to the world has its equally important
analogue in religion. As regards sense perception, I am thinking of
the kind of critical realism that was represented by such American
philosophers as R. W. Sellars, Arthur Lovejoy, A. K. Rogers and J. B.
Pratt. They took full account of the conceptual and interpretative
element in sense perception, and regarded our ordinary perceiving
as a complexly mediated awareness of a real physical world of
which we, as bodily organisms, are part. They held that the sensory
content of which we are directly aware (or, as they often said, which
we intuit) is private to the perceiving consciousness, but that by
means of this we are nevertheless able to live successfully in a real
physical world which transcends our own consciousness. Thus Sellars,
for example, wrote passages such as the following:

> Perceiving involves more than sensing. . . . There is belief, con-
> struction and interpretation, all this leading to what is taken to be
> the awareness of things . . . [We need] to distinguish between the
> intuition of the sensory appearance, which alone is given, and the
> denotative selection of a thing-object which is believed in and
> characterized. . . . In short, all sorts of facts about the thing per-
> ceived . . . influence our perceptual experience. . . . Attitudes,
> expectations, memories, accepted facts, all operate interpretatively.
> . . . There is, if you will, stimulus and complex interpretative
> response.[1]

Since the time, two or three generations ago, when the critical
realists were writing we have become even more conscious of the
subjective interpretative contribution to all awareness of our environment, including that ultimate environment – if such there be –
of which the religions speak. There is of course still, and probably
always will be, a naïve realism in religion as in ordinary life. The
philosophically unsophisticated person, who has not been troubled
by the sorts of questions that epistemologists raise, is a naïve realist
in relation to the physical world – though probably without having
encountered either this notion or its alternatives. He or she simply
assumes that the world around us is as it seems to be; and likewise

the ordinary unsophisticated religious person, of whatever tradition, has normally been a naïve religious realist. What is believed in this way is, of course, almost endlessly variable, for naïve religious realism is not a creed but a way of thinking – namely, assuming that what is spoken about in the religious language that one has learned is just as described in this language, understood literally. And by 'literally' I simply mean 'straightforwardly, rather than as metaphor or myth'. It may very well be that, as many argue today, the literal and non-literal uses of language are not distinct in kind but rather form a continuum of legitimate usages. But a continuum can contain large differences and there is often a large difference between, for example, understanding a biblical story literally and understanding it as myth. Thus a naïve Christian realist might, on reading Chapter 3 of the Book of Genesis and treating it as authoritative, believe the human race to have consisted originally of a single pair, who lived in a locality called the Garden of Eden until they were expelled for disobedience. In contrast to this, a critical Christian realist might regard Genesis 3 as a mythic story picturing the state of moral and spiritual disorder into which each generation is born. Or again the naïve Christian realist may perhaps think of God as a great super-human person looking down upon us from the sky. A contrasting critical religious realism can take a number of forms. The form which I favour myself thinks of, say, the Jahweh of Israel as the particular historical *persona* that has been jointly formed by the universal presence of the ultimately Real and the culturally specific thought-forms of the Jewish people. The Jahweh *persona* developed over the centuries from the tribal warrior god of the earliest layers of the tradition to the Holy One, blessed be he, of rabbinic Judaism. Both divine presence and human projection have accordingly been at work in the formation of the figure of Jahweh; and likewise of the heavenly Father of the New Testament, of the Allah of the Qur'anic revelation, of Shiva, of Vishnu and so on; and again – looking further afield – in the formation of the various *impersonae* of the Real – Brahman, the Dharmakaya, the Tao and so on.

If we distinguish – as we should – between, on the one hand, the psychological, anthropological and social insights of the psychologists, anthropologists and sociologists of religion, and on the other hand, the naturalistic presuppositions which have so often accompanied them, the former (though not the latter) can be fully integrated into a contemporary religious realism. This can readily accept, to take a simple and basic example, that God thought of as the heavenly Father is manifestly a conception of the divine in human terms; but will reject the naturalistic dogma which authorises the inference in the minds of many social scientists that the heavenly Father is *nothing but* a human projection.

Thus a critical religious realism affirms the transcendent divine reality which the theistic religions refer to as God; but is conscious that this reality is always thought of and experienced by us in ways which are shaped and coloured by human concepts and images. We see the Real always and only through the spectacles of our religious categories; and these, as we are acutely aware today, vary significantly from one culture to another.

Thus critical religious realism differs importantly both from the naïve religious realism which assumes that the divine reality is just as spoken about in the language of some one tradition, and from the religious non- or anti-realism which rejects the idea of a transcendent divine reality existing in addition to and independently of we human beings.

IV

It is time now to specify further the non-realist religious point of view. This also can take a wide variety of forms. But centrally it interprets religious language, not as referring to a transcendent reality or realities, but as expressing our emotions, or our basic moral insights and intentions, or our way of seeing the world, or as referring to our moral and spiritual ideals. The premiss, either open or concealed, that lies behind the non-realist understandings of religion is the naturalistic conviction – or indeed faith – that the realm of material things and living organisms, including the human organism with its immensely complex brain, is the only realm there is; and that God exists only as an idea in the human mind/brain – *in mente* but not *in re*. The classic statement remains that of Ludwig Feuerbach, whose *Essence of Christianity* was first published in German in 1841. He held that the idea of a loving God is a projection onto the cosmos of our ideal of love. The heavenly Father is love personified and deified in the religious imagination. Today Feuerbach's spiritual descendants likewise start from a denial of 'objective theism', that is, of the conviction that God is a reality *a se* whose existence accordingly does not consist only in being conceived or imagined by human beings. They then develop their alternative account of religion, which moves along one or other of two paths. For some, strongly influenced by Wittgenstein, and represented today by Dewi Phillips, God is not so much an idea in our minds as an element in our language, the central element, indeed, of the realm of theistic language. This is in turn one dimension of something more many-sided, namely the theistic way or form of life. From this point of view, that God exists means that the concept of God operates effectively in the distinctive expressions and communications of religious people. For others, of whom Don Cupitt is a leading representative, God is an imaginary personification of our spiritual ideals. These ideals have intrinsic validity and are to be served, and served with all our strength, for their own sake. However, the imagined God figure, although sometimes giving psychological reinforcement to these ideal requirements, has also operated in all sorts of restricting and harmful ways and is today better discarded. Whereas Phillips has not, in his writings, emphasised the negative implications of this position, Cupitt has been anxious to have us all face them so that we can proceed to live consciously in a post-realist religious world.

It is important, in line with that last phrase, to recognise that these contemporary non-realist accounts of religion constitute religious, not anti-religious, interpretations. Although in an important sense atheistic, they differ from the atheism of such philosophers as A. J. Ayer, Antony Flew, Paul Edwards and many more, who reject the whole realm of religious language and practice as, at best, the experience of a delusion and hence as valueless or, less favourably, as positively harmful. In contrast to this, the stream that runs from Feuerbach through such thinkers as Santayana, Dewey and Randall in the United States, and Julian Huxley, R. M. Hare and now Dewi Phillips and Don Cupitt in Britain, sees religious language as expressing something of great value, even though its value is fundamentally different from that which religious people have generally supposed. A good way to bring out the positive character of non-realist religious thought is to note the analogy with Kant's move in declaring ethics to be autonomous. For Kant, the claim of morality upon us has an intrinsic authority, not dependent upon any external source or power, not even God. We are to do the right simply and solely because it is right. Action to gain a reward or avoid a penalty is sub-moral. Analogously, the non-realist religious thinkers are saying that the religious life, including its distinctive language and practices, has intrinsic value and authority. It is to be engaged in for its own sake, as inherently the best way to exist; and its value does not depend upon any factor or circumstance beyond itself. The activity of 'worshipping God', for example, does not gain its value, even in part, from there being (objectively) a God to be worshipped. Rather, in 'worshipping God' we are celebrating the ideals which we have personified and deified in our own imaginations. The reality of God is the reality of our ideals, and the 'life of God' consists in the living out of those ideals. And so we find that the religious non-realist can use the whole range of religious language, and can participate in the established liturgies, recite the creeds and prayers, listen to the scriptures, sing the hymns and receive the sacraments, but all within the invisible brackets of the belief that this activity is an autonomous end in itself, rather than a response to an ultimate transcendent reality in relation to which lies our final good.

What has led the religious non-realists to this radical reinterpretation?

Negatively, they have been persuaded of the validity of the twentieth-century positivist critique of religion. They regard talk of God or of eternal life, understood realistically, as either meaningless or utterly implausible. Thus the first chapter of Phillips's *Death and Immortality* echoes closely Antony Flew's arguments against any form of survival of bodily death – as indeed Flew has pointed out. And Cupitt's rejection of the idea of God, realistically understood, echoes that of many contemporary sociologists and psychologists, who assume without argument that God is wholly a projection of the human imagination. This naturalistic assumption of much of the social science community is all the more powerful for operating as an unquestioned dogma which renders inaudible the counter-arguments propounded today by such considerable figures as, for example, Richard Swinburne, Alvin Plantinga, William Alston and many others.

Nevertheless, it is in this area – in the perennial debate between (realist) religion and naturalism – that the main argument has to take place. For only if there are good reasons to reject religious realism is there any need to develop a non-realist alternative. Having pointed this out, however, I am not going to proceed with that debate here. For the distinctive contribution of the non-realist religious thinkers has not in fact been in this area: here they have simply merged with the widespread contemporary rejection of the idea of the Transcendent, and evidently feel little need to offer arguments in support of it. (Even that opening chapter to which I referred in Phillips's *Death and Immortality* is little more than perfunctory.)

The other and more positive consideration behind religious non-realism is the sense that the religious life, as a totality which includes a language and its correlative practices, is not an aberration but, on the contrary, the most valuable and ennobling aspect of our human existence. The thinkers we are considering therefore want to retain the religious life; and they seek to do so by emptying it of its, to them, unacceptable cosmic and metaphysical implications. They accordingly reject the conception of religion as the varied range of human responses to the Transcendent, and reinterpret it as a purely human activity, having its value as an end in itself.

V

Before seeking to evaluate this non-realist proposal we must isolate the central issue; and to that end we need to strip away other associated issues which might be confused with it. One such issue, which figures prominently in some of the literature, concerns the autonomy or heteronomy of ethics. Some of the most eloquent polemics in the non-realist literature attack the basing of morality upon the hope of divine rewards or fear of divine punishment, whether in this life or in the life to come. The authors make the point that action so motivated is not genuinely ethical, and draw the conclusion that a realist belief in God substitutes self-regarding prudence for authentic morality. And it must be admitted that this has happened on quite a large scale in the history of religion. The nineteenth-century Archdeacon William Paley – who has in the late twentieth century embarked upon a second career as one of our standard sources of erroneous views – wrote that virtue is 'the doing good to mankind, in obedience to the will of God, and for the sake of everlasting happiness'.[2] But this is today something of a museum-piece. Most critical religious realists accept Kant's view of the autonomy of ethics, holding that we are so constituted (and, ultimately, divinely constituted) that morality is intrinsic to our nature as social beings. And indeed long before Kant religious thinkers were teaching that we should love God for God's sake and not for any hope of reward. Both the Muslim Rabia and the Christian St Francis Xavier have been credited with the prayer: 'O God, if I worship thee for fear of hell, burn me in hell; and if I worship thee in hope of paradise, exclude me from paradise; but if I worship thee for thine own sake, withhold not thine everlasting beauty.' And, earlier still, it was Plotinus who said, 'If a man desires the good life except for itself, it is not the good life that he desires.' I suggest, then, that whilst the autonomy of the moral life may still be an issue between religious non-realists and some naïve religious realists, it is not the issue that they have to debate with contemporary critical religious realists.

Nor, I suggest, is another topic that is much stressed in some of the non-realist literature, namely the socially conditioned and culturally relative character of all religious phenomena. That, for example, settled agrarian societies in the ancient world tended to think of the divine in female terms, and nomadic herd-keeping societies in male terms – together with a hundred and one other correlations between the circumstances of human life and the religious practices and beliefs that occur within them – has been a matter of increasingly public knowledge since at least the work of Max Weber. This knowledge does indeed undermine a naïve religious realism; but it is fully accepted by modern critical religious realists. This, again, is not the point at issue between them and religious non-realists.

VI

What then is the real issue? It concerns the nature or structure of the universe in which we find ourselves. Is this, from our human point of view, good, or bad, or indifferent? Whereas pre-axial (or, in Eliade's terminology, archaic) religion was centrally concerned to keep human life on an even keel, enduring or enjoying it as it occurred, post-axial religion, embodied in what we call today the great world faiths, is centrally concerned with salvation – with the transformation of human existence. It sees ordinary human life as radically defective: as a fallen life in a fallen world, or as immersed in egocentric illusion and pervasively subject to *dukkha*. But it proclaims at the same time a limitlessly better possibility, and teaches a way to receive or to attain this – for some have found that it is given from beyond and others that it ripens from within. According to the great traditions, each human being is able sooner or later to go through the gateway of transformation, entering the kingdom of God or attaining *moksha* or *nirvana*. And these traditions proclaim, in terms of their very different conceptualities, that the structure of the universe is such that this limitlessly better possibility is actually available, and can even be entered upon now. For the transcendent Real towards which the religions point is not an entity or a person that might be directly observed or encountered, but that source or ground of everything, including the experienced deities and absolutes, in virtue of which the universe is, from the point of view of we human beings, ulti-mately benign or gracious. And so – according to the great post-axial religions – to live consciously in relation to that ultimate Reality in which is our final good is not to nurture an empty hope or a sustain-ing illusion, as the naturalistic thinkers believe, but is to be living in accordance with reality. In thus affirming the good, or to-be-rejoiced-in, nature of the Real, the great world faiths are forms of cosmic optimism. This ultimate optimism is, however, linked with an immediate pessimism which sees our ordinary existence as in desperate need of radical transformation. It is true that within each tradition, taken as a vast historical totality, there is also a subsidiary strand of ultimate pessimism. In Christianity this has taken the form of belief in a hell in which many – indeed, according to St Augus-tine,[3] a majority – are to be eternally damned. And it is implicit within that modern development within Buddhism which rejects the traditional belief in a long series of rebirths leading eventually to universal *nirvana*; so that only for those few who are fortunate enough to be able to attain or at least approach *nirvana* in the present life can the universe be said to be truly good. But from the standpoint of the normative interpretation of religion which I have adopted here, these strands of thought run contrary to the central and dominant message of their respective traditions.

Now the cosmic optimism of the great world faiths depends upon a realist interpretation of their language. For it is only if this universe is the creation or expression of an ultimate overarching benign reality, and is such that the spiritual project of our existence continues in some form beyond this present life, that it is possible to expect a fulfilment that can justify the immense pain and travail of the journey. If, on the contrary, such notions as God, Brahman, Dharmakaya, rebirth, eternal life, are figments of our imaginations, we must face the grim fact that the marvellous human spiritual potential will only be fulfilled to the very fragmentary extent that it is in fact fulfilled in this world – none at all in some, a little in most of us, and a great deal in a very few. Thus a non-realist interpretation of religion inevitably entails a profound pessimism. From the point of view of a fortunate few it constitutes good news, but from the point of view of the human race as a whole it comes as profoundly bad news.

The issue between religious realism and non-realism, then, is the issue between two fundamentally opposed conceptions of the nature of the universe as it affects our human existence in its world-wide and history-long totality. The non-realist faith starts from and returns to the naturalistic conception that we are simply complex animals who live and die, the circumstances of our lives happening to be fortunate for some and unfortunate for others. Probably half or more of the children who have been born throughout human history and pre-history have died in infancy, their potentialities almost entirely undeveloped. Of those who have survived to adulthood, great numbers have lived under oppression or in slavery, or have experienced many other forms of suffering, including anxious fear of starvation or of slaughter by enemies. And amidst these harsh pressures the human potential, of which we glimpse aspects in the saints, artists, thinkers and creative leaders, has only been able to make a very small beginning towards its fulfilment in the majority of human lives. If the naturalistic vision is correct, that potentiality can never be fulfilled in the great majority, for at death they have ceased to exist. And it would be Utopian to expect that our situation on this earth is about to become radically different. Thus the non-realist forms of religion, presupposing this naturalistic interpretation of the human situation, abandon hope for humankind as a whole. However, one seldom sees any awareness of this in the writings of our non-realist colleagues. They could, in my view, learn at this point from Bertrand Russell, who faced unflinchingly the harsh implications of his naturalistic philosophy – as in this well-known passage:

That Man is the product of causes which had no prevision of the end they were achieving; that his origin, his growth, his hopes and fears, his loves and his beliefs, are but the outcome of accidental collocations of atoms; that no fire, no heroism, no intensity of thought and feeling, can preserve an individual life beyond the grave; that all the labours of the ages, all the devotion, all the inspiration, all the noonday brightness of human genius, are destined to extinction in the vast death of the solar system, and that the whole temple of Man's achievement must inevitably be buried beneath the debris of a universe in ruins – all these things, if not quite beyond dispute, are yet so nearly certain, that no philosophy that rejects them can hope to stand. Only within the scaffolding of these truths, only on the firm foundation of un-yielding despair, can the soul's habitation henceforth be safely built.[4]

The language here is somewhat florid, as indeed Russell himself noted in a letter some 40 years later. But, he added, 'my outlook on the cosmos and on human life is substantially unchanged'.[5] And this, surely, is where a candid religious non-realist should start. He or she can then rejoice with the élite few whose heredity or environment or both are such that they are able to attain to personal blessedness, purity, the eternal quality of life, *moksha, nirvana, satori*, before death extinguishes them. But if they are deeply concerned for their less-fortunate fellows they may well conclude with Omar Khayyam:

> Ah Love! could thou and I with Fate conspire
> To grasp this sorry Scheme of Things entire,
>   Would not we shatter it to bits – and then
> Re-mould it nearer to the Heart's Desire!

In contrast to this, the great world traditions see the universe as, from our human point of view, ultimately good. As William James put it, religion 'says that the best things are the more eternal things, the things in the universe that throw the last stone, so to speak'.[6] This does not mean that present pain and suffering, injustice, unfulfilment and tragedy are not appallingly real. But it does mean that they are not the universe's last word. The total process of the universe, whether visualised in Judeo-Christian-Islamic or in Buddhist or Hindu terms, has at its heart a Reality that is conceived as the limitless love or grace of God, the being-consciousness-bliss (*satchitananda*) of the Brahman which lies in the depths of our own being, or the infinite outflowing compassion of the eternal Dharmakaya.

I do not believe that it is possible, on the basis of our present limited experience, either to prove or to disprove the truth of this religious vision, construed in a critical realist way; nor even to show it to be either overwhelmingly probable or improbable. The universe can be interpreted in both realist-religious and in naturalistic terms, the way that one interprets it philosophically reflecting the way that one interprets and inhabits it experientially. The non-realist construal of religious language becomes an option if one has entered into the widespread contemporary naturalistic state of mind. And the basic disagreement with religious realists occurs at that point. I cannot pursue this fundamental issue here. This chapter aims only to make clear what the central question is. And my contention is that the debate between religious realists and non-realists is a new form of the old debate between religious (which has in the past always meant realist religious) and naturalistic interpretations of the universe.

VII

Let me ask in conclusion, however, whether we are really faced with an either/or choice between religious realism and non-realism? May there not also be intermediate possibilities? I think not. There can be endlessly different and endlessly complex and subtle variations on either theme, no doubt with all manner of new options yet to be developed. But in the end they will all fall on one or the other side of the distinction between naturalistic and supra-naturalistic understandings of the universe. Unfortunately we lack both an agreed and an agreeable terminology for this distinction. 'The natural and the supernatural', which was the title of a famous book by John Oman published more than 50 years ago, is no longer in vogue. In addition to natural/supernatural and natural/supra-natural we have natural/transcendental and natural/non-natural None of these is, I think, entirely felicitous. So we have to speak infelicitously. Using the term 'non-natural', Robert Adams has defined a non-natural fact as 'one which does not consist simply in any fact or complex of facts which can be stated entirely in the language of physics, chemistry, biology, and human psychology'.[7] We should, I think, add to the naturalistic languages that of sociology. The crucial question, then, concerning an understanding of the universe is whether it includes or excludes reference to any (putative) non-natural facts or realities. In the non-realist interpretations all such apparently non-natural realities as God, Brahman, the Dharmakaya and so on are describable entirely in psychological and sociological terms. They are held to refer to ideas in our minds and/or to modes of human behaviour, including linguistic behaviour. In realist interpretations, on the other hand, (some of) these 'transcendent realities' are non-natural, not describable entirely in physical, psychological or sociological terms.

According to critical realism they are indeed all phenomenologically describable in the terms provided by the anthropological sciences; for religious experience, as a psychological phenomenon, is constructed from the same (culturally variable) elements as the rest of our experience. But it is held by the realist to be at the same time, and in varying degrees, a cognitive response to a non-natural reality or realities. Non-natural or supra-natural reality is impinging upon us; though the form that it takes in our conscious thought and experience depends upon the concepts and images with which our minds are furnished.

And whether religious language is entirely about natural realities, wholly describable in physical, psychological and sociological terms, or is also about non-natural realities mediated through human concepts, does seem to be a matter of genuine contention. We seem to be faced with a real either/or, which there is no point in concealing.

Notes

1. R. W. Sellars, 'A Statement of Critical Realism', *Revue internationale de philosophie,* vol. I (1938–9) pp. 474–7.
2. William Paley, *Moral and Political Philosophy,* 2nd edn (Boston, Mass.: West & Richardson, 1817) p. 36.
3. St Augustine, *Enchiridion,* 24:97.
4. Bertrand Russell, *Mysticism and Logic* (1918) pp. 47–8.
5. Bertrand Russell, *Autobiography,* vol. III (London: Allen & Unwin, 1969) pp. 172–3.
6. William James, *The Will to Believe and Other Essays* (New York and London: Longmans Green, 1905) pp. 25–6.
7. Robert Adams, *The Virtue of Faith* (New York and Oxford: Oxford University Press, 1987) p. 105.

2

Religious Experience: Its Nature and Validity

If we start from ordinary usage, we can say that interpretation is concerned with meaning, and presupposes that there is something (using that term in its most comprehensive sense to include entities, statements, actions, complex situations or indeed the universe as a whole) whose meaning is not indisputably self-evident to us. There is accordingly ambiguity, making room for alternative contruals, some of which will normally be misconstruals.

Ordinary usage thus suggests a dichotomy between objective facts (statements, actions, entities, situations, the universe as a whole) and subjective interpretations of them. However, at this point we need to distinguish between the two main families of meanings of 'meaning': on the one hand the various kinds of semantic meaning (that is, the meaning of linguistic utterances) and on the other, the kinds of what I shall call dispositional meaning (that is, the practical meaning, for the interpreter, of objects, events and situations). In the case of semantic meaning there is indeed a dichotomy between a linguistic entity – a sentence, an exclamation, a command, and so on – and an interpretation of it. But dispositional meaning is importantly different. The world is indeed there, and is as it is; but we do not have access to it as it is in itself, unperceived by us. We are aware of it only as it impinges upon us and is perceived and inhabited by us in terms of many kinds and levels of dispositional meaning. The dispositional meaning of an object, event or situation consists in the practical difference that it makes, currently and/or potentially, to the meaning-perceiver. For example, I perceive what is before me as an orange. In so doing I am recognising or identifying something by means of the concept *orange*. And my recognising it as an orange consists in part in my being in a dispositional state in relation to it which is appropriate (as I take it) to its being an orange rather than something else. Such a dispositional state usually cannot be fully spelled out. But it includes in this case being liable in certain circum-

17

stances to eat the orange; and it excludes, for example, expecting it to talk or grow wings or prove to be as heavy as lead. Thus when I see or, using all the relevant senses together, when I experience this as an orange my total dispositional state includes a sub-range of dispositions that is appropriate to this thing being an orange. And the same holds for everything else that I recognise, that is, am aware of as being some particular kind of thing or, in other words, as instantiating some concept.

The dispositional meaning of events is more complex than that of individual objects, being usually an aspect of the yet more complex and comprehensive significance of a situation. A situation is composed of objects but has its own dispositional meaning over and above the separate meanings of its constituent objects. Consider, for example, the situation which we describe as a session of an academic conference. The participants, having been prepared by invitations, programme and other documents, are automatically experiencing what is going on around them as a session within, let us say, a philosophical conference. They are in a dispositional state to behave appropriately – by listening to the paper, being ready to raise questions and to discuss after the paper has been read, and so on. And this rather complex readiness to behave in certain kinds of ways and not in others presupposes an extensive network of concepts which are part of our modern western academic culture. But if we can imagine a Stone Age person suddenly being brought into an academic conference, such a person would not perceive what is going on as having the same character or meaning. The Stone Age person would not have the concepts of conference session, academic discussion, scholarly paper, philosophy, or most of the wider conceptual field to which these belong, and would accordingly experience the same physical configuration as having some quite different meaning to which a quite different dispositional state would be appropriate.

Human life is normally lived at this situational level of complexity. And whereas the dispositional meaning for us of natural objects, such as oranges, consists in our practical adaptation to the physical world, situational meaning is largely a cultural construct. For our inhabited world of meaning – corresponding to the *Lebenswelt* of the phenomenologists – depends upon our corporate systems of concepts, which have formed over the decades, centuries or even millennia, and are embodied in our developing languages. Our experienced and inhabited world accordingly varies considerably through time and across cultures.

Returning now to our imagined conference, its participants, although intent upon the business before them, are at the some time potentially within a range of other situations. On one level (in a sense of 'level' to be indicated in a moment) they are not only at the gathering in, let us say, San Francisco, but also in the larger situation of the life of that city and the still wider situation of the earthquake region of California. And if an earthquake were suddenly to occur their situational awareness would at once shift to this new context of meaning, evoking a different dispositional state, expressing itself in appropriately different patterns of behaviour.

In such a case the new focus of attention would supersede the previous one. And it is a feature of situations of this kind, on what I am calling the same level, that they are more or less mutually exclusive, so that we can usually only live effectively in one at a time. But we can, and often do, live simultaneously in relation to different levels of meaning – levels in the sense that a higher includes but transcends a lower level. The three such levels that have long been recognised in western thought are the physical, the ethical and the religious. Note that in each case meaning has an essential behavioural aspect: the meaning of an object, event or situation is defined in terms of the practical dispositional state in which one is in virtue of recognising that object, event or situation as having that particular character. ('Recognise' here of course includes 'misrecognise', for when we make mistakes in identifying what is before us or around us we still respond by varying our dispositional state in relation to it, though this is then an inappropriate instead of an appropriate variation.)

On the physical level of meaning are all the ways in which we experience material objects, events and situations as being such that it is appropriate for us to behave in relation to them, or within them, in one range of ways rather than another. To experience this as a pen, that as a table and that over there as a mountain, and to experience a conference, a family meal, walking on a sidewalk, driving a car and so on, as we do, are examples of our continuous awareness of meaning at this basic level. It is because we perceive our environment as having meaning in this dispositional sense that we are able to live from moment to moment and year to year within it.

Such a dispositional analysis of recognition in terms of concepts presupposes, of course, some basic aim or desire on our part, such that this rather than some other set of readinesses for action becomes appropriate. Roughly, in relation to our physical environment, the

basic aim that renders a particular dispositional response appropriate is the aim of surviving and, beyond this, of flourishing in terms
of such basic natural values as health and contentment.

Our ordinary everyday consciousness of our physical environment is thus normally a continuous consciousness of it as having
various kinds of meaning in virtue of which we have some notion of
how to behave within it in order to fulfil our basic aim as animal
organisms. This everyday consciousness normally occurs at the
situational, rather than the object, order of complexity. All this applies to the lower as well as to the human forms of animal life,
though with two differences; the situations of which we humans are
conscious can have a much greater temporal extension; and what are
in the lower animals simply recognitional capacities have been abstracted by the human mind as concepts fixed by language.

It is within our human situational awareness that the next level of
meaning, the ethical, arises. I shall say very little about this here,
since it is not the primary concern of this chapter. But situations of
which other persons are constituents always have actual or potential
ethical meaning for us. That is to say, they may render appropriate
some action or range of actions determined, not by the aim of surviving, but by a moral principle. In my view Kant successfully
identified the basic nature of the distinctively moral aim as that of
treating oneself and others equally as ends in ourselves. In terms of
this basic aim, interpersonal situations can take on a further meaning, whose appropriate dispositional response may be at variance
with, and claim to override, that rendered appropriate by their purely
physical meaning. Thus anyone who incurs death or pain or even
discomfort or inconvenience in order to treat others as ends rather
than as means is responding to the distinctively ethical character of
some situation. The physical situation remains unchanged, but the
way in which it is experienced has changed, in that it is now perceived as also having moral significance.

Now let us turn to the religious level or order of meaning. Here
we apply religious concepts both to external objects, events and
situations and to the events and states of our inner life. On the face
of it some forms of religion are more concerned with the inner and
others with the outer realm. However, we must not make the mistake of characterising whole traditions in these terms – for example,
as exclusively 'prophetic' or exclusively 'mystical'. For the various
kinds of religious experience constitute, I shall argue, a continuum

ranging from the purely 'external' to the purely 'internal', the entire spectrum being present in varying proportions within each large and long-lived tradition. Further, I shall argue that religious experience throughout this continuum consists – if understood religiously – in the presence of a transcendent divine Reality coming to consciousness in terms of our human concepts. Because the different ways of being human have produced a variety of such conceptual systems, with their associated spiritual practices, the transcendent Reality (which I shall refer to simply as the Real) postulated by a religious understanding of religion is experienced in a variety of ways which have become enshrined in the different religious traditions.

I have spoken of the presence of the Real coming to consciousness in us as our awareness of the Real. In the case of physical realities, their presence to us comes to consciousness by means of their impact upon our sense organs, which is somehow translated into modifications of consciousness that are endowed with dispositional meaning by the system of physical-object and physical-situation concepts in terms of which we live. In contrast to this, the presence of the Real affects us by a non-physical impact, which comes to consciousness in forms that are endowed with dispositional meanings supplied by our system of religious concepts.

This occurs in a range of ways. At one end of the spectrum – where most moments of religious awareness are concentrated – our attention is directed upon the material environment, but we experience this not only in terms of physical concepts but at the same time on another level, in terms of religious concepts, so that some object or event or situation is experienced as mediating the divine presence to us. At the other end of the spectrum the divine presence is experienced independently of the physical environment, in forms supplied by the mystic's religious concepts. Between these extremes are various mixed modes, as I shall indicate in a moment.

Let us note some examples along this spectrum. The kinds of objects that are experienced as having religious significance include icons, images and idols (such as are found in Orthodox and Catholic churches and Hindu temples), symbolic objects (such as a cross or the star of David or the bread and wine in the eucharist), and also holy places (such as Mecca, Jerusalem, Bethlehem, Vrindaban, Benares, Bodh Gaya). To experience these as having religious significance is to be in a dispositional state in relation to them that can be broadly characterised as reverence, a receptivity through which (on a religious interpretation of religion) the Transcendent is mediated to us.

However, religious experiencing-as more commonly occurs in the awareness of situational than of object-meaning. Thus at the situational level the religious consciousness may find a further order of meaning in the moral life, interpreting the ethical requirements of the interpersonal world as mediating either the external claim of God or the internal requirement of Dharma, leading one to act or refrain from acting in this or that way. But it may also find a religious meaning in any or all of the events of individual life and corporate history. Thus in Hebrew religious consciousness it has embraced the entire national story, seen as a living out of the covenant with Yahweh. For the understanding of history expressed in the Hebrew scriptures is one in which crucial events have a religious significance. The exodus from Egypt, the wandering in the desert, the settlement in Canaan, the exile in Babylon, the return, are all presented as happenings in and through which God was guiding, disciplining or caring for God's chosen people. Much of the story, as it is told in the Hebrew Bible, has reached mythic proportions, and we do not know precisely to what extent it is rooted in history. But in some of the prophetic writings we come closer to history as it was taking place and was experienced at the time as having religious significance. For example, it seems that Jeremiah in the sixth century BCE experienced the Babylonian army marching on Jerusalem as being wielded by Jahweh to punish faithless Judah.

It is in such historical events that we find the foundational religious experiences that have given rise to the three Abrahamic religions. Each is based upon special revelatory moments in which historical events were experienced as divine epiphanies. Thus Moses' experience at the 'burning bush', and in receiving the Law on Mount Sinai, and again the communal experience of the exodus from Egypt, were foundationally revelatory events for Judaism. Jesus' intense experience of God as *abba*, Father, expressed in his life, teaching and death, including the unknown event that has come to be called his resurrection, is the foundationally revelatory event for Christianity. And the prophet Muhammad's experience, over a period of some 20 years, of hearing a heavenly voice reciting the words that became the Qur'an, is the foundationally revelatory event for Islam.

Each of these required an appropriate interpretation, or mode of experiencing-as, in order to have the character of revelation. Considered simply as historical events each is capable of being construed both religiously and naturalistically. When someone – Moses, Jesus, Muhammad – reports that they were conscious of a divine presence or heard a divine voice, it is always open to the sceptic to grant that they had the experiences that they report but to hold nevertheless that these were hallucinatory in character, being projections of their own unconscious minds. Thus sceptics have held that Moses was deluded; that Jesus' intense communion with God was a religious hallucination; and that the suras of the Qur'an are purely the produce of Muhammad's own mind, without any transcendent input.

We are noticing here an aspect of what we can call the religious ambiguity of the universe – the fact that, from our present standpoint within it, the universe is capable of being intellectually understood and concretely experienced in both religious and naturalistic way. I shall come later to the question whether, and if so how, this ambiguity may be resolved. But first let us look more widely at the religious way of experiencing what it happening around us and within us.

Within the theistic traditions the broadest term for the dispositional aspect of this mode of experiencing-as is worship. But this includes much more than specific acts of prayer and liturgical behaviour. It includes a centring of one's existence in God, expressed in obedience and trust and in a consequent release from self-centredness and a freedom to love others; and also in an ultimate confidence that (in Lady Julian's words) 'all shall be well, and all shall be well, and all manner of thing shall be well'.

To depict in this way a life lived in the conscious relationship to God that we call worship is, of course, to picture an ideal. Most of us live most of the time in forgetfulness of God and with our existence centred in ourselves. Nevertheless this God-centred form of life remains the ideal that we see embodied in a considerable degree in some of the great saints of our different traditions, and in many lesser degrees in many ordinary believers. When such a believer reports the 'sense of the presence of God', or perhaps better the sense of being in God's presence, she is experiencing her total situation as mediating the divine reality. This mode of experiencing-as may be triggered in many ways – by a feeling of finitude, contingency and absolute dependence; by a moment of deep appreciation of the gran-

deur and beauty of the natural world; by gratitude for life's goodness, or by the fellowship of suffering in time of disaster or tragedy;
by reflection on 'the starry heavens above and the moral law within';
or indeed by all manner of individual promptings. When such a
'trigger' operates, there is an apperceptive switch analogous to that
which occurs when, looking at a puzzle picture, we suddenly see a
face where before we saw only a confusion of lines. The religious
person is now experiencing-as in a new and importantly different
way.

Such an apperceptive switch can produce a fairly focused sense,
momentary or prolonged, of being in the divine presence. But it can
also produce a more general or diffused awareness of the world as
manifesting the divine and thus as having a new meaning and value.
Speaking metaphorically, the light of God's presence now shines
through it. Two well-known examples will suffice to illustrate this
mode of experience. George Fox, the founder of Quakerism, recorded in his *Journal* that 'All things were new; and all the creation
gave another smell unto me than before, beyond what words can
utter',[1] and Jonathan Edwards, the New England theologian, tells
how 'The appearance of everything was altered; there seemed to be,
as it were, a calm, sweet cast, or appearance of divine glory, in
almost everything. God's excellency, his wisdom, his purity and
love, seemed to appear in everything; in the sun, moon and stars; in
the clouds and blue sky; in the grass, flowers and trees; in the water
and all nature. . . .'[2]

But religious experiencing-as is not of course always theistic.
Within the Mahayana tradition of Buddhism there is the startling
claim that *samsara*, the ordinary process of human life, pervaded as
it is by *dukkha* ('suffering', 'unsatisfactoriness'), is identical with
nirvana. That is to say, experienced from the point of view of the self-
concerned, grasping ego, life involves the ineradicable anxieties and
fears engendered by our vulnerability to unpredictable chances and
to the inevitability of decay and death. But experienced from the
standpoint of the 'true' or 'original' self, found by transcending ego-
centredness and realising one's own universal Buddha nature, life is
free from these deep human anxieties. Although still finite, vulnerable and mortal, the 'awakened one' rejoices to be part of the ever-
changing flow of *pratitya-samutpada*, the unitary interdependent life
of the universe. Father Heinrich Dumoulin quotes this description of
the *satori* experience by a contemporary Zen priest:

Enlightenment is an overwhelming realization which comes suddenly. Man feels himself at once free and strong, exalted and great, in the universe. The breath of the universe vibrates through him. No longer is he merely a small, selfish ego, but rather he is open and transparent, united to all in unity. Enlightenment is achieved in *zazen* [meditation], but it remains effective in all situations of life. Thus everything in life is meaningful, worthy of thanks, and good – even suffering, sickness and death. . . .[3]

So far, then, we have been noting that there are religious ways, theistic and non-theistic, of experiencing both particular objects, events and situations, and our total existence in the world – all these being, on a religious understanding of them, modes of response to the universal presence of the Real.

As we move along the spectrum from the external to the internal, we come next to types of religious experience in which the mystic – for at this point that term begins to be commonly used – whilst being outwardly aware of the world is also inwardly aware of the Transcendent, and projects the latter awareness as a vision or audition or photism. There are numerous examples of this in the scriptures and in the post-scriptural histories of the various traditions. One example that well illustrates this mixture of the inner and the outer is the experience of the mystic, Julian of Norwich, whom I quoted earlier, as she lay apparently dying and looking at a crucifix which a priest was holding before her. Her awareness of the Real came to her in distinctively Christian terms as a sense of the divine love manifested in Jesus' death on the cross, and so fused with her perception of the wooden figure that 'suddenly I saw the red blood trickling down from under the crown, all hot, flowing freely and copiously, a living stream, just as it seemed to me that it was when the crown of thorns was thrust down upon his blessed head'.[4] Her receptiveness at this moment to the presence of the Divine, the Real, was given form (I am suggesting) by the religious ideas instilled in her by her tradition, thus creating this vivid experience.

Moving yet further along the spectrum, there are forms of religious experience in which the outer world plays no part. The mystic is in a state of deep meditation or trance, unconscious of the external environment. 'To one who is entering this state', says Evelyn Underhill, 'the external world seems to get further and further away; till at last nothing but the paramount fact of his own existence remains.'[5]

In this form of religious experience as in the others, I am suggesting, the mystic's mind is being directly affected by the divine Reality; and this impact (or, in the cybernetic sense of the term, this 'information') comes to consciousness in forms provided by the constructive imagination of the recipient, fed by the concepts and symbols of his or her tradition. If there is (as I think that in fact there is) the kind of mental impact of one human mind upon another that is called telepathy, this provides a partial analogy to the impact of the presence of the Real upon human minds. In the case of visions and auditions the telepathic analogue is that of 'crisis apparitions'. The literature of parapsychology from the days before radio communication contains numerous cases of this. Typically, a man travelling or working abroad, say in India, is unexpectedly killed in some accident. It takes two or three weeks for the news to reach his wife in England by the normal channels. But during the night immediately after the accident she has a vivid dream or a waking vision that symbolises his death. This may take a variety of forms: a dream or an apparition of her husband looking still and deathlike, or of a coffin or other symbol of death, or of receiving an announcement of his death, and so on.[6] In such a case it seems reasonable to suppose that in the moment of crisis the husband's state of mind telepathically affected that of his wife at an unconscious level and that (usually) at night, when her attention was withdrawn from the outer world, this 'information' came to her consciousness by means of the mechanism by which ordinary dreams are created. In the case of mystical experiences, however, the source of the 'information' is the universal presence of the Transcendent, the Divine, to which the mystic is exceptionally open; and this impact comes to consciousness through the basic religious concepts and the specific concrete symbols of the mystic's tradition.

What, however, of unitive mysticism? Does not this fall outside any analysis of religious experience as involving the interpretative concepts of the experiencer? For it would seem that here, without the mediation of the world or of either outer or inner visions, there is a direct experience of being absorbed into or becoming one with God, the One, the Divine. As Meister Eckhart, perhaps the greatest of the Christian unitive mystics, expressed it, 'when the divine light pours into the soul, the soul is united with God, as light blends with light'.[7] Reflecting on such experiences Eckhart says, 'If I am to know God directly, I must become completely He and He I: so that this He and this I become and are one.'[8] And so he says that 'God and I are One

. . . I am the unmoved Mover, that moves all things.'[9] This parallels the famous *Ana 'l-Haqq* (I am the Real, that is, God) of the great Muslim mystic al-Hallaj.

From the standpoint of orthodox Christian or Muslim theology, the mystic's sense of union with God can only be subjective. For the creature remains for ever ontologically distinct from and dependent for existence upon the Creator. Thus Bernard of Clairvaux, speaking of the 'unitive' state, says, 'How can there be unity where there is plurality of natures and difference of substances? The union of God and man is brought about not by confusion of natures, but by agreement of wills. Man and God, because they are not one substance or nature, cannot be called "one thing" . . . but they are with strict truth called "one spirit" if they adhere to one another with the glue of love.'[10] Thus the language of total and unqualified unity is, from this point of view, either rhetorical exaggeration or heresy. In the cases of Eckhart and al-Hallaj their respective political-religious authorities persecuted them for these statements and al Hallaj was even executed.

On the other hand, parallel statements by advaitic Hindu mystics are entirely acceptable within their tradition. Thus in the *Crest Jewell of Discrimination* (*Viveka-Chudamani*), attributed to Shankara, we read: 'The ego has disappeared. I have realized my identity with Brahman . . . My mind fell like a hailstone into that vast expanse of Brahman's ocean. Touching one drop of it, I melted away and became one with Brahman.'[11]

However, this notion of a direct unitive experience of the Real, the One, the Divine, gives rise to an epistemological dilemma. An experience that is reported, and that has therefore been remembered, even if it cannot be adequately captured in words, was by definition an episode in the history of the reporter: the mystic undergoes the experience and is subsequently able to remember having had it. But in that case it seems that the mystic must never have ceased to exist as a distinct stream of consciousness. There can have been no losing of identity through becoming totally merged into the Infinite. For if the finite consciousness of the mystic had been dissolved in the Infinite, like a drop of water becoming part of the ocean, there would be no continuous thread of finite consciousness such as is required for an individual memory of the experience. We therefore seem driven to conclude either that the remembered 'unitive experience' was not truly unitive or that, if the mystic was indeed absorbed into a truly unitive state, this cannot have been properly speaking an experience undergone by the mystic, since he or she could then have no memory of it.

It therefore seems to me that the remembered experience, which is subsequently spoken of as unitary, must have been the experience of a continuing finite consciousness, though one in which the entire field of consciousness became filled, in the case of a theistic mystic, by the presence of God, and in the case of the advaitic mystic, by the universal reality of Brahman. For it would seem that when a human self has attained to a sufficient transcendence of the ego and its concerns it may become so open to the Divine, the Real, the Ultimate as to undergo moments in which the consciousness is totally occupied with the transcendent Reality. But the fact that this 'unitive' experience takes both theistic and non-theistic forms (and sub-varieties of each) suggests that the finite consciousness of the mystic has carried with it into this moment the basic conceptual structure whereby it experiences the Real, in some cases as a personal, and in other cases as a non-personal, reality.

I am suggesting, then, that religious experience in all its forms is a mode of consciousness that occurs when someone is freely (though not necessarily by conscious volition) open and responsive to the universal presence of the transcendent Reality. The impact of this presence comes to consciousness as a mode of experience whose specific forms are provided by the experiencer's religious concepts and symbols. This of course would explain how it can be that Christians have distinctively Christian forms of religious experience, Muslims distinctively Islamic forms, Hindus distinctively Hindu forms, and so on.

But let us now look at the same range of phenomena from a naturalistic point of view, which denies that there is any transcendent Reality to evoke these forms of experience. A naturalistic philosophy must hold that religious experience is internally generated. Instead of religious concepts being used to give form to our awareness of a transcendent impact upon us, they are being used to shape the products of our own imaginations, the (unconscious) motive behind their production being primarily reassurance in the face of our inescapable finitude, vulnerability and mortality.

Since the same reported experiences occur on either a religious or a naturalistic view, wherein lies the difference between situations in which the one or the other of these views is true? What is the difference between there being and there not being a transcendent divine Reality which is a factor, in collaboration with our human conceptual systems, in the genesis of religious experience? The answer must lie, not in the nature of the experiences themselves as describable phenomena, but in the implications of their rival construals for the larger structure of the universe considered as entailing the possibility of further experiences. If a religious account of the universe is true, the universe is so structured as to give rise to further human experiences in the future which will not occur if a naturalistic account is true. For each of the great traditions teaches that our present earthly life is only a small segment of our total existence. Each tradition speaks of an ultimate eschatological state, variously pictured as heaven or hell, paradise, oneness with the infinite consciousness of Brahman, or as a nirvanic state beyond individual ego-existence. Whilst there are these, and yet other, pictures and symbols, strong strands of each tradition regard the ultimate state as lying beyond the range of our earthly concepts. However, each also speaks in more concrete terms of the pareschaton (the phase or phases between this life and that ultimate state) in which we continue to exist as individual persons, being either resurrected or reborn in this or other worlds, or going through some kind of purgatorial experience or 'continued sanctification after death'. We do not have to choose between these different pareschatologies in order to see that if any one of them is correct, a purely naturalistic understanding of the universe must be incorrect. Indeed, this is still the case if none of them is correct in its specific expectations and yet all are correct in their common affirmation of continued personal existence beyond the present life. It could further be the case that as we proceed into whatever unexpected form our continued existence takes we find that a religious, as distinguished from a naturalistic, understanding of the universe is progressively confirmed whilst the particular conceptualisation of that religious understanding is itself being progressively revised or transcended. It is at any rate clear that the wider sets of beliefs and expectations that cohere respectively with a religious and with a naturalistic construal of religious awareness are very different and cannot both be compatible with the full range of human experience.

Needless to say, I have only touched in these last remarks upon a very large field for speculation. There can be a variety of possible complications of this picture, modifying naturalism in the religious direction. But I am only concerned here to make the general point that the rival understandings of religious experience are integral to radically different conceptions of the larger character of the universe, involving different expectations concerning the context and the content of future human experience.

The claim that religious experiences connect with expectations of some kind of life after death does nothing, of course, to establish now the truth of this larger conception of the universe. It does however show that, whilst religious and naturalistic believers grant that the various reported forms of religious experience occur, and are thus far in agreement, their different understandings of those experiences are such that if the religious understanding turns out to be correct the naturalistic understanding will thereby have been shown to be false.

In the meantime the two construals of religious experience – as cognitive in humanly varying ways of a transcendent Reality, and as purely a product of the human imagination – connect with different forms of life, different ways of inhabiting the world. These often have considerable overlap on the physical and ethical levels of meaning. But they differ basically in their understanding of the overall character of the universe and hence of what is going on in and through the entire phenomenon of human existence.

Each of these global interpretations constitutes an act of faith; the religious and the naturalistic believer must both be said to 'walk by faith'. The religious believer is living in terms of a meaning which may prove to be substantially true or may be an illusion; and the naturalistic believer is living in terms of a meaning which may be true or may prove to be an illusion. And we have to say that both are at present entitled to believe as they do, and that each is taking a cognitive risk in so doing.

And so the appropriate form of defence of the rationality of religious belief is not the traditional one that seeks to prove or to show it to be more probable than not that God exists. For the universe, as we can presently observe it, is ambiguous in the sense that it is capable of being experienced and comprehensively described in both religious and naturalistic ways. The appropriate form of religious apologetic is accordingly one that seeks to show instead that it is fully rational for the person who experiences life, or some aspect of it, religiously to form beliefs on the basis of that mode of experience. In other words, the general empiricist principle that it is rational to form beliefs on the basis of experience is here extended to include religious as well as sensory experience.

More precisely, beliefs that reflect our experience are *prima facie* justified. But there may of course be all sorts of circumstances that tell against this *prima facie* justification, thereby reducing the degree of rationality of such believings, perhaps even to zero. In the case of beliefs reflecting religious experience the main 'defeater' that offers itself consists in a broad contrast with beliefs reflecting sensory experience. Sense experience is universal among human beings whereas religious experience is not. Consequently sense reports are in general subject to public confirmation, whereas religious experience reports are not. And sense experience is processed through a largely common set of concepts, whereas religious experience is processed through a number of different sets of concepts operating within different religious traditions.

The proper response to these differences, from the point of view of a religious believer, is, I suggest, that they arise from differences between the ostensive objects of sensory and religious experience respectively. As animal organisms moving about in a material environment it is necessary for our survival and flourishing that we should all experience it as it affects creatures such as ourselves, and thus basically in the same way. We are accordingly forced to experience it correctly, eventually on pain of death. But our relationship to the more ultimate environment of which the religions speak is importantly different. This latter confronts or surrounds or undergirds or envelops us as the bearer of ultimate value, and value differs from matter in leaving us free to recognise and respond to it or not. We are not forced to be aware of the Transcendent as we are forced to be aware of our physical surroundings. Consequently the religious mode of experiencing is not, at any given time, universal. We are free to respond or fail to respond religiously to the ultimate mystery of the universe and of ourselves as part of it. Accordingly the claim to experience the Transcendent is not subject to public checks, except within the borders of a given tradition; although I have already argued that it is subject to an ultimate eschatological confirmation or disconfirmation. And again, the religious response to the universe can occur in terms of different conceptual schemes, giving rise to different forms of religious experience within the different religious traditions.

Given these inbuilt differences, I suggest that it is as rational for one who, in a powerful and compelling way, experiences life religiously to believe in the reality of the Transcendent as for all of us to believe in the reality of the physical world.

Notes

1. *The Journal of George Fox* (1694; London: J. M. Dent; New York: E. P. Dutton, 1924) p. 17.

2. Quoted by William James, *Varieties of Religious Experience* (1902; London: Collins; New York: Mentor Books, 1960) p. 248.

3. Heinrich Dumoulin, *A History of Zen Buddhism*, trans. Paul Peachey ([1959]; New York: Random House, 1963) p. 275.

4. *Showings*, short text, trans. Edmund Colledge and James Walsh (New York: Paulist Press, 1978) ch. 3.

5. Evelyn Underhill, *Mysticism* (1911; New York: New American Library, 1955) p. 318.

6. For actual accounts see, for example, F. W. H. Myers, *Human Personality and its Survival of Bodily Death* (1903; New York: Arno Press, 1975).

7. *Meister Eckhart*, trans. Raymond B. Blakney (New York: Harper & Row, 1941) Sermon 14, p. 163.

8. Sermon 99, quoted by Underhill, *Mysticism*, p. 420.

9. *Meister Eckhart*, Sermon 28, p. 232.

10. Bernard of Clairvaux, *Sermons on the Canticles*, Sermon 71. See also St John of the Cross, *Ascent of Mount Carmel*, Book II, ch. 5; and John Tauler, 'First Sermon for the Second Sunday of the Epiphany', in A. Poulain (ed.), *The Graces of Interior Prayer* (St Louis, Mo.: Herder, 1950) Part II, ch. 18.

11. Shankara, *Crest Jewell of Discrimination*, trans. Swami Prabhvananda and Christopher Isherwood, 3rd edn (Los Angeles: Vedanta Press, 1978) p. 113.

Part II
Christ and Christianity

3

An Inspiration Christology

Where should we begin? With the man Jesus of Nazareth, who lived
in Palestine 19 centuries ago and who became the founder of the
Christian religion – though, paradoxically, without intending to do
so since he apparently expected the end of the age within a few
years? Or with the Christ figure of developed Christian theology and
faith, the eternal Second Person of a divine Trinity, who once lived a
human life and now reigns as Lord of all?

There is a dilemma here. On the one hand it would seem that an
incarnational faith, rooted in history, must go back to the historical
Jesus; yet the modern study of the New Testament documents has
shown how relatively little certain knowledge we have of him. The
idealised Christ, on the other hand, is unaffected by the defects of
historical evidence, so that we can glorify him without limit. The
result is an absolute figure who is the one and only way, truth and
life for the whole human race and whose totalitarian claim thus
clashes with our contemporary awareness of God's saving grace
within other streams of religious life.

I shall return later to the relation between Jesus and the non-
Christian majority of human beings. In the meantime I propose to
resolve the methodological dilemma by beginning with the historical Jesus. Although our assured information about him is very
limited, the New Testament obviously reflects the existence of a real
person, who was critically important to many who encountered him
and whose existence has been of ultimate significance for hundreds
of millions since. On the basis of this we can at least try to imagine
ourselves as first-century persons encountering Jesus of Nazareth.
Imagine is the right word, even though it must be imagination under
the broad control of historical evidence. This evidence is drawn from
the New Testament, from other documents of the same period, and
from wider information concerning the ancient world. Because we
are trying to imagine a distinctively religious personality we shall, in
interpreting the evidence, also use our knowledge of other religiously impressive people of whom we have read or whom we have

encountered. For those of us who are Christians, the figure of Jesus has profoundly affected us by meeting our own spiritual needs, so that the pattern of those needs has inevitably influenced our perception of him. Accordingly, imaginative reconstructions of the historical Jesus are bound to differ because we use partially different ranges and selections of historical information and also because we bring to that information different experiences of religiously impressive humanity and our own varying spiritual needs. Indeed, because of this last element our respective pictures of Jesus will say something about us as well as something, hopefully something that is historically well-founded, about the Jesus who was a part of public human history.

Before exposing my own imaginative reconstruction, let me note a possible objection. It might be said that for Christian faith, Jesus was not a 'religiously impressive man' but was God incarnate and as such absolutely unique, not comparable – even remotely – with great religious figures such as the founders of other religious traditions or with such religiously impressive persons as we ourselves may have had the good fortune to encounter.

From a Christian point of view this would, I think, be a mistaken objection. The traditional doctrine of the incarnation affirms that Jesus was truly man as well as truly God. As man he belonged to our earthly history and is to be accepted as an authentic human being. And if he was a man, who preached a religious message, influencing his hearers so powerfully that many became his disciples, and through them a new world religion came into being, it seems safe to say that he must have been a religiously very impressive person. If so, we can, in forming our imaginative pictures of him, appropriately draw not only upon our all-too-scanty historical information but also upon our knowledge of other religiously impressive persons.

I see Jesus as dominated, at least in the most important moments of his life, by his awareness of the overwhelmingly evident reality and presence of God – the God of whom he had learned from his Jewish tradition. He was aware of God as both limitlessly gracious and limitlessly demanding – both as the loving heavenly *Abba* who welcomes home the prodigal son (Luke 15:11–24) and also as the holy and righteous one who makes a total and absolute claim upon human beings. So powerful was Jesus' awareness of the heavenly Father in comparison with the awareness of those around him, including the official religious leaders of his time, that he was aware of a unique calling and responsibility to communicate the reality of

God by proclaiming the imminent coming of the divine kingdom and the insistent divine claim upon each man, woman and child. He must thus have been conscious of a special role in God's dealings with the people of Israel in those last days before the kingdom came in power and glory. Inevitably he would, as God's voice to his contemporaries, have had a central position, in his own mind and in the minds of those who responded to him, within the crisis of the end time in which he and they believed themselves to be living.

When we seek to imagine ourselves as Jesus' contemporaries, we must of course remember that we would not be the same persons that we now are; we would be first-century Palestinian Jews. As far as our individual relationship to God is concerned we can perhaps assume that we might nevertheless be at heart essentially the same persons. Although in that society we could never have doubted, intellectually, the existence of God, we would not necessarily on that account be living consciously in God's presence either more or less than we are today. There would therefore be an immense contrast between Jesus' powerful and pervasive sense of the divine Thou, with his consequent absolute certainty of God's reality, and our own feeble and intermittent God-consciousness. We may know from our own experience something of what it is to encounter a person who is much more powerfully aware of the divine presence than we are ourselves and the shape of whose life embodies a response to the claims of the divine reality. To encounter such a person is to be profoundly challenged. For the very existence and presence of an authentic saint focuses the liberating divine claim in turn upon others. And if that claim should be specifically articulated and directed to oneself, the impact must be all the greater. I envisage a first-century encounter with Jesus as having this deeply challenging and disturbing quality, demanding a radical reordering of one's existence: 'The time is fulfilled, and the kingdom of God is at hand; repent, and believe in the gospel' (Mark 1:14); 'Unless you turn and become like children, you will never enter the kingdom of heaven' (Matthew 18:3); 'Another of the disciples said to him, "Lord, let me first go and bury my father." But Jesus said to him, "Follow me, and leave the dead to bury their own dead"' (Matthew 8:21–2); 'He who finds his life will lose it, and he who loses his life for my sake will find it' (Matthew 10:39); 'If any man would come after me, let him deny himself and take up his cross and follow me. For whoever would save his life will lose it, and whoever loses his life for my sake will find it' (Matthew 16:24–5); 'One thing you still lack. Sell all that you have and distribute to the poor, and you will have treasure in heaven; and come, follow me' (Luke 18:22); 'You have heard that it was said, "You shall love your neighbour and hate your enemy'. But I say to you, Love your enemies and pray for those who persecute you, so that you may be sons of your Father who is in heaven' (Matthew 5:43–5); 'You cannot serve God and mammon. Therefore I tell you, do not be anxious about your life, what you shall eat or what you shall drink, nor about your body, what you shall put on' (Matthew 6:24–5). All these may well not be Jesus' *ipsissima verba*, but nevertheless they clearly reflect something of the impact of his challenging demands upon his hearers. Such challenges are also moments of judgement in which we turn toward or away from God. If we turned to God, as God's claim was mediated to us through Jesus' words, our lives would begin to be reordered around a new centre; and the divine love would shine in our hearts, creating a joyful trust and releasing a new love of our neighbours.

But the historical Jesus whom we are imagining ourselves as encountering was not only a preacher of God's love and claim but also a healer, expressing the divine love in action. It seems that when a human being is sufficiently attuned to the life of God, divinely established psychic laws can come into operation to produce 'miraculous' healings and providential coincidences. This was strikingly evident in the life of Jesus. Because he was so open and responsive to God's presence, the divine creativity flowed through his hands in bodily healing and was present in his personal impact upon people, with challenging and re-creating power.

I conceive, then, that a close encounter with Jesus in first-century Palestine would be a conversion experience. It would perhaps begin by our witnessing or hearing of one of his healing 'miracles'. It would continue as a deeply challenging call, a claim threatening to revolutionise our life, shattering our self-centred world of meaning, and plunging us into the vast unknown universe of God's meaning. And it would grow into a profound sense of the sovereign goodness and love of God, relieving us of anxiety for ourselves and empowering us to love and serve others, gladly bearing witness to the divine power that had thus changed us.

This or something like this would, as I see it, be Jesus' 'existential' impact upon us. And this impact would be bound up with a body of ideas that we would accept on Jesus' authority and assimilate with a greater or lesser degree of comprehension.

Perhaps the most important such idea would be the one already mentioned – the apocalyptic conviction of living in the last days of the age. The end was about to come in catastrophic judgement, to be followed by a new age, the kingdom of God on earth, in which all things would be made new. This seems to have been a powerful theme in the teaching of Jesus (Mark 9:1; 13:30; Matthew 10:23; 16:28; 23:36; Luke 9:27) and consequently in the outlook of the early Christian community (1 Peter 4:7; Peter 3:3–10; James 5:8–9; Heb. 10:25; John 21:22; 1 John 2:28; 1 Thessalonians 2:19; 3:13; 4:15; 5:23; I Corinthians 4:5; 7:29; 11:26; 15:51; Romans 13:11–12).[1] But looking back across 19 centuries and knowing that the Christian expectation gradually faded as the end failed to arrive, we may suppose that Jesus was so intensely conscious of God's surrounding presence and power that he expected this to become publicly manifest in the immediate future. His sense of the kingdom knocking on the door of the present moment reflected, I am suggesting, his own vivid sense of God's immanent presence. Immanence, we could say, was expressed as imminence.

Jewish tradition in Jesus' time offered at least two images of the one who was to fulfill the role of the last prophet, the herald of the end that also was to be God's great beginning. One was that of the Messiah, who was to be of the royal line of David and to reign as king in the new age in which Jerusalem would be the centre of the world and in which God's will would be done on earth. The other was that of the Son of man in the Danielic prophecy:

> and behold, with the clouds of heaven
>   there came one like a son of man,
> and he came to the Ancient of Days
>   and was presented before him.
> And to him was given dominion
>   and glory and kingdom,
> that all peoples, nations, and languages
>   should serve him;
> his kingdom is an everlasting dominion,
>   which shall not pass away,
> and his kingdom one
>   that shall not be destroyed.
>   (Daniel 7:13–14)

Both these images were used by the early Church, though they were probably adopted initially in different places, perhaps the Messiah image in Jerusalem and the Son of man image elsewhere in Palestine or Syria.[2] It is clear that Jesus used the term *son of man*, though possibly not as a title but simply as an accepted way in which a man could refer to himself. It also seems that others sought to thrust the title Messiah upon him, though it does not seem that he himself accepted it. We know that his powerful sense of the divine presence and his experience of the divine power working in his own healings signified to Jesus the presence of God's transforming rule: 'If it is by the finger of God that I cast out demons, then the kingdom of God has come upon you' (Luke 11:20). In the understanding of the early church it was a natural development to identify him either as God's Messiah or as the Son of man who was to come again with the clouds of heaven. Note, however, with a view to the later Christian doctrine of the incarnation, that neither the Messiah nor the Son of man was, in Jewish thinking, divine. Each was a human, or perhaps even superhuman, figure who was to be God's servant and instrument in ushering in the kingdom. This role was clearly very special, indeed unique, but it was emphatically not equivalent to being God incarnate.

It seems to have been Jesus' proclamation of the imminent inbreaking of God's rule, a message that the Roman occupying power feared might spark a revolt (such as occurred in 66 and 132 CE), which led to Jesus' death at the instigation of the religious authorities and at the hands of the Roman occupying power.[3] The words of the disciples in the postresurrection Emmaus story indicate what kind of hopes had centred upon Jesus in the minds of many of his followers. Their thoughts had been 'concerning Jesus of Nazareth, who was a prophet mighty in deed and word before God and all the people, and how our chief priests and rulers delivered him up to be condemned to death, and crucified him. But we had hoped that he was the one to redeem Israel' (Luke 24:19–21). But such hopes of redeeming Israel from Roman captivity were politically dangerous, and it is not surprising that anyone who evoked them was marked in the eyes of the establishment. The ecclesiastical authorities were no more desirous of revolution and disorder than were their Roman overlords.

It seems that Jesus foresaw his own coming martyrdom and also foresaw that it would take place in the Holy City: 'for it cannot be that a prophet should perish away from Jerusalem' (Luke 13:33). It also seems that he understood his death as a sacrifice for the good of the people (Mark 10:45; Matthew 20:28). This was in line with the current Jewish belief that the sufferings of the righteous – particularly, in the immediately preceding period, the sufferings of the Maccabean martyrs – worked for the good of Israel. As John Downing concluded, in his study of this aspect of first-century Judaism, 'people thought in terms of human beings making atonement for others by means of their sufferings and death'.[4] The idea is also illustrated by the following quotation from the second-century rabbi Shim'on:

> When the righteous are seized by disease or affliction, it is in order to atone for the world. Thus all the sins of the generation are atoned for. When the Blessed Holy One wants to bring healing to the world, He strikes one righteous human among them with disease and affliction; through him He brings healing to all.[5]

But the later Christian notion that Jesus, in his death, was our substitute in bearing God's just punishment, or otherwise appeasing the divine wrath or satisfying the divine justice, and so enabling a righteous Creator to forgive his sinful creatures is – it seems to me – far removed from the spirit and teaching of Jesus himself. His own understanding of the divine forgiveness is expressed in, for example, the parable of the prodigal son. The earthly father clearly represents the heavenly Father. When his erring son repents and returns home, the father does not say, 'Because I am a just father I cannot forgive you until I have first killed my other son to atone to me for your sins.' He calls for the best robe and has a great feast prepared, 'for this my son was dead, and is alive again; he was lost, and is found' (Luke 15:24). Again, in the Lord's Prayer, Jesus taught his disciples to speak to God directly, as their heavenly Father, and to ask for forgiveness. There is here no mediator, no atoning sacrifice; only the profound and far-reaching requirement that we forgive one another.

After Jesus' death came his resurrection. It is impossible for us today to know the precise nature of the resurrection event. The New Testament evidences are too fragmentary and conflicting to permit more than speculative reconstructions. The only first-person account that we have of an encounter with the risen Jesus, that of Paul on the Damascus road (Acts 26:12–18; cf. 9:1–7), described a bright light and a voice but no physical body. The earliest surviving reference to the resurrection appearances (1 Corinthians 15:3–8) includes this Damascus road encounter, and the list is entirely compatible with a series of photisms, luminous phenomena that might take a variety of forms, including that of visions of the glorified Jesus.[6] Later strata of the tradition speak of the empty tomb (Mark 16:6; Matthew 28:6; Luke 24:2–3; John 20:2–9), and of the physical presence of Jesus (Matthew 28:9–10; 16–20; Luke 24:13–49; John 20:14–29; 21:1–22), though aspects of some of these manifestations – sudden appearances and disappearances (Luke 24:31, 36; John 20:19, 26) and difficulties in recognising Jesus (Matthew 28:17; Luke 24:16) – consist better with visions than with the presence of his raised physical body. In the lengthening tradition the resurrection faith of the church seems to have developed from a certainty of the living presence of Jesus, perhaps mediated by lights or visions or voices, to the story of the return of his physical body to life, his physical presence on earth for 40 days (Acts 1:3), and his final bodily ascension into the sky (Luke 24:51; Acts 1:9–11).

However, visions on the one hand and a resuscitated physical body on the other are not the only possibilities. Another is exemplified in at least two recorded resurrection encounters with religiously significant individuals within the past hundred years. These have been recounted by Paramahansa Yogananda (the founder of the still active Hindu movement in the West known as the Self-Realization Fellowship) in his *Autobiography of a Yogi*, first published in 1946.[7] Yogananda wrote in the florid Victorian English that was the literary style of many Indians of his own and earlier generations, but clearly this does not in any way entail that what he said is false. Yogananda's guru, Sri Yukteswar, died on 9 March 1936. Yogananda says that on 19 June of the same year Sri Yukteswar appeared to him in a hotel bedroom in Bombay. He was roused from his meditation by a bright light.

> Before my open and astonished eyes, the whole room was transformed into a strange world, the sunlight transmitted into supernal splendor. Waves of rapture engulfed me as I beheld the flesh and blood form of Sri Yukteswar! 'My son!' Master spoke tenderly, on his face an angel-bewitching smile. For the first time in my life I did not kneel at his feet in greeting, but instantly advanced to gather him hungrily in my arms. Moment of moments! The anguish of past months was toll I counted weightless against the torrential bliss now descending . . . . (pp. 414–15)

According to Paramahansa Yogananda, Sri Yukteswar spoke with him for two hours before vanishing from his sight, and he has relayed much of what his guru told him during that time (ch. 43). His sudden appearing and bodily presence would seem to have been very like the one attributed to Jesus in the upper room in Jerusalem (John 20: 19, 26).

The other resurrection recorded by Paramahansa Yogananda, that of Sri Yukteswar's guru, is said to have occurred in 1895.

> Lahiri Mahasaya's beautiful body, so dear to the devotees, was cremated with solemn householder rites at Manikarnika Ghat by the holy Ganges. The following day, at ten o'clock in the morning, while I was still in Banaras, my room was suffused with a great light. Lo! before me stood the flesh and blood form of Lahiri Mahasaya. It looked exactly like his old body, except that it appeared younger and more radiant. . . . (p. 349)

Again, the resurrected guru spoke and eventually disappeared.

Whatever the nature of Jesus' resurrection, inaccessible to us as it is, it launched the Christian church as we know it. Whether without this event Jesus' disciples would have begun again to preach his message and whether that message would have been recorded in Gospels and would have spread far and wide, we cannot know. For it was in fact the conviction of Jesus' continued life as their glorified Lord that inspired his disciples to form a faith-community that was able to capture the Roman Empire and has come to constitute one of the great religious traditions of the world.

In a very early phase of the apostolic preaching, St Peter is reported to have proclaimed,

> Men of Israel, hear these words: Jesus of Nazareth, a man attested to you by God with mighty works and wonders and signs which God did through him in your midst, as you yourselves know – this Jesus, delivered up according to the definite plan and foreknowledge of God, you crucified and killed by the hands of lawless men. But God raised him up, having loosed the pangs of death, because it was not possible for him to be held by it. (Acts 2:22–24)

But later apologists have come to see Jesus' resurrection as a proof of his deity. So self-evident is this connection in popular Christian thought that it must seem paradoxical to question it. Yet the connection is far from self-evident. If we argue that anyone who, being dead, returns to life, is divine; Jesus returned to life; therefore, Jesus is divine, the difficulty will be that according to the Christian scriptures many other people have also returned to life (for example, John 11:1–44; Luke 7:11–17; 8:49–56; Mark 5:35–43; Matthew 11:5; 27:52–3; Hebrews 11:35). If we then argue that among those who have returned to life Jesus was unique in that he was raised directly by God, we shall be faced with the fact that the early Church, who believed that Jesus was indeed raised directly by God, did not infer that he was divine ('a *man* [italics mine] attested to you by God with mighty works and wonders and signs', Acts 2:22). If we now move to what happened to Jesus after his resurrection and argue that he was unique in that, whereas others who had risen from the dead had resumed an ordinary life and eventually died, Jesus did not die but was raised bodily into heaven, we must consider Elijah, who was not divine but who was also taken up bodily into heaven (2 Kings 2:11–12), and the post-biblical story of the bodily assumption of Moses into heaven.[8] Can we then argue that although neither having been raised by God from the dead nor being taken up bodily into heaven indicates divinity, the combination of the two does? Perhaps, but perhaps not. The connection is by no means beyond question.

How then did the historical Jesus develop, in the mind of the church, into the exalted Christ of what was to become traditional Christian faith? The subject is large and complex. The orthodoxy of a century ago and earlier held that no development was necessary; the historical Jesus, as depicted in the fourth Gospel, was already consciously divine, and his message was a summons to be saved by believing in him: 'You are from below, I am from above; you are of this world, I am not of this world. I told you that you would die in your sins, for you will die in your sins unless you believe that I am he' (John 8:23–4). This Christ-centred message was for many centuries the foundation of Christian orthodoxy. Since I shall be diverging from that older tradition, on the basis of modern biblical scholarship, I shall cite acknowledged experts in this field.

First, the problem. Students of the New Testament agree that it is extremely unlikely that Jesus made for himself the claims that later Christian thought made for him. To quote Wolfhart Pannenberg:

In the quest for the historical Jesus, Jesus' self-consciousness was long regarded as the root of his claim to authority; at the same time the self-consciousness of Jesus was understood in a very special sense as the objective knowledge of his own place of honor and community with God. In the Gospels such a self-consciousness is attributed to Jesus. This is done the most clearly in the 'I' sayings of John's Gospel. The most important of this group of sayings with respect to content and the clearest in its absence of the usual figurative language is John 10:30; 'I and the Father are one.' . . . After D. F. Strauss and F. C. Bauer, John's Gospel could no longer be claimed uncritically as a historical source of authentic words of Jesus. Consequently, other concepts and titles that were more intimately connected with Jesus' relation to God came into the foreground of the question of Jesus' 'Messianic self-consciousness'. However, the transfer of these titles to Jesus . . . has been demonstrated with growing certainty by critical study of the Gospels to be the work of the post-Easter community. Today it must be taken as all but certain that the pre-Easter Jesus neither designated himself as Messiah (or Son of God) nor accepted such a confession to him from others.[9]

Again, Hans Küng accurately summarised contemporary research when he said that 'even more conservative exegetes conclude that Jesus himself did not assume any title implying messianic dignity: not "Messiah", nor "Son of David", nor "Son", nor "Son of God" '.[10] Yet the Christian tradition came, in a process that was finally completed in the fifth century, to see Jesus as the eternal pre-existent Son of God, Second Person of a divine Trinity, living a human life. How did this happen? There is no single comprehensive answer. In general it seems that the early Christians, seeking to understand and communicate the significance of their Lord, grasped at concepts and titles within their culture and that these developed under the pressures of preaching and controversy. Consider, for example, the 'Son of God' language. The title 'son of God' was common in the ancient world. Oscar Cullmann wrote:

> The origin of the 'son of God' concept lies in ancient oriental religions, in which above all kings were thought to be begotten of gods. . . . In the New Testament period also the Roman emperors were entitled *divi filius*.
>
> But in Hellenism the expression is by no means limited to rulers. Anyone believed to possess some kind of divine power was called 'son of God' by others, or gave himself the title. All

miracle workers were 'sons of God,' or, as one also said, θεῖοι ανδρες; Apollonius of Tyana, for instance, whose life is described by Philostratus in a form which is often reminiscent of our Gospels; or Alexander of Abonoteichus, whom we know through Lucian. Used in this sense, the title was quite common. In the New Testament period one could meet everywhere men who called themselves 'sons of God' because of their peculiar vocation or miraculous powers.[11]

And within Judaism:

> In the Old Testament we find this expression used in three ways: the whole people of Israel is called 'Son of God'; kings bear the title; persons with a special commission from God, such as angels, and perhaps also the Messiah, are so called.[12]

In particular the ancient Hebrew kings became sons of God by divine adoption – 'You are my son, today I have begotten you' (Psalms 2:7); 'I will be his father, and he shall be my son' (2 Samuel 7:14). Clearly, this was metaphorical (or mythological) language. And it is not in the least surprising that Jesus, as a spirit-filled prophet, a charismatic healer, perhaps as Messiah, believed to be of the royal line of David, should have been thought of and should have thought of himself as, in this familiar metaphorical sense, a son of God. What happened, as the gospel went out beyond the Hebraic millieu into the Greek-dominated intellectual world of the Roman Empire, was that the metaphorical son of God was transformed into the metaphysical God the Son, to support which status Jesus had eventually to be declared to have two complete natures, one human and the other divine. As Pannenberg said,

> At first the Son of God concept did not express a participation in the divine essence. . . . Only in Gentile Christianity was the divine Sonship understood physically as participation in the divine essence. In the Jewish, also in the Hellenistic-Jewish, sphere, in contrast, the expression 'Son of God' still retained the old meaning of adoption and of God's presence through his Spirit which was bestowed upon Jesus for a long time. In Mark's Gospel the basic concept of Jesus as the epiphany of the Son of God begins, but represents a conversion into the Hellenistic way of thinking.[13]

Purely Jewish concepts, such as the throne (*Merkabah*), may have provided stepping-stones toward deification. The basic motivation of the early Christian group was to absolutise the one whose impact had so profoundly changed their lives, the one for allegiance to whom they were being persecuted, and later, the one in whose name the Church had become co-ruler of the empire. It was indeed in this latter period of Christian political ascendancy that the christological and trinitarian doctrines received their fullest scope and became dogmatically solidified as basic articles of faith; the triumphant Lordship of the church was reflected in and validated by the absolute status and authority of the Church's Lord.

Notice the parallel in the absolutisation of the founder of the Buddhist tradition. Gautama was a human teacher, though one who had attained perfect enlightenment and who accordingly spoke with the authority of firsthand knowledge. After his death he was spoken about in the developing Buddhist literature in exalted terms, frequently as the Blessed One and the Exalted One. Stories of his many previous lives became popular, and legend attributed to him a supernatural conception, birth and childhood. In later literature he was called *devatideva* ('God beyond the gods', 'God of gods') and *Tathagata*. Of this last title T. R. V. Murti says, 'The Tathagata as the Perfect Man . . . is the ultimate essence of the universe. His position is analogous to that of God of Rational Theology (*ens realissimum*).'[14]

The later Mahayana doctrine of the Trikaya is comparable with the Johannine doctrine of the Logos and its development of the incarnation idea. As Jesus was the incarnation of the pre-existent Word/Son, who was of one substance with the Father in the eternal Trinity, so Gautama was the earthly manifestation of a heavenly Buddha, and all the Buddhas are one in the ultimate reality of the eternal Dharmakaya. Thus, the developed Buddhology of the Mahayana, some five centuries after the death of Gautama, parallels the developed Christology that reached its completion at the fifth-century Council of Chalcedon.

Although comparisons between past events and alternative possibilities are always fraught with danger – for they profess to know what can never be known – a strong case can be made for the functional value of the Nicene/Chalcedonian Christology to the church at that stage of its history. It could well be that its deification of Jesus helped the early Christian community to survive its period of intermittent persecutions and that subsequently, if the church

was to be spiritual, moral and cultural director of the Roman
Empire, and thus of Western civilisation, it needed the prestige of a
founder who was none other than God, in the person of the eternal
Son, who came down from heaven to institute a new human society
and who gave to its officers the fateful 'keys of the kingdom'. However, we are now living in a very different period of history.
Christianity has long since ceased to consist of a small persecuted
minority – except in certain marginal situations. It has also, since the
Enlightenment of the eighteenth century and the rise of modern
science, ceased to be the supreme spiritual and intellectual authority
within western civilisation. It is now seen as one religion among
others in a manifestly pluralistic world. In this very different era
the traditional absolutist Christology has become subject to serious
criticism, for it now hinders an unqualified acceptance of what is
today, within God's providence, the reality of our human situation.
In claiming that the life of Jesus was the one and only point in history
at which God has been fully self-revealed, it implicitly sets Christians apart from the rest of humanity. In declaring that God has lived
a human life on earth, so that here and here only men and women
were able to meet God face to face, to hear God speak and to respond
to God in faith, Christianity declares that these fortunate few and
their successors have a highly privileged access to the Creator. In the
words of Emil Brunner during the high tide of neoorthodoxy, 'Only
at one place, only in one event, has God revealed Himself truly and
completely – there, namely, where He became man.'[15] It follows that
the Christian religion and it alone was personally founded by God.
Must God not then wish all human beings to become part of the
church, the body of the redeemed, the saved community? Is not
Christianity thus singled out as the one religion that God has authorised, and hence uniquely superior to all others? Christian history is
indeed full of this assumption – and of its practical outworkings in
colonialism, anti-Semitism, the burning of 'heretics' and the western
political and cultural superiority complex.

    To a growing number of Christians this assumption no longer
seems self-evidently valid. On the contrary, many now see in it a
group of human beings consciously or unconsciously asserting their
own in-group superiority over the rest of the human race. Further,
such exclusivism is now recognised as religiously regressive, for it
turns the Lord of the whole universe into the tribal god of Europe
and the United States and their spiritual colonies. There is accordingly a move to go behind the projections of the Christian past and

to try to recover a more basic and authentic form of Christian aware-ness. This move is strongly supported by the results of the historical study of the scriptures and of Christian origins, which show that the Nicene/Chalcedonian Christology lacks the dominical authority that it had so long been assumed to have and that so long constituted the main reason for accepting it.

And so the first major point being made in the contemporary deconstruction of the traditional Christology is that it was not au-thorised by Jesus himself. And the second major point – also histor-ical – is that we can discern, at least in very general terms, when and how the deification of Jesus came about and can appreciate that in that religious-cultural milieu it provided a natural way of expressing the legitimate Lordship of Jesus over against the 'many gods' and many 'lords' (1 Corinthians 8:5) of the Roman Empire.

The third major point is conceptual rather than historical; the developed dogma – that Jesus of Nazareth was both God and man, that he was the Second Person of a divine Trinity living a human life, and that he had two natures, one human and the other divine – has never been shown to have any precise meaning. Every attempt made in the great period of the Christological debates to spell out the meaning of the God–man formula proved unacceptable because of incompatibility either with Jesus' Godhead or with his full human-ity. For example, one of the most constructive of the early theo-logians, Apollonius, at the end of the fourth century, holding with a tradition going back to Plato that a human person consists of spirit (*nous*), soul (*psyche*) and material body (*sarx*), suggested that in Jesus the eternal divine Logos functioned as his spirit, whereas his soul (or mind) and body were human. This theory made intelligible the claim that Jesus was both human and divine. But it had to be de-clared heretical for the convincing reason that without a human spirit Jesus would not have been genuinely human. All of the many other attempts to give specific meaning to the idea of divine incarna-tion likewise had to be rejected. No way has in fact been found of understanding the literal God-manhood of Christ. All that is left is a 'mystery' – in the sense, in this case, of an impressive form of words without any specifiable meaning. The definitive formulation of the mystery adopted by the Council of Chalcedon affirms of our Lord Jesus Christ that he is 'truly God and truly man', 'consubstantial with the Father in his divinity, consubstantial with us in his human-ity': 'We declare that in his divinity he was begotten of the Father before time, and in his humanity he was begotten in this last age of Mary the Virgin. . . . We declare that the one selfsame Christ, only-begotten Son and Lord, must be acknowledged in two natures without any comingling or change or division or separation; that the distinction between the two natures is in no way removed by their union but rather that the specific character of each nature is preserved and they are united in one person and one hypostasis.' But of course this does not explain anything. As has recently been said by a historian of that period, 'Chalcedon has proved less a solution than the classic definition of a problem which constantly demands further elucidation.'[16]

In recent times some theologians – but a decreasing number of those writing in Christology – have continued to affirm the two-natures Christology of Chalcedon; many others have been acutely conscious of its difficulties and have looked for new approaches. These new approaches move in two different directions. One, seeking to remain faithful to the God–man conception that Chalcedon tried to articulate, speaks of God's *kenosis* or self-emptying in Jesus. In this theory the historical Jesus did not have the divine qualities of omniscience, omnipotence, omnipresence, eternity, self-existence, creatorship or even – in the latest versions – the consciousness of his own deity. For the eternal Son, or Logos, divested himself of these attributes in becoming human. This concept of *kenosis* has appealed to a number of contemporary theologians. The difficulty, however, parallels the difficulty of the Chalcedonian formula, namely that no one has yet succeeded in spelling it out intelligibly. How can God cease to have God's attributes? What can it mean to say that the eternal, self-existent Creator of everything that exists other than God was for some 30 years not eternal, not self-existent, not the Creator of everything that exists other than God? Does it perhaps help to make a distinction and say that although God the Son laid aside his 'metaphysical' attributes in becoming a man, he retained his 'moral' attributes: goodness, love, wisdom, justice, mercy? At first this sounds more promising. But again questions arise. What does it mean to say that the human Jesus of Nazareth was infinitely loving, good, wise, just, merciful? Let us simplify matters by assuming that all these qualities are aspects of the one central attribute of love, *agape*. What then does it mean to say that Jesus embodied infinite love? Very great love, yes, but *infinite* love? How can a human being embody, incarnate, exhibit, love, or indeed any other quality, to an infinite degree? Surely we must say rather that the historical Jesus possessed, exhibited, incarnated, as much of the infinite divine love as could be expressed in and through an individual human life.

At this point, however, we have come close to the other possible new direction in Christology. If Jesus' life expressed, incarnated, embodied, very great but not infinite *agape* – and if, as we may surely add, all authentic *agape* is a finite reflection of the infinite divine *agape* – we have reached the position that in the life of Jesus the eternal and infinite *agape* of God was mirrored, expressed, lived out, made flesh, incarnated, within the limitation of a particular human life lived at a particular time and place. It is this approach that a number of recent Christologies have sought to make intelligible. Two representative examples are the paradox-of-grace Christology of Donald Baillie and the inspiration Christology of Geoffrey Lampe.

Baillie's book *God Was in Christ*[17] was described by Rudolf Bultmann as 'the most significant book of our time in the field of Christology'.[18] In this book Baillie proposed that we should understand incarnation in terms of what he called the paradox of grace. This is the paradoxical fact that when we do God's will it is true both that we are acting freely and responsibly and that God's supernatural grace is acting through us. The paradox is summed up in St Paul's words: 'it was not I, but the grace of God which is with me' (I Corinthians 15:10). As Baillie said, the essence of the paradox

> lies in the conviction which a Christian man possesses, that every good thing in him, every good thing he does, is somehow not wrought by himself but by God. This is a highly paradoxical conviction, for in ascribing all to God it does not abrogate human personality nor disclaim personal responsibility. Never is human action more truly and fully personal, never does the agent feel more perfectly free, that in those moments of which he can say as a Christian that whatever good was in them was not his but God's. (p. 114)

Baillie then used this paradox of grace as the clue to the yet greater paradox of the incarnation: that the life of Jesus was an authentically human life and yet that in and through that life God was at work on earth.

> What I wish to suggest is that this paradox of grace points the way more clearly and makes a better approach than anything else in

our experience to the mystery of the Incarnation itself; that this paradox in its fragmentary form in our own Christian lives is a reflection of that perfect union of God and man in the Incarnation on which our whole Christian life depends, and may therefore be our best clue to the understanding of it. In the New Testament we see the man in whom God was incarnate surpassing all other men in refusing to claim anything for Himself independently and ascribing all the goodness to God. We see Him also desiring to take up other men into His own close union with God, that they might be as He was. And if these men, entering in some small measure through Him into that union, experience the paradox of grace for themselves in fragmentary ways, and are constrained to say, 'It was not I but God', may not this be a clue to the understanding of that perfect life in which the paradox is complete and absolute, that life of Jesus which, being the perfection of humanity, is also, and even in a deeper and prior sense, the very life of God Himself? If the paradox is a reality in our poor imperfect lives at all, so far as there is any good in them, does not the same or a similar paradox, taken at the perfect and absolute pitch, appear as the mystery of the Incarnation?   (pp. 117–18)

In other words the union of divine and human action that occurs whenever God's grace works effectively in a man's or a woman's life was operating to a total extent in the life of Jesus.

Baillie's suggestion offers some degree of understanding of what it means to say that the life of Jesus was a divine as well as a human event. Of course, in making the idea of incarnation intelligible in this way Baillie had to discard the traditional Chalcedonian language of Jesus' having two natures, human and divine, and of his being in his divine nature of one substance with the Father. This language has long since lost its meaning for the modern mind, and the kind of reinterpretation that Baillie offered is an attempt to bring the doctrine of the incarnation to life in our time, giving it meaning as a truth that connects with our human experience and that is at least to some extent intelligible in contemporary terms. Although few people today use the ancient Hellenic concept of 'substance' or find the idea of a person with two natures other than grotesque, all Christians have some experience and appreciation of the reality of divine grace operating in human life. Further, they can connect this reality with the extraordinary events of the New Testament.

In an essentially similar way Geoffrey Lampe, in his book *God as Spirit*,[19] used as his clue or model for the understanding of Christ the activity within human life of the Holy Spirit, the Spirit of God, which is, he said, 'to be understood, not as referring to a divine hypostasis distinct from God the Father and God the Son, or Word, but as indicating God himself as active towards and in his human creation' (p. 11). The principal activity of God as Spirit in relation to humanity is inspiration; accordingly, the Christology that Lampe presents is 'a Christology of inspiration' (p. 96):

> the concept of the inspiration and indwelling of man by God as Spirit is particularly helpful in enabling us to speak of God's continuing creative relationship towards human persons and of his active presence in Jesus as the central and focal point within this relationship. (p. 34)

Again, 'The use of this concept enables us to say that God indwelt and motivated the human spirit of Jesus in such a way that in him, uniquely, the relationship for which man is intended by his Creator was fully realized' (p. 11). On this view the Spirit of God has always been active within the human spirit, inspiring men and women to open themselves freely to the divine presence and to respond in their lives to the divine purpose. Indeed 'God has always been incarnate in his human creatures, forming their spirits from within and revealing himself in and through them' (p. 23). We must accordingly 'speak of this continuum as a single creative and saving activity of God the Spirit towards, and within, the spirit of man, and of his presence in the person of Jesus as a particular moment within that continuous creativity' (p. 100).

This kind of Christology, centring on the activity of the gracious divine Spirit in and through the human Jesus, is in effect the kind that Pannenberg characterised as 'probably the oldest attempt to express God's presence in Jesus', namely 'by the concept of the Spirit'.[20] Before Jesus became deified in the Christian mind and the trinitarian doctrine developed to locate him within the Godhead, the earthly Lord was thought of as a man filled with the Spirit, beginning the fulfilment of the prophecy that in the last days the Spirit would be poured out again. As Pannenberg has said, 'Through the Spirit, Jesus is not only connected with particular figures of Jewish expectation, with the prophet of the last times, the Son of Man, the

Servant of God, or the Messiah, but directly with God himself.'[21] Jesus' life was a direct response of obedience to the divine Spirit. It was a special case of divine immanence.

In this inspiration Christology we have not only a return to the original understanding of Jesus in the very early church but an advance to an understanding of him that makes sense in our consciously religiously plural world as it moves toward the twenty-first century.

Both Baillie and Lampe assumed in traditional Christian fashion the 'uniqueness' of Christ; they held that in Jesus the paradox of grace was 'complete and absolute' (p. 117), or that the working of the Spirit in Jesus was 'a perfected form of inspiration' (p. 12).[22] They accordingly assumed the centrality and superiority of Christian within God's providence. However, their major new departure (of the full extent of which they may not have been conscious) is that the dogma of the unique superiority of Jesus and of the Christian religion no longer follows from the idea of divine incarnation as such. If, with Baillie and Lampe, we see in the life of Jesus a supreme instance of that fusion of divine grace/inspiration with creaturely freedom that occurs in all authentic human response and obedience to God, then uniqueness, supremacy, finality, can be established only by comparative historical evidence. We are no longer speaking of an intersection of the divine and the human that occurs, by definition, only in this unique case but of one that occurs in different ways and degrees in all human openness and response to the divine initiative. Thus the primacy of the Christian revelation no longer follows as a logical corollary from either Baillie's or Lampe's Christology. To see Jesus as exemplifying in his own special degree the paradox of grace, or the inspiration of God as Spirit, is to leave open the further question as to how this particular exemplification stands in relation to other exemplifications, such as those in some of the other great religious traditions. Baillie and Lampe believed that the grace/inspiration in the life of Jesus was unique because it was total and absolute. But the point to be stressed is that such a belief ceases, in the light of this type of Christology, to be a necessary inference from the concept of incarnation itself but must be a judgement based upon historical information. The main question that arises, for any Christian who is familiar with the modern scholarly study of the New Testament, is whether we have sufficient knowledge of the historical Jesus to make such absolute statements as that his *entire* life was a *perfect* exemplification of the paradox of grace or of divine inspiration.

The inevitable verdict is that we do not have, and indeed cannot have, the volume and quality of historical knowledge that would entitle us responsibly to affirm such absolute qualities. On this issue I quote the New Testament scholar Dennis Nineham. Speaking of such claims as 'It is in Jesus, and Jesus alone, that there is nothing of self to be seen, but solely the ultimate, unconditional love of God',[23] Nineham asks:

> Is it, however, possible to validate claims of the kind in question on the basis of historical evidence? To prove an historical negative, such as the sinlessness of Jesus, is notoriously difficult to the point of impossibility. . . . [T]he sort of claims for Jesus we are discussing could not be justified to the hilt by *any* historical records, however full or intimate or contemporary they might be, and even if their primary concern was with the quality and development of Jesus' inner life and character.[24]

In the kind of Christology exemplified in Baillie's and Lampe's work – the basic ground plan of which is also evident in the work both of the older liberal theologians, such as Harnack, and of such recent and contemporary Protestants as the New Testament scholar John Knox and the systematic theologians Maurice Wiles and Norman Pittenger, and also, though much more guardedly and obscurely, in the work of such Roman Catholic thinkers as Karl Rahner, Edward Schillebeeckx and Hans Küng – there is, I suggest, the basis for an authentically theocentric development of Christianity that is compatible with genuine religious pluralism.

An exposition of the kind of Christian theology of religions that is made possible by such an inspiration Christology lies beyond the scope of this essay, and I have in any case attempted that elsewhere.[25] My purpose here is to present the outline of a Christology or, more precisely, of an understanding of the religious significance of Jesus of Nazareth. I define a Christian as one who affirms one's religious identity within the continuing tradition that originated with Jesus. From its inception this tradition has included a range of Christologies, the kind of inspiration Christology to which I subscribe being one of the earliest, possibly the earliest. A return today, in our pluralistic age, to this simplest, least theoretical or speculative, and most directly experiential understanding of Jesus seems to me to offer great gains, both for the Christian community and for the wider human family.

Notes

1. The Q material, believed to reflect the earliest Christian tradition, is highly apocalyptic. See Howard Clark Kee, *Jesus in History: An Approach to the Study of the Gospels*, 2nd edn (New York: Harcourt Brace Jovanovich, 1977) ch. 3.
2. See Helmet Koester, *History and Literature of Early Christianity*, vol. 2 (Philadelphia: Fortress, 1982) p. 89.
3. See Norman Perrin, *The New Testament: An Introduction* (New York: Harcourt Brace Jovanovich, 1974) pp. 42–3.
4. John Downing, 'Jesus and Martyrdom', *Journal of Theological Studies*, n.s., vol. 14 (1963) p. 284.
5. *Zohar* 3:218a. Quoted by Daniel Chaman Matt, trans., *Zohar: The Book of Enlightenment* (New York: Paulist, 1983) p. 19. For a list of similar passages, see ibid., p. 196, n. 50.
6. See William James, *The Varieties of Religious Experience* (New York: New American Library, 1958) pp. 201–6.
7. Paramahansa Yogananda, *Autobiography of a Yogi*, 11th edn (Los Angeles: Self-Realization Fellowship, 1971).
8. R. H. Charles, *The Apocrypha and Pseudepigrapha of the Old Testament in English*, 2 vols (Oxford: Clarendon Press, 1913) vol. 2, pp. 408–9.
9. Wolfhart Pannenberg, *Jesus – God and Man*, trans. Lewis L. Wilkins and Duane A. Priebe (Philadelphia: Westminster, 1968) p. 327.
10. Hans Küng, *On Being a Christian*, trans. Edward Quinn (Garden City, N.Y.: Doubleday, 1976) p. 289.
11. Oscar Cullmann, *The Christology of the New Testament*, rev. edn, trans. Shirley C. Guthrie and Charles A. M. Hall (Philadelphia: Westminster, 1963) pp. 271–2.
12. Ibid., pp. 272–3.
13. Pannenberg, *Jesus – God and Man*, p. 117.
14. T. R. V. Murti, *The Central Philosophy of Buddhism*, 2nd edn (London: George Allen & Unwin, 1960) p. 40.
15. Emil Brunner, *The Scandal of Christianity: The Andrew C. Zenos Memorial Lectures* (Philadelphia: Westminster, 1951).
16. Frances M. Young, *From Nicaea to Chalcedon: A Guide to the Literature and its Background* (Philadelphia: Fortress, 1983) p. 178.
17. D. M. Baillie, *God Was in Christ: An Essay on Incarnation and Atonement* (New York: Charles Scribner's Sons, 1948). This book was written when Baillie was a professor of systematic theology at the University of St Andrews.
18. Quoted by John Baillie, in Donald M. Baillie, *The Theology of the Sacra-*

ments and Other Papers, with a Biographical Essay by John Baillie (New York: Charles Scribner's Sons, 1957) p. 35n.

19. G. W. H. Lampe, *God as Spirit: The Bampton Lectures, 1976* (Oxford: Clarendon Press, 1977). This book was written when Lampe was Regius Professor of Divinity at Cambridge University.
20. Pannenberg, *Jesus – God and Man*, p. 116.
21. Ibid.
22. Lampe's thought is more complex than this quotation alone suggests. He did hold 'that Christ is the centre and climax of the entire work of God throughout history' (*God as Spirit*, p. 104); but *Christ* does not mean the historical Jesus but 'the complex of Jesus and his interpreters, a complex to which many minds have contributed' (p. 27) – in fact, virtually the Christian tradition as a whole.
23. John A. T. Robinson, *Honest to God* (Philadelphia: Westminster, 1963) p. 74.
24. Dennis Nineham, 'Epilogue' in *The Myth of God Incarnate*, ed. John Hick (London: SCM Press; and Philadelphia: Westminster, 1977) p. 188.
25. John Hick, *God Has Many Names* (Philadelphia: Westminster, 1982); Hick, *God and the Universe of Faiths: Essays in the Philosophy of Religion* (London: Macmillan, 1973); Hick, *Problems of Religious Pluralism* (London: Macmillan; and New York: St Martin's Press, 1985).

4

The Logic of God Incarnate

The most important recent philosophical treatment of Christology is that of Thomas V. Morris in *The Logic of God Incarnate*,[1] defending the high-orthodox position that 'Jesus of Nazareth was one and the same person as God the Son, the Second Person of the divine Trinity' (p. 13) against the charge that the characteristics of deity and humanity are non-compossible in one person at one time, so that it is a contradiction to attribute both sets of qualities to the historical Jesus of Nazareth. I believe that Morris's defence, impressive though it is, does not succeed but on the contrary provides yet another illustration of the thesis that any attempt to spell out the idea of divine incarnation as a metaphysical theory, rather than as religious metaphor or myth, is bound to be unacceptable or, in traditional terminology, heretical.

Morris's defence is in two stages. The first (Chapter 3) seeks to establish the general logical possibility of a being having both ontologically higher and lower characteristics; and the second (Chapters 4–6) seeks to show more particularly that there is no reason why the distinctively divine and human characteristics should not coinhere in Jesus.

II

Morris first points to the distinction between individual-natures and kind-natures. An individual nature, that is, the nature or essence of a particular individual, consists of 'the whole set of properties individually necessary and jointly sufficient for being numerically identical with that individual' (p. 38). Thus the individual-nature of John Smith consists of the characteristics without which John Smith would not be the unique individual that he is. A kind-nature, on the other

hand, consists of 'a shareable set of properties individually necessary and collectively sufficient for membership of that kind' (p. 39).
Thus, for example, the nature or essence of the quadruped kind
consists of having four feet. An individual sheep shares in this. But
it also shares in other kind-natures, such as mammality. And so the
distinction between individual and kind natures produces at once a
sense in which the same individual may have, or share in, two
different natures, that is, different kind-natures. As Morris says, 'No
individual has more than one individual-nature. But of course it
does not follow from this that no individual has more than one kind-
nature. The conception of a kind-nature certainly does not in itself
rule out by definition the possibility that there be a single individual
with two such natures. And it is two natures of this sort which
orthodox doctrine ascribes to Christ' (pp. 40–1).

Morris now introduces the idea of an ontological hierarchy, and at
the same time distinguishes between having a kind-nature 'fully'
and having it 'merely':

> Consider a diamond. It has all the properties essential to being a
> physical object (mass, spatiotemporal location, etc.). So it is fully
> physical. Consider now an alligator. It has all the properties es-
> sential to being a physical object. It is *fully* physical. But, there is
> a sense in which we can say that it is not *merely* physical. It has
> properties of animation as well. It is an organic being. In contrast,
> the gem is merely physical as well as being fully physical. Now
> take the case of a man. An embodied human being, any one you
> choose, has mass, spatiotemporal location, and so forth. He is thus
> fully physical. But, again, there is a sense in which he is not
> merely a physical object, he has organic and animate properties as
> well. So let us say he is fully animate. But unlike the alligator he
> is not merely animate; he has rational, moral, aesthetic, and spir-
> itual qualities which mere organic entities lack. Let us say that he
> belongs to a higher ontological level by virtue of being human,
> and if, like you and me, he belongs to no ontological level higher
> than that of humanity, he is merely human as well as being fully
> human.   (pp. 65–6)

Morris next applies this to Christology:

> according to orthodox christology, Jesus was fully human with-
> out being merely human. He had all the properties constitutive of

human nature, but had higher properties . . . A philosophical anthropology developed from a distinctively Christian point of view will categorize all human properties logically incompatible with divine incarnation as, at most, essential to being *merely human*. And, again, the Chalcedonian claim is not that Jesus was merely human. It is rather that he was, and is, fully human in addition to being divine.   (p. 66)

At this point Morris considers certain human characteristics: 'possibly coming into existence, coming to be at some time, being a contingent creation, and being such as to possibly cease to exist' (p. 67). These are selected as properties which, it would seem, cannot be acquired by God, even with the aid of what Morris calls the manoeuvre of kenosis or self-emptying (p. 61). They appear on the contrary to be essential human properties which are incompatible with the individual who has them being God. However, Morris denies this, claiming that although they are 'common human properties' they are not 'essential to being human. They, or some of them, may be essential to being *merely* human, but they can be held, in all epistemic and metaphysical propriety, not to be essential to being *fully* human, so exemplifying the kind-essence of humanity' (p. 67). There is thus in principle no reason why there should not be fully human beings who are eternal, uncreated and non-contingent. It is true that they would not be *merely* human. They would rather be human plus – more than merely human without ceasing to be fully human, as a crocodile is more than merely physical without ceasing to be fully physical.

This completes the first phase of Morris's argument. If it is sound it opens up the possibility of a Chalcedonian Christology, although still requiring essential work to be done in the second phase. But before turning to that let us examine what has already been said.

Although recent discussions of the concept of individual identity and of essences have shown how complex these notions are, I see no reason for our present purposes to question the distinction between individual-natures and kind-natures. Nor is there any difficulty about the fact that an individual can (and nearly always does) instantiate more than one generic characteristic. But, equally obviously, not *all* kind-natures are capable of being instantiated in the same individual at the same time. Squareness and roundness, for example, cannot both characterise the same plane figure. And the Christological puzzle is whether the distinctively human and divine natures are such that they could be co-instantiated in the person of Jesus of Nazareth.

Morris's linked distinctions between common or 'merely *x*' properties, and essential or 'fully *x*' properties, and his notion of the instantiation in the same individual of kind-natures on different levels, are intended to open a door in this direction. At each step, as we ascend the ontological ladder from inanimate matter to matter endowed with life, and then to life endowed with intellectual and spiritual qualities, the essential (or 'fully *x*') characteristics of the lower type are carried forward onto the next higher level. If we extrapolate further to the divine level we come to a being who has all the essential (that is, 'fully *x*') qualities of existence at the lower levels – being physical, animate and intelligent and so on – plus the essential qualities of deity; and this is Jesus Christ. The point of this progression is that since the idea makes sense of a higher-level being having some of the essential properties of beings on the lower levels, so *ipso facto* does the idea of a higher-level being becoming incarnate as a lower-level being. I say '*ipso facto*' because no connecting argument is offered. Morris must be assuming that if it is coherent to speak of progressively higher beings having lower characteristics, it must automatically be coherent to speak of progressively lower beings having higher characteristics – for this is the principle presupposed by the idea of God coming to have all essential ('fully *x*') human characteristics.

But does the possibility of a higher-level being also having lower-level characteristics really entail the contrary possibility of a lower-level being also exhibiting higher-level characteristics? A higher-level entity can indeed share characteristics with a lower-level entity without thereby losing its higher-level status – thus a living crocodile can (and indeed must) also be a physical object. And having the human characteristics of intelligence and spirituality does not exclude also having the lower characteristics of organic life and materiality. But does it follow that it is possible for the crocodile, considered now as a lower-level being, to take on the additional higher-level characteristics of humanity without ceasing to be a crocodile? Let us try the appropriate thought experiment. Let us imagine a human soul or spirit – with intelligence and aesthetic, moral and spiritual qualities – becoming incarnate as Morris's crocodile. (We have to specify a human soul, rather than body, because the idea of incarnation seems to presuppose this.) We are now imagining a man-crocodile, a humanly intelligent and spiritual creature of the species *crocodilidae*. Such an animal, it might be said, would have all the essential ('fully *x*') but not all the common ('merely *x*') character-istics of a crocodile. Of course, given the existing laws of nature such a thing is empirically, or causally, impossible. It would require the crocodile to have a brain of the size and complexity found only at the human level of evolution; and since the brain is integral to the nervous system as a whole, and this in turn to the entire bodily structure and circulatory and metabolic functioning, it would pre-sumably not be possible for a crocodile body to sustain a distinc-tively human brain. And in the case of an incarnation of God as a human being there would be analogous contrary-to-natural-law dif-ficulties. How could a finite human brain receive, process and retain the infinitely extensive information possessed by omniscience? How could a finite human physique be able to exert infinite power? These seem to be legitimate questions. But more basically, it has (as Morris notes) been very naturally and persuasively held that in the case of biological kinds, such as crocodiles and humans, it is an essential characteristic to have a certain type of genetic origin. From this point of view human beings are, by definition, the offspring of human beings, part of the ongoing stream of life that we describe as human. This is itself part of the larger stream of life that has evolved over hundreds of millions of years, proliferating through gradual changes into its innumerable species. To be human is thus to be both part of the total evolutionary process of life on this earth, and within this of the particular sub-strand known as *homo sapiens sapiens*. Clearly, if this is a basic requirement for being human it presents difficulties for the traditional belief that Jesus had a human mother but no human father; for he would then have carried only half of the full human genetic complement. However, given a strong enough motive, or presupposition, namely a commitment to the Chalcedonian Christology, it is possible to waive such problems by ruling both that the human physical structure belongs to the common rather than the essential set of human characteristics, and also that genetic origin is not essential to natural kind identity, at least in the case of human-ity. This latter is what Morris does; he says that

> a Christian committed to the orthodox doctrine of the incarnation will need to hold that there are no stable generalization about natural origins for the kind-nature of humanity. Only if this is true will there be no difficulty on this count with the orthodox

claim that Jesus was fully human even though he had no human paternity, and moreover, in the strictest sense never came into existence at all. (p. 69)

It is possible to make such rulings; although of course they are arbitrary and such that others are under no obligation to accept them. However, Morris goes on to make what may well be the mistake, from his point of view, of supporting his ruling with arguments. One is that if, in order to be human, one has to have human parents, then

> Suppose we hold, for simplicity's sake, that God directly produced Adam *ex nihilo* along with an entire universe to boot. Then . . . Adam was not a human being or the sort of human precursor allowed by standard evolutionary theory, since he did not have the requisite sort of natural origin. But then what would that make us, as his descendants? (p. 68)

Such an appeal would link the doctrine of the incarnation with a fundamentalist use of the scriptures in a way which many modern-minded Chalcedonians would not welcome. However, it is true that *if* humanity began with the special creation of a fully-formed Adam and Eve we should have to amend the definition of humanity to 'being Adam and Eve or a descendant of Adam and Eve'. On the other hand, if there was no prehistoric Adam, created by God *ex nihilo*, no such amendment is needed. But in neither case is the question of Jesus' humanity affected. Morris's other supporting argument seems to me no stronger. He says

> suppose that in some laboratory of the future, scientists were to accomplish the astounding task of concocting *from scratch* (from basic chemicals, etc.) a being with the constitution, organs, appearance, mannerisms, and cognitive abilities of a normal human adult male. Suppose he acts like a human, marries a woman, fathers a child, takes a job, and cultivates many close and satisfying friendships. Would this creature *be* human or not? Intuitions may possibly vary on this, but I think it most reasonable to say yes. And if so, this provides the sort of metaphysical view which is needed to support not only a doctrine of *creatio ex nihilo*, but an orthodox doctrine of the Incarnation. (p. 69)

But if an orthodox Christology requires Morris's confessedly optional intuition at this point, is it not thereby weakened rather than strengthened? Certainly, to test this intuition in its most sensitive form, if we learned that Jesus himself was such a fabricated creature, made in a laboratory, would we not feel that this was a setback rather than a support to the doctrine that he was genuinely human? For who knows what special powers – such as a capacity to resist temptations – might have been programmed into him?

However, let us for the sake of the argument grant Morris the right to make such rulings. We shall then hold that, in the case of the human being incarnate as a crocodile, its bodily structure is among the common rather than the essential properties of a crocodile. There might accordingly be a crocodile that is differently internally structured so as to be able to include a human-type brain. And it is true that in a wide enough universe of discourse what one counts as essential to being a crocodile is to some extent flexible. We can go into the realms of the imagination and encounter, in fairy stories and myths, intelligent talking animals – even sometimes very wise and good ones. But our concern here is to test the idea of divine incarnation as a human being within ordinary earthly history. And within ordinary earthly history such a contrary-to-natural-law phenomenon as a man-crocodile, with powers of intelligence, speech, moral judgement and spiritual awareness, would be so utterly astonishing as to shake accepted biology to its foundations. The presence of such a marvel would be, to say the least, sensational. In other words, the incarnation of a higher kind as a lower kind would inevitably break the ordinary mould of the lower kind.

Coming, then, to the case with which we are directly concerned, the question is whether, or in what sense, the second person of the Trinity could become a human being without breaking the human mould. Would not a man endowed with omnipotent and omniscient powers and all other essential divine qualities be someone whom no one could mistake for an ordinary or merely human being? And yet Jesus of Nazareth was perceived by his contemporaries as precisely that. He was not, indeed, regarded as ordinary in the sense of being average or unremarkable. In that sense he was a most extraordinary human being. He was not, however, seen by his disciples (let alone by others) as God, but rather as 'Jesus of Nazareth, a man approved of God among you by miracles and wonders and signs, which God did by him in the midst of you' (Acts 2:22). He was thus regarded as a very special and significant human being, perhaps even uniquely significant as the last prophet before the coming of the kingdom, but still as a human being and not as God. And so Morris's argument for the general possibility of a higher-level being becoming incarnate as a lower-level being does not tend to render plausible the belief that Jesus was God incarnate, but on the contrary tells against it. For such an incarnation would be a manifest prodigy, a walking miracle; and the historical evidence indicates that Jesus was not this.

Can we perhaps, however, save matters by distinguishing between Jesus *having* omnipotence, omniscience and so on, and his both having *and exercising* these powers? If he had exercised them, he would indeed have been a manifest prodigy, a walking miracle; but if he possessed them without ever exercising them, surely no one would have noticed any difference in these respects between himself and ordinary human beings. No doubt the possession of such unused powers is possible. But nevertheless we have to ask whether someone who has unlimited power, but consciously refrains from using it, can be said fully to share our human nature and condition. Would not the awareness of one's divinity and one's omnipotence and omniscience impart a certain play-acting character to one's dealings, for example, with opponents? For whereas an ordinary man or woman is genuinely vulnerable to superior force, an omnipotent Jesus would only be able to be crucified if he permitted it. Again, a consciously divine being, aware that he is uncreated and indestructible, would not fear death as ordinary human beings do. The kind of picture that emerges approaches the Fourth Gospel icon of a Christ who is physically but not spiritually and psychologically human, a God-man walking the earth in conscious divinity.

Morris, with his admirable clear-sightedness, is conscious of this danger lurking within his line of thought. He accordingly concludes this phase of his discussion with an acknowledgement that thus far the argument seems to present us with an unacceptable picture:

> On the resultant picture, will it not follow that Jesus was omniscient, omnipotent, necessarily existent, and all the rest, as well as being an itinerant Jewish preacher? And is not this outlandish to the greatest possible degree? . . . How could such a view possibly be squared with the biblical portrait of Jesus as a limited man among men? How could such a being possibly be said to have shared our human *condition*? (p. 70)

And so we have to face – as Morris proceeds to do in the second phase of his argument – the question of the compossibility of divine and human attributes in the same individual. More specifically, are such distinctively divine qualities as eternal self-existence, being the creator of everything other than God, omniscience, omnipotence, and omnipresence, compatible with being a human being? It will not at this point do to say that the Christian knows by observation – namely, observation of Jesus Christ – that they are compatible. For when we look at Jesus through our best historical lenses we do not see these divine attributes. To all appearances he was a remarkable man. And the acceptability of the doctrine, developed by later generations, that this remarkable man was the second person of a divine Trinity incarnate, depends in part upon the compatibility of the divine and human attributes. If any pair of these is incompatible then the doctrine, in its strong Chalcedonian form, must be a human mistake. And so we now have to look directly at this issue of compatibility.

III

The question, then, is whether it makes coherent sense to hold that Jesus Christ had both all essential divine and all essential human attributes, so as to be both fully God and fully man. On the face of it, this does not make sense. For how could anyone have both divine omniscience and human ignorance, divine omnipotence and human weakness, divine goodness and human temptability, divine omnipresence and a finite human body? Clearly if it is to be reasonable to believe that Jesus was a God-man having all these pairs of apparently incompatible attributes, some rather sophisticated theory will be required.

The theory most readily at hand in the present state of Christological discussion is kenoticism, the suggestion that in becoming incarnate God the Son temporarily divested himself of such divine attributes as are incompatible with being genuinely human. Theories of this kind were developed in the latter part of the nineteenth and the earlier part of the twentieth centuries and have recently been revived by several contemporary theologians. Morris has an interesting discussion of the kenotic idea, showing how it can be formulated in more as well as in less plausible ways. However, in the end he concludes that even the most plausible form is shipwrecked on the rock of divine immutability, this being understood by him in a novel way, which has much to commend it, as 'a property, or modality, of the exemplifications of all those attributes constitutive of deity, kind-essential for divinity. In brief, any individual who has a constitutive attribute of deity can never have begun to have it, and can never cease to have it. He has it, rather, immutably' (p. 97). Given this conception of immutability, kenoticism is excluded. Morris's precise conclusion is not that the kenotic possibility is entirely ruled out, but that it is very hard to sustain and that such a difficult manoeuvre is rendered unnecessary by the availability of a more satisfactory theory. I shall therefore not follow Morris through the various stages of his clarification and eventual rejection of kenoticism, but move directly to his own preferred alternative, which is the two-minds view of Christ.

This is the view that

in the case of God Incarnate, we must recognize something like two distinct ranges of consciousness. There is first what we can call the eternal mind of God the Son with its distinctively divine consciousness, whatever that might be like, encompassing the full scope of omniscience. And in addition there is a distinctly earthly consciousness that came into existence and grew and developed as the boy Jesus grew and developed. It drew its visual imagery from what the eyes of Jesus saw, and its concepts from the language he learned. The earthly range of consciousness, and self-consciousness, was thoroughly human, Jewish, and first-century Palestinian in nature. We can view the two ranges of consciousness (and, analogously, the two noetic structures encompassing them) as follows: The divine mind of God the Son contained, but was not contained by, his earthly mind, or range of consciousness. That is to say, there was what can be called an asymmetric accessing relation between the two minds. Think, for example, of two computer programs or informational systems, one containing but not contained by the other. The divine mind had full and direct access to the earthly human experience resulting from the Incarnation, but the earthly consciousness did not have such a full and direct access to the content of the overarching omniscience proper to the Logos, but only such access, on occasion, as the divine mind

allowed it to have. There thus was a metaphysical and personal
depth to the man Jesus lacking in the case of every individual who
is merely human.   (pp. 102–3)

In further explication of the idea of two minds, one enclosed
within the other, Morris offers at this point three further analogies.
One is that of a dreamer, participating in the stream of dream events
and yet aware at some overarching level that it is all a dream. Here
the 'overarching' consciousness corresponds to the divine and the
dream material to the human mind. A second analogy is that of the
'levels' of consciousness referred to in standard psychological theory:
'The postulated unconscious, or subconscious, mind would stand in
an asymmetric accessing relation to the conscious mind somewhat
parallel to that postulated between the divine consciousness and the
earthly consciousness of God Incarnate' (p. 105). And a third is that
of the two consciousness in a case of 'multiple personality':

> in some cases of multiple personality, there exists one personality
> with apparently full and direct knowledge of the experiences had,
> information gathered, and actions initiated by one or more other
> personalities, a sort of knowledge which is not had by any other
> personality concerning it. In other words, there seem to exist
> asymmetric accessing relations in such cases, interestingly though
> of course not perfectly parallel to the sort of relation claimed by
> the two-minds view to hold between the divine and human minds
> of Christ.   (p. 106)

What all these analogies have in common is that they are concerned with the *cognitive* relationship between the two minds, divine
and human. These are seen as repositories of information, as noetic
structures or belief-systems; and the theory is concerned with the
way in which and the extent to which each mind is conscious of the
contents of the other. But such a view of mental life is abstract and
one-dimensional. (As such, it is consonant with Morris's general
treatment of a religion as consisting essentially in a set of beliefs – a
western post-Enlightenment view which has more recently come
under serious criticism.)[2] For a living consciousness is not only a
noetic structure but a dynamic activity, processing information received through the senses, continuously exercising a power of choice
and decision, adopting attitudes, exerting itself volitionally; and it
perceives the world with varying affective tones, and feels emotions,

which are sometimes powerful and determining. This difference between Morris's one-dimensional conception of the mind and the multi-dimensional reality is important. I shall argue that, on the one hand, a purely noetic account of the relation between the divine and human minds cannot amount to a religiously significant sense of 'incarnation', but that on the other hand if we expand it to include volition and emotion, Morris's two-minds Christology becomes unacceptable for another reason – to which I shall come presently.

Let us proceed in stages. Consider first the case of *complete* asymmetry of access. Here there are two streams of consciousness. A and B, one including the other in the sense that A is aware of everything occurring in the B stream of consciousness while B is unaware of the contents of the A consciousness. Thus God the Son could know all that was going on in the consciousness, and also in the unconscious mind, of Jesus whilst Jesus was entirely unaware that the Son was thus monitoring him, or even unaware of the Son's existence.

Now this – as Morris himself notes (pp. 158–9) – is something that the doctrine of divine omniscience (without having to specify the Son as the omniscient mind) already entails. For an omniscient God must be aware of the contents of every stream of human consciousness. But such asymmetrical cognitive accessing would not constitute divine incarnation in any religiously significant sense. For if incarnation consists in God's full one-way awareness of a human consciousness, God is incarnate, and incarnate to an equal extent, in everyone. But this is not a morally acceptable idea. For God must be as fully aware of what is going on in the most wicked and depraved as in the most holy of human mentalities and therefore, on the view we are considering, equally incarnate in them all. Thus the notion of a unique divine incarnation in Jesus could not be sustained by such exclusively one-way cognitive accessing alone. I shall return presently to Morris's response to this point. But first we should note that his theory does not in fact postulate such an exclusively one-way access between the two minds. It is, for him, at least partly and spasmodically two-way. He says:

> The divine mind had full and direct access to the earthly, human experience resulting from the Incarnation, but the earthly consciousness did not have such full and direct access to the content of the overarching omniscience proper to the Logos, but only such access, on occasion, as the divine mind allowed it to have. There

was thus a metaphysical and personal depth to the man Jesus
lacking in the case of every individual who is merely human.
(p. 103)

The nature of the limited access of the human to the divine mind
postulated here needs to be specified more fully. I can see two rather
different ways of spelling it out. One involves the possibility of
mutual relationship and interaction between the two minds, divine
and human. That is to say, at certain times and to a certain degree the
human mind of Jesus became conscious of being an object of awareness of the vaster encompassing consciousness of God the Son. He
became conscious of being in a state of mutual I–Thou awareness
with the second person of the Trinity. In these moments he was
conscious of being in the presence of God the Son and at the same
time aware that God the Son was conscious of him. Such a picture
would seem to fit the New Testament indication of Jesus' consciousness – except of course that the encompassing divine presence of
which he was so vividly aware was not the second person of a
Trinity but simply God, known as *Abba*, father. But, further, Jesus'
relationship to God, as reflected in the synoptic gospels, involved
not only a cognitive but also a conative or volitional aspect. Not only
was he (at least during the period of his public ministry, and possibly earlier as well) overwhelmingly conscious of the reality and
presence of God, but he was in an active relationship in which he
prayed to God, heard God's voice, and responded in his action to
God's will for him. His life was continuously guided by his sense of
God's purposes for human life on earth.

Now this kind of interaction, in which a person is overwhelmingly conscious of God's presence, speaks to God, hears God's voice
(whether inwardly or outwardly), is aware of God's will, is one in
which many men and women have participated in varying degrees.
Outstanding examples include Moses, Jeremiah, the Isaiahs,
Muhammad, Guru Nanak, St Francis, Kabir, Rumi, and many others
down to our own day. This kind of openness and responsiveness of
the human to the divine is the basis for the understanding of Jesus'
relationship to God proposed by the grace or inspiration christologies
of such recent theologians as Donald Baillie and Geoffrey Lampe.
According to them Jesus was conscious of the environing divine
presence and responsive to God's will to such an extent that God's
love could be said (in a natural metaphor) to be incarnated on earth
in his words and deeds. However, this is not the kind of spelling out

of the two-minds idea that Morris intends; for he wants it to carry the same weight as the Chalcedonian two-natures Christology.

Another possible way of spelling out a limited access of the human to the divine mind is in terms, not of occasional consciousness–consciousness interaction, but of occasional consciousness–consciousness unity. That is to say, from time to time, and perhaps in varying degrees, the human mind of Jesus became conscious of its identity with the divine mind of God the Son. The picture here is of the smaller human consciousness of Jesus existing within the larger divine mind of the Logos, which is aware of everything happening in the human consciousness whilst the latter is normally unaware that it is the object of this superior consciousness. But from time to time the divine mind enables the human mind to be conscious of this. In these moments Jesus was aware that he was God the Son incarnate. He was consciously divine. Such a picture is consonant with the interpretation of Jesus offered in the Fourth Gospel – except that there Jesus is presented as believing that the divine presence with whom he was in unity was God the Father: 'I and my father are one' (John 10:30), 'he that hath seen me hath seen the father' (John 14:9).

This option assimilates Jesus' God-consciousness to that reported in unitive mysticism. Normally, in theistic mysticism, a final distinction is preserved between the human consciousness of the mystic and the divine Being. Occasionally, however, such mystics – Jewish, Christian and Muslim – have at least seemed to transcend this distinction. But it is in Hindu advaitic thought that the identity of the purified human consciousness with the divine Reality is most explicitly taught. According to this teaching, when we transcend egoity we discover in a moment of salvific illumination that we are one with the infinite and eternal Brahman: *Tat tvam asi*. Several Hindu philosophers[3] have pointed out the analogy between the claim of the Fourth Gospel Christ to unity with the Father and this ancient Vedantic idea that only our false individual egohood conceals from us our own identity with the absolute reality of Brahman.

The limitation of such an interpretation of the two-minds idea is that it fits the divine Christ of the Fourth Gospel much better than the human Jesus of the Synoptics. One can rule, by stipulative definition, that a man who is consciously God is still to be counted as fully human. But such a one would nevertheless not be one of us, sharing our common human condition. Even if he was only aware on special occasions of his identity as God the Son, he would at other times presumably remember and live in terms of these all-important moments. Thus even if one were to grant the possibility of God becoming incarnate, on the Fourth Gospel model, as a physically human being who is at least sometimes conscious of being divine, eternal, omnipotent and omniscient, this would not be the Jesus whom historical research has glimpsed through the synoptic gospels.

Let us now return to Morris's response to the point that a one-way cognitive access account of incarnation amounts to no more than the fact of God's omniscient awareness, not only of Jesus' consciousness but of all human consciousness. Morris says:

> Consider a case of telepathy. Person A has telepathic access to the mind of person B. Suppose if you like that A telepathically has complete access to the mind of B. Does it follow that B's thoughts are A's thoughts, that B's mental states are A's mental states? Of course not. From B's believing that it is raining outside and A's having perfect telepathic access to the mind of B, it does not follow that A believes it is raining outside, for A can have independent reason to think that B is wrong. The accessing relation itself does not alone constitute ownership. So from God's standing in a perfect accessing relation to all our minds it does not follow that all our minds *are* his mind or that all our thoughts are his thoughts. And so of course it does not follow that each of us is God Incarnate.   (p. 159)

One might well think from this passage that the divine mind's access to the human mind is only to count as incarnation if there is also an identity of ownership. However, Morris goes on to point out that, in view of our historical picture of Jesus, identity of ownership would not in fact be an asset. For 'most theologians who take seriously the real humanity of Jesus, however orthodox they might be, will want to allow . . . the possibility of the earthly mind of Jesus containing some false beliefs, beliefs, for example, concerning the shape of the earth, or the nature of the relative movement of the sun and the earth, among other things' (pp. 159–60). Have we then now, with this timely correction, arrived at last at an adequate concept of incarnation, namely as God the Son's complete accessing of the contents of Jesus' earthly mind, but being aware in so doing that some of Jesus' beliefs are mistaken? No; for this model will apply not only to Jesus but equally to all other human minds. And so Morris at this stage accepts that his original account of incarnation as consisting in 'an asymmetric accessing relation between the two minds' (p. 103) is not sufficient. Some additional factor is required. The additional factor, says Morris, is a unity of 'causal and cognitive powers'. In the case of two human beings, A and B, A having telepathic access to B's mind, the state of B's mind at a given time is a result (at least in part) of B's exercise of her own causal powers, whilst A's accessing of her mind is an exercise of his own causal powers. Two numerically distinct sets of causal powers are thus involved. But the case of Jesus was different and unique:

> He was not a being endowed with a set of personal cognitive and causal powers distinct from the cognitive and causal powers of God the Son. For Jesus was the same person as God the Son. Thus, the personal cognitive and causal powers operative in the case of Jesus' earthly mind were just none other than the cognitive and causal powers of God the Son. (pp. 161–2)

These 'cognitive and causal powers' are clearly now crucial to Morris's final theory. What are they? Presumably our cognitive power is our capacity to cognise, whilst our causal power is our capacity to initiate changes, in other words our will. That causal power, in the case of a mind, is volitional, is evident in Morris's text from the fact that he speaks of a person attaining to a given mental state 'as the result of the exercise of her own cognitive and causal powers' (p. 161). For, clearly, it is by the exercise of her will, thereby making choices, that she comes at that particular time to be in this particular mental state rather than some other.

Let us then consider the implications of the idea that the volitional activity in virtue of which the human mind of Jesus was at each moment in the state in which it was, was the volitional activity of God the Son. Morris, with his exclusive attention to the cognitive relation between the two minds, only applies this principle to their belief-systems or noetic structures. He says that the results of the operation of the cognitive and causal powers of God the Son 'through the human body, under the constraints proper to the conditions of a fully human existence, were just such as to give rise to a human mind, an earthly noetic structure distinct from the properly divine noetic structure involved with the unconstrained exercise of divine powers' (p. 162). But to take account only of noetic structures is to operate with the inadequately one-dimensional, purely intellectual, view of the mind that we noted earlier. In reality the will operates not only in forming beliefs but also in the person's agency in the world in relation to other people. And here a unitary will, which is the will of God the Son, would mean that when Jesus decided to say or do anything, God the Son was so deciding; and likewise when Jesus resisted temptation the will that resisted was that of God the Son. Morris is, in other words, at this point embracing the view that Jesus had no human will and that the will operative in his life was the divine will of God the Son.

However, throughout his book Morris is very good at recognising difficulties and trying to meet them. And he is aware that the idea that the will whereby Jesus made his choices from moment to moment was the will of God the Son was condemned as the monothelite heresy by the sixth Ecumenical Council, meeting at Constantinople in 680–1. The Council was concerned to preserve Jesus' full humanity, including his human will, and appealed to such texts as 'I seek not mine own will, but the will of the Father which hath sent me' (John 5:30) and 'Father, all things are possible unto thee; take away this cup from me; nevertheless, not what I will but what thou wilt' (Mark 14:36). And so in another passage Morris affirms a free human will of Jesus in addition to the divine will of the Second Person of the Trinity. The relationship between the two wills, he suggests, was that Jesus was humanly free, including being free to sin, but that if he had in fact tried to sin the divine will would have intervened to stop him. Morris asks, 'Was [Jesus'] choosing rightly a free act of his? Well, it must be admitted from the outset that he could not have chosen otherwise. His divine nature would have prevented it' (p. 150). He was thus both free and yet necessarily good. Morris helps us understand this by the imaginary case of someone, Jones, who is placed in a room and told not to leave it for two hours. Unknown to him, electrodes have been implanted in his brain which would be activated by an initial inner intention to will to leave, switching his brain to the different course of deciding to stay. Now, if in fact he never did begin to decide to leave, but remained in the room throughout entirely of his own free volition, it would then be true both that he freely obeyed the order to stay and also that it was in fact impossible for him to do otherwise. Morris says:

> Perhaps we can understand the temptations of Jesus in a some-
> what parallel way. Perhaps his divine property of being necessar-
> ily good, although it rendered impossible his having decided or

having done otherwise than he did with respect to resisting temptation, as a matter of fact played no causal role in his doing as he
did. Like Jones's unactivated electrodes, it did not act to force on
him what he did. He did it freely. As Jones was unaware of the
electrodes. . . . Jesus was unaware in his earthly consciousness
that he was necessarily good, unable to sin. Within the delibera-
tion of that earthly mind, he freely, of his own accord, decided not
to succumb to temptation. It was a choice for which, as a matter of
fact, he was fully responsible. By making such claims, I think, the
orthodox theologian avoids altogether the lurking problem of
montheletism.   (pp. 152–3)

But this proposal fails when we realise that it entails that we do
not, and cannot, know whether Jesus ever had the beginning of an
intention to sin that activated a divine overruling that prevented him
from proceeding. So far as human observation can tell, he may, on
Morris's theory, have sinned in his free human dispositions without
this ever being allowed to express itself in overt action. For all that
we can know, the human mind of Jesus may often have begun to sin,
but was always prevented by the enveloping divine mind from
carrying out those initial bad intentions. In fact, of course, we do not
even know, as historians, that Jesus never overtly sinned; for we lack
a complete record of every moment of his life. But even on the
traditional dogma that he never performed a sinful action, we cannot, within Morris's scenario, know whether this was because he
never even began to intend a sinful act, or because he did so intend
(perhaps many times) but the intention was always overruled by his
divine nature.

I suggest, then, that Morris's proposed picture does not amount to
divine incarnation in the Chalcedonian sense that he is trying to
make intelligible and believable. What we now have is a human
being, Jesus, with his own human mind and will. God the Son has
full cognitive access to Jesus' mind at all times; and if he makes a
wrong decision God the Son will prevent him from carrying it out.
That is to say, Jesus is God incarnate, not in the sense that the
personal will that was encountered by all who met Jesus was the will
of God the Son operating on earth, but in the sense that God singled
Jesus out for special treatment – namely by not allowing him to go
wrong. It follows that if God, in addition to being omnisciently
aware of the contents of someone else's mind, were also to prevent
her from making any wrong choices, that person would be another

instance of God incarnate. But has not the heart of the Chalcedonian conception now been missed out – namely the unique personal presence of God in a human life, so that those who talked with Jesus were talking with God the Son? The nearest that Morris's theory comes to this is that those who talked with Jesus were talking to a man whom God the Son was invisibly monitoring, ready to control him if he went astray.

I therefore conclude that Morris, in his two-minds hypothesis, has supplied yet another illustration of the thesis that any intelligible spelling out of the idea of divine incarnation in Jesus of Nazareth will prove to be religiously unacceptable. For the incarnational idea is essentially metaphorical. It is a natural metaphor to speak, for example, of Joan of Arc as incarnating the spirit of France or of George Washington as incarnating the will of the American people to achieve independence. And the same natural metaphor is in order when we say that Jesus was so open and obedient to God that the divine love was incarnated in his words and actions. But the Chalcedonian-type Christologies, to which Morris's intends to belong, make the mistake of converting an appropriate and powerful metaphor into an in appropriate and religiously unacceptable philosophical theory. When all literal interpretations of the God-man formula are rejected as heretical a Chalcedonian theologian can only fall back on the idea of a sacred mystery which we should not expect to be able to understand – forgetting however that the 'sacred mystery' is in reality a humanly devised form of words which has no specifiable non-metaphorical meaning!

Notes

1. Thomas Morris, *The Logic of God Incarnate* (Ithaca, N.Y.: Cornell University Press, 1986).
2. See, for example, Wilfred Cantwell Smith, *The Meaning and End of Religion* (1962; San Francisco, Cal.: Harper & Row; and London: SPCK, 1978).
3. For example, Ramchandra Gandhi, *I am Thou* (Poona: Indian Philosophical Quarterly Publications, 1984) p. 44.

5

The Non-absoluteness of Christianity

I

Ernst Troeltsch's famous book *The Absoluteness of Christianity* (1901) focused on what has always been from the point of view of the Christian church the central issue in its relationship to other streams of religious life. Until fairly recently it was a virtually universal Christian assumption, an implicit dogma with almost credal status, that Christ/the Christian gospel/Christianity is 'absolute', 'unique', 'final', 'normative', 'ultimate' – decisively superior to all other saviours, gospels, religions. Troeltsch's own intellectual journey illustrates how this implicit dogma has now come under serious question. In the lecture that he wrote for delivery at Oxford in 1923 (he died before delivering it), he criticised his own earlier position and opted for the very different view that Christianity is 'absolute' for Christians, and the other world faiths are likewise 'absolute' for their own adherents.[1] Clearly the 'relative absoluteness' of his 1923 paper is very different in its implications from the unqualified absoluteness of his 1901 book.

The Christian mind has always been composed of many segments and layers, exhibiting very different degrees of self-consciousness and self-critical reflection. But in its more intellectual hemisphere there has been, during the period since the First World War, a marked development in ways of conceiving Christianity's place within the total religious life of the world. We are now at a critical point at which that development may be halted or may proceed to its natural conclusion. The symbol of the river Rubicon, to cross which is to take a step that closes one range of options while opening another, is appropriate. In order to see where this theological Rubicon runs, we must go back for a moment to the medieval assumption – medieval, but continuing effectively until about the end of the nineteenth century – of a Christian monopoly of salvific truth and life, expressed in the doctrine *extra ecclesiam nulla salus*. This exclusivist Roman doctrine had its equally emphatic Protestant equivalent in the conviction that outside Christianity there is no salvation, so that missionaries were sent out to save souls who must otherwise have forfeited eternal life. It was a virtually unchallenged assumption that Christianity was to spread throughout the world, replacing the non-Christian traditions. Thus as late as 1913 Julius Richter defined his subject of missiology as 'that branch of theology which in opposition to the non-Christian religions, shows the Christian religion to be the Way, the Truth, and the Life; which seeks to dispossess the non-Christian religions and to plant in their stead in the soil of heathen national life the evangelic faith and the Christian life'.[2]

What has led many, perhaps most, thinking Christians during the last 70 or so years gradually to abandon this absolutist position? The full answer would be many-sided. Perhaps the most important factor has been the modern explosion of knowledge among Christians in the West concerning the other great religious traditions of the world. Between the two world wars, and even more so since the second, ill-informed and hostile Western stereotypes of the other faith communities have increasingly been replaced by more accurate knowledge and more sympathetic understanding. The immense spiritual riches of Judaism and Islam, of Hinduism, Buddhism, and Sikhism, of Confucianism and Taoism and African primal religion, have become better known in the West and have tended to erode the plausibility of the old Christian exclusivism. More about this presently. Another factor has been the realisation that Christian absolutism, in collaboration with acquisitive and violent human nature, has done much to poison the relationships between the Christian minority and the non-Christian majority of the world's population by sanctifying exploitation and oppression on a gigantic scale. I want to look here at some of the large-scale ways in which Christian absolutism has lent itself – human nature being what it is – to the validation and encouragement of political and economic evil.

That phrase 'human nature being what it is' is important. For we can imagine a very different world in which Christians have always believed their gospel to be uniquely superior to others but in which they have had no desire to dominate and exploit others. In that imagined world Christianity would have liberated its adherents from acquisitive desires, so that none of the evils that we are about to look at would have occurred. Thus the connection between Christian absolutism and these historical evils is not one of logical necessity but is a factual link via a 'fallen' human nature that Christianity has been largely powerless to redeem. But of course this very powerlessness is itself a major factor in the accounting. The picture would be very different if Christianity, commensurate with its claim to absolute truth and unique validity, had shown a unique capacity to transform human nature for the better.

It should be added at this point that the claims of other religions to absolute validity and to a consequent superiority have likewise, given the same human nature, sanctified violent aggression, exploitation and intolerance. A worldwide and history-long study of the harmful effects of religious absolutism would draw material from almost every tradition – Christianity and Islam probably providing the greatest number of examples, and Buddhism perhaps the least. However, I am writing here as a Christian specifically about our Christian attitude to other religions, and accordingly I shall be concerned with Christian rather than with other forms of religious absolutism.

II

The main destructive effects of the assumption of Christian superiority have occurred in the relationships between European and North American Christians on the one hand, and both the black and brown peoples of the world and, for an even longer period, the Jews, on the other.

As regards the Jews, there is a clear connection between 15 or so centuries of the 'absoluteness' of Christianity, with its corollary of the radical inferiority and perverseness of the Judaism it 'superseded', and the consequent endemic anti-Semitism of Christian civilisation, which has continued with undiminished virulence into and through our twentieth century. This connection has only become a matter of Christian consciousness in recent times, as also, even more recently, has the destructive effects upon Christian women of the church's traditional patriarchal system of ideas. Even less acknowledged is the way in which the Christian superiority complex supported and sanctified the Western imperialistic exploitation of what today we call the third world.

European colonisation, reaching out forcefully into Africa, India, south-east Asia, China, South America, and the Pacific Islands, and establishing white hegemony over vast brown and black populations, constitutes a complex historical tapestry woven with many and varied threads. The patterns of damage caused by organised exploitation and, within it, the elements that also occurred of incidental benefit, are well-depicted as regards one major part of the story in James Morris's three-volume history of the flourishing and fall of the British Empire.[3] Carved out by the aggressive might of western military technology, this empire at its height covered a quarter of the surface of the globe and included a quarter of its human population. It placed Britain at the centre of a vast trading network, drawing cheap raw materials to feed its nineteenth-century industrial expansion, and then exporting manufactured goods to huge captive markets. In some cases trade followed the flag, whereas in others the flag was planted to protect an already established flow of trade. The basic motives were acquisitiveness and aggrandisement – though within the structures created by these forces there was also room for shining threads of personal idealism and courage, and sometimes for a genuine, if paternalistic, spirit of service to the subject peoples.[4]

The racist attitudes that continue to poison the human community after the colonial structures have collapsed formed a powerful ingredient in the mentality that created and maintained them. For during the period when it was accepted as right that Britons, Frenchmen, Germans, Dutchmen, Spaniards, Italians and Portuguese should rule over whole black and brown populations, it was psychologically almost inevitable that they should see those whom they dominated as inferior and as in need of a higher guardianship. This categorising of black and brown humanity as inferior included their cultures and religions. Although there were individual colonial administrators – some of them remarkable and admirable men – who came genuinely to respect the people over whom they ruled, more usually their cultures were seen as barbarous and their religions as idolatrous superstitions. For the moral validation of the imperial enterprise rested upon the conviction that it was a great civilising and uplifting mission, one of whose tasks was to draw the unfortunate heathen up into the higher, indeed highest, religion of Christianity. Accordingly the gospel played a vital role in the self-justification of western imperialism. Writing of early nineteenth-century India, Morris says,

> The Indian territories were allotted by providence to Great Britain, wrote Charles Grant, the evangelical chairman of the [East

India] Company's Court of Director, 'not merely that we might draw an annual profit from them, but that we might diffuse among their inhabitants, once sunk in darkness, vice, and misery, the light and benign influence of the truth, the blessings of a well-regulated society, the improvements and comforts of active industry. . . .' James Stephen wrote of the 'barbarous and obscene rites of Hindoo superstition' and Wilberforce declared the Christian mission in India to be the greatest of all causes. 'Let us endeavor to strike our roots into their soil', he wrote, 'by the gradual introduction and establishment of our own principles and opinions; of our laws, institutions, and manners; above all, as the source of every other improvement of our religion, and consequently of our morals.'[5]

David Livingstone, the great explorer and missionary, told a British audience in 1857, 'I go back to Africa to try to make an open path for commerce and Christianity.'[6] Indeed, says Morris, 'The mission stations which, throughout the second half of the century, sprang up throughout the tropical possessions, were manned by and large by militants with no doubts – this was a Christian Empire, and it was the imperial duty to spread the Christian word among its heathen subjects.'[7] He summarises:

> The administrators of Empire, too, and very often its conquerors, were generally speaking practising Christians; the new public schools at which so many of them were educated were invariably Church of England foundations, with parson-headmasters. . . . Explorers like Speke or Grant saw themselves as God's scouts – even Stanley turned evangelist in 1875, and converted the King of Uganda and all his court to Christianity. Generals like Havelock and Nicholson slaughtered their enemies in the absolute certainty of a biblical mandate . . . and most of the imperial heroes were identified in the public mind with the Christianness of Empire – not simply humanitarianism, not Burke's sense of trusteeship, but a Christian militancy, a ruling faith, whose Defender on earth was the Queen herself, and whose supreme commander needed no identification. Every aspect of Empire was an aspect of Christ.[8]

Much more could be said. But without going into further detail it is, I think, clear that in the eighteenth and nineteenth centuries the conviction of the decisive superiority of Christianity infused the imperial expansion of the West with a powerful moral impetus and an effective religious validation without which it might well not have been psychologically viable.

A brief word should be said at this point about the missionaries themselves. Most of them were not concerned with the effects of their work on empire-building and the development of trade. They had genuinely dedicated their lives to the saving of heathen souls, and in this cause many of them willingly endured immense hardships and dangers, including the ever-present threat of fatal tropical diseases. They also usually had to accept separation from their children when these were sent back home to school. Again, although many seem to have regarded the indigenous primal or Hindu or Buddhist or Muslim religious life as valueless or even as demonic, and their adult converts as children to be commanded and instructed, there were others who developed a deep respect and affection for the people to whom they had gone; and they were able to recognise elements of profound wisdom and inspiring ideals within these alien traditions. To note the ways in which the Christian missionary imperative was used within national consciousness to motivate and validate imperialism does not require us to impugn the motives of the missionaries themselves.[9]

III

To refer to our twentieth-century awareness of the values of the other great world traditions, and to our concomitant new awareness of the pernicious side of Christian absolutism in history, is not to tell the full story of the modern erosion of theological exclusivism. But these two factors have probably been the most important. At any rate such an erosion has undoubtedly occurred. The Second Vatican Council (1963–5) highlighted and consolidated the new thinking that had been taking place for a number of years among some of the more adventurous Roman Catholic theologians. Vatican II in effect – though not of course in so many words – repealed the *extra ecclesiam nulla salus* doctrine by declaring that there *is* salvation outside the visible church; the redemption bought by the blood of Christ is offered to all human beings even without their formal entry into the church. Thus, speaking of Christ's redeeming sacrifice, Vatican II declared:

All this holds true not only for Christians, but for all men of good will in whose hearts grace works in an unseen way. For, since Christ died for all men, and since the ultimate vocation of man is in fact one, and divine, we ought to believe that the Holy Spirit in a manner known only to God offers to every man the possibility of being associated with this paschal mystery.[10]

The possibility of salvation was thus officially extended in principle to the whole world. This extension was reiterated even more strongly in the first encyclical, *Redemptor Hominis* (1979), of Pope John Paul II, in which it is declared that 'man – every man without exception whatever – has been redeemed by Christ. . . . because with man – with each man without any exception whatever – Christ is in a way united, even when man is unaware of it'.[11]

All this does not mean, however, that the old sense of Christian superiority has died out or that the traditional claim to the unique finality of the Christian gospel has been rescinded. In the past that claim took very explicit forms: Christianity alone possesses the full knowledge of God because it alone is based on and is the continuing vehicle of God's direct self-revelation; Christianity arose from and alone proclaims God's saving act in the atoning death of Christ; Christianity, despite all its historical defects, is the only religious movement to have been founded on earth by God in person. The claim has now come to be expressed in less blatant and less offensive ways.

In the modern reaction against the triumphalism of the past the Church's still cherished assumption of Christian superiority has moved discreetly into the background. In, for example, the Vatican II Declaration on the Relationship of the Church to Non-Christian Religions (*Nostra Aetate*), which was in effect addressed to the members of those other traditions, the decisive superiority of Christ/the gospel/the Church was not openly stated, although it was delicately and indirectly implied. In this document the headline-catching theme was that 'The Catholic Church rejects nothing which is true and holy in these religions.'[12] However, in the Dogmatic Constitution on the Church (significantly beginning with the words *Lumen Gentium*), in which the church was clarifying its beliefs for the benefit of its own members, it was stated openly that 'Whatever goodness or truth is found among them [that is, among "those who through no fault of their own do not know the gospel of Christ" and "those who, with-

out blame on their part, have not yet arrived at an explicit knowledge of God"] is looked upon by the Church as a *preparation* for the
gospel.'[13] And another of the Vatican II pronouncements, the Decree
on the Missionary Activity of the Church (*Ad Gentes*), emphatically
declares:

> All must be converted to [Christ] as He is made known by the
> Church's preaching. All must be incorporated into Him by bap-
> tism, and into the Church which is His body. . . . Therefore,
> though God in ways known to Himself can lead those inculpably
> ignorant of the gospel to that faith without which it is impossible
> to please Him, yet a necessity lies on the Church, and at the same
> time a sacred duty, to preach the gospel. Hence missionary activ-
> ity today as always retains its power and necessity.[14]

Protestant thinking, in so far as it has been expressed through the
World Council of Churches, has moved to a significant extent in the
same direction. The work of the Council's Subunit on Dialogue with
People of Living Faiths and Ideologies is hardly compatible with the
old exclusivist theology. At the same time, however, another powerful element within the World Council, heard at its Uppsala (1968),
Nairobi (1975) and Vancouver (1983) Assemblies, has continued to
talk in ways reminiscent of the old exclusivism. Indeed, the Catholic
scholar Arnulf Camps is probably right in his opinion, concerning
the continuing tension within Protestant thinking between a basically Barthian absolutism and a more liberal acceptance of interfaith
dialogue, that 'neither the International Missionary Council nor
the World Council of Churches has managed to get beyond this
dilemma'.[15] This being acknowledged however, it can, I think, still
be said that there has been since the early 1960s a general, even if
not wholehearted and consistent, movement within the Protestant
as well as the Catholic understanding of other religions.

The new consensus, or near-consensus, that has emerged out of
this trend away from the old exclusivism is today generally called
inclusivism. The Christian mind has now for the most part made the
move from an intolerant exclusivism to a benevolent inclusivism.
But the latter, no less than the former, rests upon the claim to Christianity's unique finality as the locus of the only full divine revelation
and the only adequate saving event. Non-Christians can be saved
because, unknown to them, Christ is secretly 'in a way united' with
them. But the saving truth unknown to them is known to the church,

which is God's instrument in making redemption known. To abandon this claim to an ultimate religious superiority is therefore to pass a critical point, entering new territory from which the whole terrain of Christian truth is bound to look different. For on the other side of this divide Christianity is seen in a pluralistic context as *one* of the great world faiths, *one* of the streams of religious life through which human beings can be savingly related to that ultimate Reality Christians know as the heavenly Father.

From one point of view, to cross this theological Rubicon seems an almost inevitable next step, following to its natural conclusion the trajectory whose path we have traced from an exclusivist to an inclusivist view of other religions. For once it is granted that salvation is in fact taking place not only within Christianity but also within the other great traditions, it seems arbitrary and unrealistic to go on insisting that the Christ-event is the sole and exclusive source of human salvation. When it is acknowledged that Jews are being saved within and through the Jewish stream of religious life, Muslims within and through the Islamic stream, Hindus within and through the Hindu streams, and so on, can it be more than a hang-over from the old religious imperialism of the past to insist upon attaching a Christian label to salvation within these other house-holds of faith? This would be like the anomaly of accepting the Copernican revolution in astronomy, in which the earth ceased to be regarded as the centre of the universe and was seen instead as one of the planets circling the sun, but still insisting that the sun's life-giving rays can reach the other planets only by first being reflected from the earth!

But the move from Christian inclusivism to pluralism, although in one way seemingly so natural and inevitable, sets Christianity in a new and to some an alarming light in which there can no longer be any *a priori* assumption of overall superiority. For the Christian tradition is now seen as one of a plurality of contexts of salvation – contexts, that is to say, within which the transformation of human existence from self-centredness to God-centredness (or a centring in the ultimately Real) is occurring. Accordingly, if it is now claimed that Christianity constitutes a more favourable setting for this transformation than the other traditions, this must be shown by historical evidence. It can no longer be established simply by defining salvation as inclusion within the scope of the divine pardon bought by Christ's atoning death. From that definition it does follow that Christianity, as Christ's continuing agency on earth, is superior to all other religions. But this kind of arbitrary superiority-by-definition no longer seems defensible, even to many Christians. Today we cannot help feeling that the question of superiority has to be posed as an empirical issue, to be settled (if indeed it *can* be settled) by examination of the facts.

IV

The observable facts – constituting the fruits of religious faith in human life – are bewildering in their variety and scope. However, two threads are available to guide us; we can look for both individual and social transformation. We find the former in its most evident form in those who are recognised as the saints of the different traditions – granting that there are different patterns of sainthood, some pursuing the inner paths of prayer, contemplation and meditation, and others the outer paths of social service and political action. But if we mean by a saint a person who is much further advanced than most of us in the transformation from self-centredness to Reality-centredness, then I venture the proposition that each of the great religious traditions seems, so far as we can tell, to promote this transformation to about the same extent. Relating this to the traditional assumption of superiority, I am thus suggesting that we have no good grounds for maintaining that Christianity has produced or is producing more saints, in proportion to population, or a higher quality of saintliness, than any other of the great streams of religious life.

A challenging recent example is set by Gandhi, recognised by hundreds of millions in India as a Mahatma or great soul. Most of us have come to see in him a human being who, in response to the claim of God on his life, realised the human moral and spiritual potential to a rare degree, inspiring many others to rise to a new level of effective self-giving love for others. Gandhi was a Hindu, and the name of God that was on his lips as he was struck down by an assassin's bullets in 1948 was not that of the Christian heavenly Father or Holy Trinity but that of the Hindu Rama. But if human salvation, or liberation, has any concrete meaning for men and women in this world, it must include the kind of transformation of human existence seen in Gandhi and, in varying ways and degrees, in the saints of all the great traditions. But this transformation, with its further influence upon other individuals and through them, more remotely, upon societies, is manifestly not confined to the Christian areas of the world. There are persons who have in varying degrees given themselves to God, or to the ultimate Reality, within each of the great traditions.

I recognise that this cannot be proved. The reason why it cannot be proved – or disproved – is that we do not at present command the conceptual precision or the exhaustive information necessary for objective comparative judgements. All that we have is a variety of overlapping concepts of saintliness and a very partial and unsystematic body of historical knowledge. Accordingly, we each have to rely upon our own working conception of a saint, our own limited range of contemporary observation, and our own reading within the vast literature of the history of religions – a literature that was not created and is not organised to answer our present question. What I am proposing on this basis, as a Christian attempting both to survey the contemporary world and to look back down the long vistas of history, is that we are not in a position to assert a greater power in Christianity than in any of the other great world faiths to bring about the kind of transformation in human beings that we all desire.

V

The thread of saintliness, then, I suggest, does not lead us to the conclusion that Christianity is manifestly superior. The other thread to be followed is that of the social outworkings of the different faiths. Here much Christian thought starts from a firm assumption of manifest superiority and, when challenged, presents a picture of the relatively affluent, just, peaceful, enlightened, democratic, northern hemisphere, owing its virtues to Christianity, in contrast to the relatively poor, unjust, violent, backward, and undemocratic southern hemisphere, held back by its non-Christian faiths. However, this picture has to be deconstructed on several levels. To begin on the surface, Buddhist-Shinto Japan is not poor or technologically backward, and several other non-Christian nations of the Pacific-rim are also rapidly becoming major industrial powers. Muslim Saudi Arabia and the other Gulf states are far from poverty-stricken; and Hindu India, which has recently produced a number of front-rank physicists, is also the largest democracy in the world. Social injustice is indeed endemic in varying degrees in all these countries; but it is, alas, endemic in virtually every country in the world, affluent as well as poverty-stricken, western as well as eastern, Christian as well as non-Christian.

And on the other side of the same coin, there are very large Christian populations that are desperately poor – particularly in the southern half of the Americas and in the southern half of Africa; there are Christian countries, in Latin America and South Africa, whose social structures are profoundly unjust and where the insignia of democracy are a mockery; there are Christian populations, in Ireland and in Lebanon, currently engaged in political violence; and others, in the United States and in most European countries, turning the earth's precious resources into weapons of destruction on an appalling scale. Again, the Amnesty International report *Torture in the Eighties*[16] impartially cites as guilty of torture a number of Muslim countries (including Turkey, Iran, Iraq, Libya, Pakistan and Bangladesh), a number of Christian countries (including South Africa, Spain, Argentina, Brazil, Chile, El Salvador, Guatemala, Paraguay and Peru), Hindu India, Buddhist Sri Lanka and Jewish Israel.

However, it remains true that the Christian, post-Christian, and post-Marxist West constitutes the relatively affluent first and second worlds, whereas the non-Christian East and partly Christian South constitutes the generally poverty-stricken third world; and also that our modern liberal ideals of political freedom and human equality have initially developed primarily in the West. And so we have to ask to what extent this affluence and these ideals are gifts of the Christian religion and evidence of its moral and intellectual superiority.

Western economic prosperity is the product of modern science and technology. It has been suggested by several authors that the birth of modern science required the intellectual environment of Christianity, with its belief in a rational creator producing an orderly and law-governed universe. And it seems clear that science needed for its birth and early growth the hospitality of a worldview that sees the cosmos as a system subject to universal laws. But all the great religious traditions in their different ways – those of Semitic and those of Indian origin – see the universe in this way. The Hindu and Buddhist cosmologies have indeed greater affinities than the traditional Christian cosmology with some major modern scientific theories. The ancient Hindu conception of the vast successive Kalpas, each leading to the conflagration of the universe and then its renewal, to go again and again through the same development, is close to one of the current scientific models of an endlessly expanding and contracting universe. And the Buddhist emphasis upon incessant process in an interdependent flux of beginningless and endless change agrees well with the physicists' picture of the universe as a field of energy undergoing perpetual transformations.

But neither Hinduism nor Buddhism, nor Christianity during the first fifteen centuries of its history, in fact gave birth to modern science. And so we have to ask what other factor entered in to enable the human mind to awaken from its long prescientific slumber. The answer seems to be the rebirth, in the European Renaissance and then in the Enlightenment, of the Greek spirit of free enquiry, gradually liberating minds from the thrall of unquestioned dogmas and enabling them to turn to observation, experimentation and reason to understand the universe in which we find ourselves. Once modern science had thus been launched, it quickly became an autonomous enterprise, of ever-increasing power, obeying its own methodological rules and emphatically asserting its independence from the religious ethos within which it had been born. This independence created painful tensions and conflicts with the religious establishment as, first, astronomy moved our world from the centre of the universe to the position of one of the sun's satellites; and then as geology established the age of the earth as enormously greater than the biblical chronology had imagined; and then finally as biology traced the place of *Homo sapiens* within the whole evolution of life, thereby erasing the biblical picture of the special creation of humanity and, as a further by-product of the scientific outlook and method, as the objective study of ancient scriptures soon began to undermine their customary literal authority.

In fact, the birth of modern science within the Christian culture of Europe reminds us of a cuckoo hatching in a thrush's nest and rapidly growing up to attack its hosts! In the science versus religion debates of the nineteenth century, as in the Church's earlier treatment of Galileo and its attempts to suppress the new cosmology, Christianity, far from seeing science as its own distinctive gift to the world, fought a long but unsuccessful battle against it! This led – despite a resurgence today of fundamentalist resistance – to a belated acceptance of the new scientific knowledge and a consequent massive rethinking of Christian doctrine. Thus Christianity can claim no proprietary interest in the modern scientific enterprise. Its special relationship consists simply in the fact that it was the first of the world faiths to be hit by the impact of the new empirical knowledge and outlook. But the same impact is now inevitably affecting the rest of the world. We may speculate that Islam will find this encounter as traumatic as has Christianity, whereas Hinduism and Buddhism may be able to adjust to it without great difficulty. But in each case the deeper effect must be, as in the Christian West, a progressive secularisation both of thought and of society. And the deeper challenge will be to develop forms of faith through which the human spirit can be transformingly related to the Transcendent within the context of our modern knowledge of ourselves and of our environment.

Similar considerations apply to the modern explosion of technology, with its fruits of hitherto undreamed-of material affluence. The firstness of the first world consists in its being the first part of the globe to have become industrialised and so to have benefited from the mass production of consumer goods. But it does not follow from this that the poor of the largely non-Christian third world would not also like to have plentiful food and a large array of consumer goods! It is true that there is a strong strand of Hindu and Buddhist teaching that is world- and wealth-renouncing, treating the ever-changing material world as ultimately unreal. Hence the famous Hindu prayer, 'lead me from the unreal to the Real.' But it is also true that there is an equally strong strand of world-renouncing Christian teaching, virtually conflating 'the world, the flesh, and the devil'. This began in the New Testament, where Jesus tells his disciples, 'If ye were of the world, the world would love his own; but because ye are not of the world, but I have chosen you out of the world, therefore the world hateth you' (John 15:19), and 'If any man come to me, and hate not his father, and mother, and wife, and children, and brethren and sisters, yea, and his own life also, he cannot be my disciple' (Luke 14:26). We read elsewhere in the New Testament that 'the whole world lieth in wickedness' (I John 5:19); and it was a widespread early Christian conviction that the earth is to be under the devil's rule until the last day. Such teaching has not, however, prevented the development of western capitalism and the general desire that it feeds for more and more possessions, including even-more-sophisticated luxuries.

Hindu teaching is no more likely to inhibit the scramble for consumer goods in a rapidly industrialising India. For the basis of

India's relative poverty in the modern period – ancient India having been fully as prosperous as Europe[17] – is the fact that its medieval phase has only now, in the second half of the twentieth century, given way to an industrial revolution. And if we ask why Britain's eighteenth- and nineteenth-century industrial transformation did not spread to India, as it did to the United States and to the white British dominions, the answer is that it was in Britain's interest to keep the Indian subcontinent as a source of raw materials and a captive market rather than encourage it to become an independent industrial competitor. To quote from Dutt's *Economic History of India*:

> It is, unfortunately, true that the East Indian Company and the British Parliament, following the selfish commercial policy of a hundred years ago, discouraged Indian manufacturers in the early years of British rule in order to encourage the rising manufactures of England. Their fixed policy, pursued during the last decades of the eighteenth century and the first decade of the nineteenth, was to make India subservient to the industries of Great Britain, and to make the Indian people grow raw produce only, in order to supply material for the looms and manufactories of Great Britain.[18]

As late as the 1920s, Gandhi was campaigning against Indians being compelled to export their raw cotton to Lancashire and then buy it back in the form of finished cloth, to the profit of the Lancashire mills and to the detriment of the Indian masses. It is only since independence in 1947 that India has begun to become industrialised on a large scale.

The general situation, then, seems to be this. The wealth-creating industrial revolution, transforming human society from its feudal to its modern phase, occurred first in Europe, and was greatly helped by the concurrent European imperial expansion, which gave privileged access to raw materials and to vast new markets. The industrial process had to begin somewhere; and if it had not started when and where it did, it would have started at some other time or place. But it does not seem possible to establish any exclusive causal connection between industrialisation and Christianity such that without Christianity industrialisation would not have occurred within human societies.

VI

The other main area in which contemporary Christianity is inclined to see itself as superior is in its adoption of the modern liberal ideals of human equality and freedom, expressed politically in democratic forms of government. These liberal ideals emerged out of the deconstruction of the medieval dogmatic-hierarchical world of thought. That they are not purely Christian ideals, but the product of a creative interaction of cultural influences, is shown by the fact that for the previous thousand years the Christian West had been strongly hierarchical, sanctifying serfdom and the subjugation of women, believing not in the rights of humanity but in the divine right of kings, burning heretics and witches, and brutally suppressing both social unrest and deviant intellectual speculation. The dawning concepts of human rights and of individual freedom and equality were initially as powerfully opposed by the church as was modern science in its early days. For example, what became in the nineteenth century the Christian campaign against slavery began as a small minority movement within the churches, opposed by many church-men acting on behalf of slave-owning interests. And the other en-deavours by such groups as the Quakers, and then by the social gospel and Christian socialist movements, to achieve greater social justice within western societies have always been an uphill struggle, generally opposed by the ecclesiastical establishments. The belated and still often wavering conversion of the churches to the ideals of human equality and freedom is a very recent development, which is now also occurring within the other world traditions.

Once again, then, Christianity does not have a proprietary interest in these powerful secular ideals of the modern world. They have a secure theoretical basis in the teachings of each of the great faiths, but in each case their emergence as a real force is largely due to the hierarchy-dissolving influences of modernity. Christianity has, how-ever, the distinction – and herein lies its genuine historical unique-ness – of being the first of the world religions to have been to a great extent transformed by modernity.

The results in the Christian West have been partly beneficial and creative; and partly harmful and destructive. On the credit side, science has made possible ever-more-advanced technologies, which have in turn spawned an immense proliferation of wealth, so that the western world now enjoys the highest material standard of liv-ing in history. This has at the same time stimulated an enormous growth and extension of education and an unprecedented explosion of cultural activity. On the debit side, the same expansion of scientific knowledge has produced ever more powerful weapons of mass destruction, culminating in nuclear and chemical missiles. Further, our modern affluence has been achieved at the expense of a galloping consumption of the earth's non-renewable resources, and of a polarisation between the over-rich northern and the desperately poor southern hemisphere, while setting up in the affluent regions social and psychological stresses and strains with frightening levels of drug addiction, suicide, divorce, crime, urban violence and a tragic sense of meaninglessness and general frustration.

VII

When we try, then, to look at the religious traditions as long-lived historical entities we find in each case a complex mixture of valuable and harmful elements. Each has provided an effective framework of meaning for millions of adherents, carrying them through the different stages of life, affording consolation in sickness, need and calamity, and enabling them to celebrate communally their times of health, well-being and creativity. Within the ordered psychic space created by a living faith, as expressed in the institutions and customs of a society, millions of men and women in generation after generation have coped with life's pains and challenges and rejoiced in its blessings; and some have gone beyond ego-domination into a transforming relationship with the Eternal. Many have responded – again, in their varying degrees – to the moral claim of love/compassion mediated by the great traditions and widely formulated as the Golden Rule: 'Let not any man do unto another any act that he wisheth not done to himself by others, knowing it to be painful to himself' (the Hindu *Mahabharata*, Shanti parva, cclx.21); 'Do not do to others what you would not want them to do to you' (Confucius, *Analects*, Book xii, #2); 'Hurt not others with that which pains yourself' (The Buddhist *Udanavarga*, v. 18); 'As ye would that men should do to you, do ye also to them likewise' (Jesus, in Luke 6:31); 'What is hateful to yourself do not do to your fellow man. That is the whole of the Torah' (Jewish *Babylonian Talmud*, Shabbath 31a); 'No man is a true believer unless he desires for his brother that which he desires for himself' (The Muslim *Hadith*, Muslim, imam 71–2).

This is the good side of the great traditions. But each has at the same time sanctified vicious human evils. Hinduism, though constituting an immensely rich and powerful universe of meaning, and pointing the way to inner liberation, also validates the hierarchical caste system of India, including the relegation of millions to the position of outcastes – an injustice which still lingers despite its official abolition in the 1947 Constitution. Hindu society tolerated the former practice of suttee and still tolerates the continuing cruel persecution and sometimes murder of brides whose dowry is deemed insufficient. Buddhism, although basically peaceful and tolerant, and suffusing millions with the ideal of unself-centred existence, has been indifferent until very recently to questions of social justice, so that many Buddhist lands have long remained in a state of feudal inequality. Islam, though calling the faithful to submission to and peace with God and promoting a Muslim brotherhood that is notably free from colour prejudice, has sanctioned 'holy wars', fanatical intolerance, and the barbaric punishments of mutilation and flogging, and still generally consigns women to a protected but narrowly confined life. Christianity, though providing in recent centuries a birthplace for modern science and a home for the modern liberal ideals of equality and freedom, has generated savage wars of religion and supported unnumerable 'just wars'; has tortured and burned multitudes of heretics and witches in the name of God;[19] has motivated and authorised the persecution of the Jews;[20] has validated systematic racism; and has tolerated the western capitalist 'rape of the earth', the misuse of nuclear energy, and the basic injustice of the north–south division into rich and poor nations.

The conclusion to be drawn seems to be that each tradition has constituted its own unique mixture of good and evil. Each is a long-lived social reality that has gone through times of flourishing and times of decline; and each is internally highly diverse, some of its aspects promoting human good and others damaging the human family. In face of these complexities it seems impossible to make the global judgement that any one religious tradition has contributed more good or less evil, or a more favourable balance of good and evil, than the others. It is of course possible that, to the eye of omniscience, one tradition is in fact, on balance, superior to the rest. But to our partial and fallible human view they constitute different ways of being human in relation to the Eternal, each with both its cultural glories and its episodes of violent destructiveness, each raising vast populations to a higher moral and spiritual level and yet each at times functioning as a vehicle of human chauvinism, greed and cruelty. We may well judge that in some respects, or in some periods or regions, the fruits of one tradition are better than, and in other respects or periods or regions inferior to, those of another. But as vast complex totalities, the world traditions seem to be more or less on a par with each other. None can be singled out as manifestly superior.

If this is so, we may begin to consider how this truth is likely to affect the ongoing work of Christian theology.

VIII

The three central doctrines of trinity, incarnation and atonement cohere together. Given a juridical conception of atonement, Jesus had to be God, as St Anselm demonstrated in his *Cur Deus Homo*? For only a sacrifice of divine, and therefore infinite, value could give adequate satisfaction for the wrong done by human sin to the creator and lord of the universe; or could meet the inexorable requirements of divine justice, thereby enabling God to regard sinful men and women as just and as fit to be received into the kingdom. And given that Jesus was God, the Godhead had to be a trinity (or at least a binity); for God was incarnate on earth as Jesus of Nazareth, and God was also in heaven, sustaining the universe, and hearing and answering prayer. It was therefore necessary to think of God as at least two in one, Father and Son, who were respectively (for a brief period) in heaven and on earth. But Christian thinking in fact went on to include the divine presence in human life outside the 30 or so years of the incarnation as a third person, the Holy Spirit. It would in theory have been possible to account for this presence with a more economic binitarian doctrine by attributing what came to be regarded as the work of the Holy Spirit to the eternal Christ-spirit or Logos; and there was indeed a period before the Holy Spirit and the Spirit of Christ had been distinguished as two distinct realities. However, eventually the trinitarian pattern became established and now pervades Christian theological and liturgical language.

Approaching this cluster of doctrines through the idea of incarnation, it is widely agreed today by New Testament scholars, including even relatively conservative ones, that the historical Jesus did not himself teach that he was God the Son, the second person of a divine

trinity, living a human life. He was intensely conscious of God as the
heavenly Father, his life (certainly during the two or three years of
his ministry) being dedicated to proclaiming the imminent coming
of God's kingdom, to manifesting its power in acts of healing, and to
teaching others how to live so as to become part of the kingdom that
was presently to be established. He probably thought of himself as
the final prophet, the one whose mission was to herald the end of the
age. He may have applied to himself either of the two main titles that
Jewish tradition offered for the fulfiller of this role – that of the Son
of man who was to come in glory on the clouds of heaven, and that
of the Messiah who was to rule the world from its new centre,
Jerusalem. Neither of these roles, it should be noted, amounted to
being God; both figures were exalted human servants of God. But it
is equally possible that Jesus refused all identifications, and that
it was his followers who bestowed these and other titles upon him.
Or he may have used the term 'son of man' simply as a Hebraicism,
a term that could be used by anyone.

The 'Son of God' title, which was to become standard in the
church's theology, probably began in the Old Testament and wider
ancient Near Eastern usage in which it signified a special servant of
God. In this sense kings, emperors, pharaohs, great philosophers,
miracle workers and other holy men were commonly called son of
God. But as the gospel went out beyond its Hebraic setting into the
gentile world of the Roman Empire, this poetry was transformed
into prose and the living metaphor congealed into a rigid and literal
dogma. It was to accommodate this resulting metaphysical sonship
that the Church, after some three centuries of clashing debates, settled upon the theory that Jesus had two natures, one divine and the
other human, being in one nature of one substance with God the
Father and in the other of one substance with humanity – a philosophical construction as far removed from the thought world and
teaching of Jesus himself as is the, in some ways, parallel Mayahana
Buddhist doctrine of the Trikaya from that of the historical Gautama.

But there have always been other strands of Christological thinking, even though the variations were officially suppressed during
the long and relatively monolithic period of medieval Christendom.
The earliest strand of language in the New Testament documents
probably expressed an inspiration Christology, seeing Jesus as a
great prophet filled with the divine Spirit. This type of Christology
has become a live option again today, some recent English-language
versions being D. M. Baillie's *God Was in Christ* (1958), several of the

contributions to *The Myth of God Incarnate* (1977), and Geoffrey Lampe's *God as Spirit* (1977).[21] The basic thought is that to speak of God's love becoming incarnate is to speak of men and women in whose lives God's inspiration, or grace, is effectively at work so that they have become instruments of the divine purpose on earth. To 'be to the Eternal Goodness what his own hand is to a man'[22] is to be a locus of divine incarnation. Incarnation in this sense has occurred and is occurring in many different ways and degrees in many different persons. Whether it happened more fully in the case of Jesus than in that of any other human being, or even perhaps absolutely in Jesus, cannot properly be settled *a priori* (though that seems to be how Baillie and Lampe settled it) but only on the basis of historical information. This means in practice that it cannot be definitively settled, for we lack the kind of evidence, touching every moment and aspect of Jesus' inner and outer life, that could entitle one to make such a judgement.

This type of inspiration or paradox-of-grace Christology falls within the range of options open to those who are not credal fundamentalists, insisting upon the verbal inspiration of the Nicene and Chalcedonian formulations. Such a Christology would seem to point out the direction – although it is not the only possible direction – in which Christology is likely to develop within those theological circles that have moved beyond inclusivism to a pluralist understanding of the place of Christianity in the total life of the world.

An inspiration Christology coheres better with some ways of understanding trinitarian language than with others. It does not require or support the notion of three divine persons in the modern sense in which a person is a distinct centre of consciousness, will and emotion – so that one could speak of the Father, the Son and the Holy Spirit as loving one another within the eternal family of the trinity, and of the Son coming down to earth to make atonement on behalf of human beings to his Father. An inspiration Christology is, however, fully compatible with the conception of the trinity as affirming three distinguishable ways in which the one God is experienced as acting in relation to, and is accordingly known by, us – namely, as creator, redeemer and inspirer. On this interpretation, the three persons are not three different centres of consciousness but three major aspects of the one divine nature. They no more resolve God into three personal beings than do the various names of God in Jewish tradition or the 99 Beautiful Names of God in the Qur'an. Such an 'economic' understanding of the trinity is as orthodox as a 'social' one and would seem to represent the direction that trinitarian thought is likely to follow in theologies that accept a pluralistic understanding of the human religious situation.

Atonement theory has also taken a number of forms, some cohering better than others with an inspiration Christology and an economic or modal trinitarianism. As in the case of Christology, the kind of atonement thinking most hospitable to religious pluralism is nearest to what appears to have been the teaching of Jesus himself. Here we find, in the familiar words of the Lord's Prayer and in such parables as that of the prodigal son, the assumption of a direct relationship to God in which all who are truly penitent can ask for and receive forgiveness and new life. The father in the parable did not require a blood sacrifice to appease his sense of justice: as soon as he saw his son returning he 'had compassion, and ran, and fell on his neck, and kissed him . . . [and said] "For this my son was dead and is alive again; he was lost and is found" ' (Luke 15:20, 24). And the only condition for God's forgiveness in the Lord's Prayer is that we also forgive one another.

This is far removed from the idea that God can forgive sinners only because Jesus has borne our just punishment by his death on the cross, or has somehow by that death satisfied the divine justice. A forgiveness that has to be bought by full payment of the moral debt is not in fact forgiveness at all. But Jesus did speak of the authentic miracle of forgiveness, a miracle not captured in the standard atonement theories. Their merit would nevertheless seem to be that they offer one way of focusing attention upon Jesus' death as an expression of the self-giving love that was incarnate in his life. And in accordance with the contemporary Jewish belief that the death of a righteous martyr somehow worked for the good of Israel, Jesus himself may well have thought of his own approaching death as a source of blessing to many (cf. Mark 10:45)[23] – as indeed it has proved to be through many different appropriations of it down the centuries.

In the case of each of these doctrines, then, the existing theological spectrum of the Christian tradition, as it has become diversified in the modern period, offers ample resources for theologies that can accept religious pluralism. What the pluralistic vision accordingly requires is not a radical departure from the diverse and ever-growing Christian tradition, but its further development in ways suggested by the discovery of God's presence and saving activity within other streams of human life. The resulting perception is that Christianity is not the one and only way of salvation, but one among several.

At the same time two other major insights – which I have not had time even to attempt to treat here – are also calling for parallel developments. One is the realisation, expressed in liberation theology, that God is at work wherever there is a costly commitment to the struggle for human justice, and is accordingly present in secular and Marxist liberation movements as much as, and sometimes more than, in the church. Indeed, too often, dominant sections of the church have been and are today on the wrong side of the liberation struggles. Whereas Christian absolutism can easily blind one to that fact, the pluralist outlook enables us to recognise it and to participate in a worldwide movement for human liberation not restricted within the borders of any one tradition. The other new insight is that expressed in contemporary feminist theology: that God is the source of life and meaning for women as truly as for men, and that our religious understanding must accordingly be brought into a new balance. Openness to the wider religious life of humankind with its rich plurality of ways – female as well as male – of symbolising the divine, can help to free us from the grip of an absolutised Christian patriarchalism.

These three concerns are today creating a new network of options for Christian thought. As in the case of the last great transformation of Christian self-awareness   its nineteenth-century response to modern science – new options will be taken up and developed in a variety of ways by some but will equally certainly be rejected and opposed by others. Our task is to try to expound and explain the new vision that is gradually coming into focus so that as many as possible can recognise in it a contemporary illumination of the Spirit, and can respond through it to God's challenging presence.

Notes

1. 'The Place of Christianity among the World Religions', reprinted in John Hick and Brian Hebblethwaite (eds), *Christianity and Other Religions* (London: Collins; and Philadelphia: Fortress, 1980).
2. Julius Richter, 'Missionary Apologetics: its Problems and its Methods', *International Review of Missions*, vol. 2 (1913) p. 540.
3. James Morris, *Heaven's Command: An Imperial Progress* (London: Faber

& Faber, 1968); *Pax Britannica: The Climax of Empire* (London: Faber & Faber, 1968); *Farewell the Trumpets: An Imperial Retreat* (London: Faber & Faber, 1978).

4. Perhaps as good an account as any of the dedicated service given by the best colonial administrators, and of their gradual realisation that paternalism must give way to independence, is that of Leonard Woolf in the second volume of his *Autobiography,* covering his years in Ceylon before the First World War, *Growing* (New York and London: Harcourt Brace, 1961).

5. Morris, *Heaven's Command,* p. 74.

6. Ibid., p. 393.

7. Ibid., p. 318.

8. Ibid., p. 319.

9. James Michener's portrait of the early nineteenth-century American missionaries in Hawaii, in part 2 of his novel *Hawaii* (New York: Random House, 1959), probably gives a fair impression of the motives and sacrifices, as well as the narrow paternalism and prejudices, of much of the missionary movement of that time.

10. Pastoral Constitution on the Church, para. 22.

11. *Redemptor Hominis* (London: Catholic Truth Society, 1979) para. 14.

12. Ibid., para. 2.

13. Ibid., chap. 2, para. 16, emphasis added.

14. Ibid., para. 7.

15. Arnulf Camps, *Partners in Dialogue,* trans. John Drury (Maryknoll, N.Y.: Orbis Books, 1983) p. 12.

16. *Torture in the Eighties* (London: Amnesty International Publications, 1984).

17. Trevor Ling, after describing the prosperous condition of northern India in the sixth century BCE adds: 'This picture of India in the Buddha's time as a land of abundant food is one which some readers may find surprising, since it is commonly believed in the West that India has an "age-old problem of poverty and hunger", to quote one recent example of this sort of ignorance. The widespread hunger of the Indian peasants, who invaded the city of Calcutta in the Bengal famine of 1943, is a relatively modern phenomenon. In 1943 the reason lay partly in distribution problems, but the long-term reason was the low productivity of Indian agriculture by the end of the British period. Under British rule a landlord system developed which led to insecurity of tenure by tenant-cultivators, in the division and redivision of plots of land, to the point where farming became uneconomical. Cultivators fell into the hands of excessively usurious money lenders. In these circumstances they had little opportunity of increasing the productivity of the land. Moreover, the rate of population increase might have been less serious in its effects had India been able to develop industrially as the Western countries themselves had done and as Japan, free from foreign rule, was able to do. India's industrial development was limited to a few enterprises which were compatible with British economic interests – railways, coal mining to supply the fuel, a small iron industry mainly for the same purpose, jute and cotton

milling, the development of which was limited by the interests of Dundee and Lancashire rivals, some sugar refining, glassware and matches. The Industrial Revolution which was needed to relieve India's growing population of its equally fast-growing poverty was not allowed to begin until independent India embarked on the first of her five-years plans in 1951' (*The Buddha* (London: Penguin Books, 1976) pp. 304–5).

18.   Romesh Dutt, *The Economic History of India*, 2nd edn, vol. I (London: Routledge & Kegan Paul, 1906) p. x.

19.   Matilda Joslyn Gage, *Women, Church and State* (New York: Arno Press, 1972; 2nd edn, 1983), says, 'It is computed from historical records that nine millions of persons were put to death for witchcraft after 1484, or during a period of three hundred years, and this estimate does not include the vast number who were sacrificed in the preceding centuries upon the same accusation' (p. 274; cited by Mary Daly, *Gyn/Ecology* (Boston, Mass.: Beacon Press, 1978) p. 183).

20.   In his history of the offence of blasphemy, Leonard Levy recalls that 'A crusader considered himself unworthy of redeeming the Holy Land from the Moslems until he first killed a Jew, for the crusader believed that avenging Christ by killing Jews earned a crusader remission of his sins. . . . During the Shepherd's Crusade in 1251, almost every Jew in southern France was slaughtered' (*Treason Against God* (New York: Schocken Books, 1981) p. 115). See also Rosemary Radford Ruether, *Faith and Fratricide* (New York: Seabury Press, 1979).

21.   It is also to be found, though in guardedly obscure forms, in such pioneering Catholic writers as Karl Rahner, Edward Schillebeeckx and Hans Küng. On Rahner's Christology, see my *Problems of Religious Pluralism* (London: Macmillan, and New York: St Martin's Press, 1985) ch. 4.

22.   *Theologica Germanica*, trs. Susanna Winkworth (London: Macmillan, 1937) p. 32.

23.   Cf. John Downing, 'Jesus and Martyrdom', *Journal of Theological Studies*, vol. 14 (1963).

Part III
Hints from Buddhism

6

The Buddha's Doctrine of the 'Undetermined Questions'

In considering the 'conflicting truth claims' of the different religions we need not only a theory of religious knowledge but also a theory of religious ignorance. And I think that we have a very good start to such a theory in the Buddha's doctrine of the *avyakata* or, as the term is often translated, the undetermined questions.

Let us begin by looking at what the Buddha had to say. There are two main texts in the Pali scriptures, Sutta 63 and Sutta 72 of the *Majjihima Nikāya,* and in each Sutta we have the same list of ten propositions or 'views' (*ditthi*):

1. The world is eternal.
2. The world is not eternal.
3. The world is (spatially) infinite.
4. The world is not (spatially) infinite.
5. The soul (*jiva*) is identical with the body.
6. The soul is not identical with the body.
7. The Tathagata (that is, a perfectly enlightened being) exists after death.
8. The Tathagata does not exist after death.
9. The Tathagata both exists and does not exist after death.
10. The Tathagata neither exists nor does not exist after death.

Each of these propositions can be readily supplied with the question to which it functions as a response so that we can speak either of the unresolved issues or the unresolved questions.

The issues dealt with under these ten propositions fall, under examination, into two categories, which I shall call respectively unanswered questions and unanswerable questions. (Whether this distinction was in the mind of Guatama, or in the minds of the editors

105

of the Pali canon, I do not profess to know.) The first group is exemplified in Sutta 63 and the second in Sutta 72. But first let us hear the fundamental point — which means in the case of the Buddha's teaching the soteriological point – which he was concerned to make about both categories; namely, that to know the answers to these questions is not necessary for liberation and that to treat them as though they were soteriologically important will only hinder our advance toward liberation. He told the parable of the man pierced by a poisoned arrow. If he insists, before receiving medical treatment, on knowing who shot the arrow, and of what clan he is, what kind of bow he was using, what the bow string and the shaft of the arrow were made of, from what kind of bird the feathers on the arrow came, he will die before his thirst for knowledge is satisfied. Likewise, if we distract ourselves from the path to enlightenment by trying to settle these disputed cosmological and metaphysical issues we may well fail to be healed from birth, ageing, dying, grief, sorrow, suffering, lamentation and despair. And so these matters are set aside by the Buddha because such knowledge 'is not connected with the goal, is not fundamental to the Brahma-faring, and does not conduce to turning away from, nor to dispassion, stopping, calming, super-knowledge, awakening not to nibbana'.[1]

This fundamental soteriological point applies to both of the two kinds of issues. The difference between them is, however, of considerable interest. The first, consisting of what I am calling the unanswered questions, are questions to which there is a true answer although we do not in fact know that answer. The example in Sutta 63 is the eternity or non-eternity of the world. The monk Malunkyaputta complains,

> If the Lord knows that the world is eternal, let the Lord explain to me that the world is eternal. If the Lord knows that the world is not eternal, let the Lord explain to me that the world is not eternal. If the Lord does not know whether the world is eternal or whether the world is not eternal, then, not knowing, not seeing, this would be honest, namely to say, 'I do not know, I do not see.'[2]

On the face of it Malunkyaputta's request is reasonable. The world must be either eternal or not eternal. He reckons that if the Buddha has attained insight into all things he will know which. And indeed it may be that the Buddha does know; this is not clear from the Pali scriptures. But whether he knows or not, he insists that the answer is not necessary for liberation and that to treat the question as soteriologically important would only distract Malunkyputta from a single-minded striving to attain *nirvana*.

The second category of issues is illustrated in Sutta 72 by the question, asked by the monk Vaccagotta, about the state of the Tathagata after death. A Tathagata is a fully enlightened being, a Buddha, and the question concerns the ultimate conclusion of the process of finite human existence. This is not the question of the fate after death of ordinary unenlightened individuals; the Buddha's answer to that question was the doctrine of rebirth. In response to Vaccagotta's question he rejects as inapplicable the entire range of possible answers in terms of which the question was posed – namely, by specifying in what kind of world the Tathagata arises after death:

'Arise', Vaccha, does not apply.
Well, then, good Gotama, does he not arise?
'Does not arise', Vaccha, does not apply.
Well then, good Gotama, does he both arise and not arise?
'Both arises and does not arise', Vaccha, does not apply.
Well then, good Gotama, does he neither arise nor not arise?
'Neither arises nor does not arise', Vaccha, does not apply.[3]

Vaccha then expresses his bewilderment and disappointment, and the Buddha responds, 'You ought to be at a loss, Vaccha, you ought to be bewildered. For Vaccha, this dhamma is deep, difficult to see, difficult to understand, peaceful, excellent, beyond dialectics, subtle, intelligible to the wise . . .'[4] – referring all the time to the mystery of *nirvana* beyond this life. It is misleading to say that after death the Tathagata exists, or does not exist, or both exists and does not exist, or neither exists nor non-exists.[5] The Buddha then illustrates the idea of a question which is so put that it has no answer by speaking of a flame that has been quenched. In which direction has the flame gone – east, west, north or south? None of the permitted answers applies. Likewise what happens after the bodily death of a Tathagata cannot be expressed in the categories that we have available. For the analogy of the quenched flame is not intended to indicate non-existence. 'Freed from denotation by consciousness', Gautama says, 'is the Tathagata, Vaccha, he is deep, immeasurable, unfathomable as is the great ocean.'[6]

The difference, then, between the two kinds of *avyakata* is this. The unanswered questions are legitimate questions to which there are presumably true answers, but to which we do not in fact know the answers. It is not excluded, in logic, that human beings might some day come to know the truth of these matters. But it would still be the case that salvation/liberation does not depend upon such knowledge and that the search for it is not conducive to salvation/liberation. In distinction from these, the unanswerable questions are about realities transcending the systems of categories available in our human thought and language. They are matters which, in St Paul's words, 'No eye has seen, nor ear heard, nor the heart of man conceived'.[7] It seems appropriate to refer to the subject matter of these unanswerable questions as mysteries, matters that are beyond human comprehension and expression. But once again we do not, according to the Buddha, need to be able to penetrate these mysteries in order to attain to liberation; and to feel that we must hold a dogmatic view concerning them is soteriologically counterproductive.

Although this thought was first presented to the world by the Buddha, it should not be regarded as an exclusively Buddhist insight but rather as one that is available on its merits to us all. It could be that the universe, like a modern spy operation, is conducted on a 'need to know' basis and that what, religiously, we need to know is soteriological rather than metaphysical. If so, the metaphysical differences between the different religious traditions, responding in their distinctively different ways to the various unanswered and unanswerable questions, will not affect the all-important matter of salvation/liberation. This is the possibility that I now want to explore a little.

Let us put to one side for a moment the distinction between the unanswered and the unanswerable questions, together with the thought that it is not necessary for liberation to know the truth concerning them, and turn to the other half of our subject, the 'conflicting truth claims' of the different religious traditions. These are of three kinds which are, in ascending order of importance, first, historical issues; secondly, what I shall call (for want of a better name) trans-historical issues; and thirdly, conceptions of that ultimate reality to which the religions are, on a religious interpretation of them, different responses. I want to suggest (though with different qualifications and complications in each case) that these three sets of issues all concern either unanswered or unanswerable questions, which naturally evoke theories and guesses, but concerning which knowledge is not necessary for salvation/liberation.

Consider first conflicts of historical truth-claims. (I mean 'historical' here in the basic sense of referring to alleged past events of such a kind that if they occurred it would have been possible, had the necessary technology been available, to record them with camera and/or microphone.) There are in fact very few conflicts of this kind between the different traditions. In general the historical affirmations of the religions refer to different and non-overlapping strands of history, and the doctrines of tradition A have nothing to say, either positively or negatively, about the distinctive historical beliefs of tradition B. For example, Judaism tells the story of the conflict between Elijah and the priests of Baal, whilst the Hindu, Buddhist, Confucian and Taoist scriptures are not concerned either to confirm or deny this – it belongs to a different universe of discourse from their own. Indeed the only instances I have been able to identify of direct inter-traditional conflicts of historical beliefs are the Christian belief that Jesus died on the cross versus the Muslim belief that he only appeared to die, and the Jewish belief that it was Isaac, versus the Muslim belief that it was his brother, Ishmael, who was nearly sacrificed on Mount Moriah. What are much more common are historical disagreements *within* a tradition, producing splits between rival subtraditions – for example, the Mahayana–Theravada dispute as to whether the latter preserves the original teaching of the Buddha; the Catholic–Protestant dispute as to whether Jesus appointed Peter as head of his church and whether the popes are Peter's successors in this office; and the Sunni–Shia dispute as to whether Muhammad appointed Ali as his successor in the leadership of the Muslim Ummah.

Such historical issues – both inter- and intra-traditional – can only be settled by historical evidence. In practice, however, such questions are not usually today definitively settleable because the historical evidence is no longer available. The historian, *qua* historian, has to be content to live with uncertainty. These, then, are examples of unanswered questions – questions to which there are true answers although we do not, and indeed may perhaps never, know with certainty what those answers are.

However, it is possible to hold that even though we lack conclusive evidence, such beliefs nevertheless are so integral to a whole religious system that it is necessary for salvation/liberation to hold certain views as a matter of faith. Thus some Christians would hold that if Jesus did not die on the cross, then (a) the New Testament records are unreliable, and (b) Jesus' subsequent resurrection is denied; and that either or both of these implications would be fatal to the system of Christian doctrine. If it is then added that it is necessary for salvation to accept the system of Christian doctrine, it will follow that only those who believe by faith that Jesus died on the cross are able to receive salvation.

This particular question of Jesus' death raises well some of the issues that we have to look at. As a historical question it is fairly nonthreatening to Christian faith. For the historical evidence is distinctly one-sided. Although the documents come from two generations after the event, they all concur in indicating a death, and the only basis on which this is denied in the Qur'an is the theological inference that God would not allow so holy a prophet to be killed. But this inference does not constitute historical counter-evidence. Any strictly historical question mark is a very slight and shadowy one arising merely from the general fact that we cannot attain one hundred per cent certainty about any historical details of the remote past. So there is (in my view at least) no serious historical dispute here.

But if we go on to affirm that it is necessary for salvation to believe this historical fact because it is an integral part of a system of belief the acceptance of which is essential for salvation, we create difficulties of the most profound and disturbing kind. I do not know how such a position could be disproved. It does, however, have alarming implications concerning the character of a God who could institute such an arrangement. But there have always been those who are apparently untroubled by such implications. For my part, I find the idea that God has ordained a scheme under which the large majority of the human race are, through no fault of their own, condemned to perdition, so morally repulsive that it would undermine the Godness, or worship-worthiness, of any being who was said to be God. It would thus be a religiously self-refuting view. I shall therefore pass on to the next type of conflict of belief.

This consists of matters of what I am calling, for want of a better name, trans-historical fact. I mean by this, matters of fact which are not settleable, even in principle, by historical or other empirical evidence. Some within this category are unanswered questions whilst others are unanswerable. The Buddha's own example, whether the universe is eternal, is of the former kind, for regressive description must either terminate or not terminate in an initial state. At the moment we do not know which. It is possible, indeed likely, that the scientific cosmologists will one day be able to settle the matter. Within the framework of the big bang hypothesis, the critical issue is whether the volume of matter in the universe is or is not sufficient to generate a gravitational pull that will reverse the present expansion. But the Buddha's point was that it is not necessary for, or conducive to, liberation to know whether the universe is infinite in time and/or infinite in space. I would go further and say that no scientific knowledge can in itself be religiously significant except in so far as the religions unwisely adopt dogmatic views, as they have some times done, on questions in astronomy, geology, biology, astrophysics or any other of the special sciences. For the physical universe is religiously ambiguous, in the sense that everything we know or can conceive of knowing about its physical structure and workings is capable of being construed both religiously and naturalistically. Thus if the big bang of some 15 billion years ago was unique, it does not necessarily follow that there is a God who created it; and on the other hand if the universe is going through an infinite succession of expansions and contractions, it does not necessarily follow that it is not a divine creation. Nor is there any objective sense of probability in which scientific discoveries can render the existence of God either more or less probable. The only way to pull a divine rabbit out of the scientific hat would be to reduce the concept of God to that of an aspect of the physical universe – either to a relatively precisely definable aspect, such as energy (which figures in Einstein's basic relativity formula), or to such vaguely defined aspects as life, order, creativity or complexification. Certainly, if we choose to mean by God the fact of life, or the fact of evolution, or the fact of creativity (that is, the emergence of new features), or some other aspect of the physical universe, then science can indeed lead us to God. But it will be arbitrary and gratuitous to call this aspect of the universe God, and the move will inevitably be objectionably reductionistic from the point of view of the traditional monotheistic faiths.

The doctrine of reincarnation or rebirth is another response to an unanswered trans-historical question. Of course, the Buddha himself did not classify it in this way. It seemed obvious to all within his religio-cultural world that human life is part of a vast karmic process involving repeated rebirths in this and other worlds. But this is nevertheless not universally obvious. So far as the West is concerned the idea of reincarnation conflicts both with traditional Jewish, Christian and Muslim beliefs and with contemporary western naturalism. Thus looked at on the world scale, we have to categorise reincarnation as one of the *avyakata* or undetermined issues. And if we accept the Buddha's basic soteriological insight, we shall conclude that it is neither necessary for salvation/liberation to know whether reincarnation occurs nor conducive to salvation/liberation to devote one's energies to establishing such knowledge.

Let us turn now to an instance not of an unanswered but an unanswerable question. Here the Buddha's example was the state of a Tathagata – that is, a perfected human being – after death. This is the question of the ultimate state to which the projectory of human spiritual growth finally leads. And the Buddha said that this cannot be described in our present set of human concepts. None of the options of which we can conceive is applicable. The notion of a self existing does not apply; but neither does the notion of a self not existing. What lies beyond what we now think of as the self cannot be expressed in our present conceptual system or pictured with our present imaginative resources: 'Freed from denotation by consciousness is the Tathagata, Vaccha.' And once again the Buddha's point was not only that we cannot at present know what the ultimate state is but also that we do not at present need to know and that it would not be conducive to salvation/liberation to speculate – and still less (I think we may add) to insist that everyone must accept our speculation.

I shall come presently to the third level of disagreement, which concerns conceptions of the ultimate. But let us pause here to draw some interim conclusions. The belief systems of the great world faiths consist very largely of assertions regarding what I have called matters of trans-historical fact. I shall consider some Christian examples, though each of the other world faiths deals in the same or similar issues. The traditional Christian dogmas include: that the universe began through an act of divine creation; that the first human beings fell from grace, so that all human beings since have been sinners; that we can be forgiven by God only as a result of his Son dying on the cross; that Jesus had a virgin birth and a bodily resurrection and ascension into the sky; that after death we go either to heaven or to hell (or to heaven via purgatory); that the Bible is the divinely inspired and therefore authoritative Word of God to humanity; that there is no other way in which humans can be saved except by faith in Christ. These are dogmas which nearly all Christians from about the end of the second to about the end of the eighteenth century confidently believed. However, during the last 150 years or so, thoughtful Christians have been treating this belief system as more pliable and open to development than was possible during the ages of dogmatic faith. When one way of construing a basic concept leads to mounting difficulties, it is now regarded as possible to explore other construals of it. The cumulative result has been gradually to disentangle the Christian life from commitment to particular dogmatic answers to both the unanswered and the unanswerable questions. This is the direction in which Christian theology has been going for more than a century and in which it seems likely to continue. Accordingly, forms of Christian theology which leave open the unanswered questions, and which respond with what are accepted as myths to the unanswerable questions, are at present being experimentally developed. It will, however, be a long time before a new consensus develops, and when it does, it may well prove to be not another monolithic consensus at all but rather a pluralistic range of differing theoretical frameworks for the same soteriological process.

Let us now consider how the Buddha's doctrine of the unanswered and the unanswerable questions might apply to the developments in Buddhist thought after his time. I would suggest that any doctrine that generalises dogmatically beyond the scope of experience, including within experience the experience of enlightenment, will be affected by it.

Thus, first, to say that we find ourselves to be part of a vast continuous process of interdependent change (*pratitya samutpada*), in which there is no aseity, or self-existence, but everything is mutually co-constituted by everything else, is to affirm a doctrine based upon experience and the analysis of experience. But to go beyond this to affirm that this continuum of *pratitya samutpada* is uncreated and not structured towards any end or fulfilment is to go beyond the witness of experience. Indeed, the Buddha himself included the eternity or non-eternity of the world in his own list of *avyakata*. And likewise the existence of a creator is not dogmatically denied, according at least to some well-known scholars of Buddhism. Thus Edward Conze, who was himself a Buddhist, wrote:

Buddhist tradition does not exactly deny the existence of a creator, but it is not really interested to know who created the universe. The purpose of Buddhist doctrine is to release beings from suffering, and speculations concerning the origin of the universe are held to be immaterial to that task.'[8]

I suggest that dogmatic insistence upon the nonexistence of a creator, and again a dogmatic insistence that the universe does not have a teleological structure moving towards what we can refer to, in Buddhist language, as universal *nirvana*, would be to go beyond what is known within Buddhist experience. And to insist that this 'more' is the truth which everyone needs to know in order to find liberation would be soteriologically counterproductive.

But further, concerning the doctrine that the ultimate reality indicated by the term *sunyata* is identical with *pratitya samutpada*, the world process: is this a truth necessary for liberation, or is it an optional speculative view? One possible Buddhist position, I suggest, is that the ultimate reality, *sunyata*, is manifested within Buddhist experience as *pratitya samutpada*, but is not exhausted by or limited to the world process. Rather, it is itself beyond all concepts, including the concept of *pratitya samutpada*, being empty of everything that human thought might attribute to it. Thus Masao Abe in his very important paper 'A Dynamic Unity in Religious Pluralism: a Proposal from the Buddhist Point of View'[9] suggests that *sunyata*, which is ultimate reality, the Real, is manifested as the various personal Gods, and presumably also (though he does not say this) the nonpersonal Absolutes, of the world religions. It is the ground of these different experienced manifestations of it within human consciousness. If he were to add that the absolute of distinctively Buddhist experience, namely *pratitya samutpada*, is also a manifestation of *sunyata*, we would then have what would in principle be a field theory of religion. We would be saying that the ultimate reality, in itself inexperienceable and beyond the scope of human conceptuality, is experienced in a range of different ways made possible by the different spiritual disciplines and systems of religious thought. There are Jewish, Christian, Muslim and Hindu and other theistic experiences of *sunyata* as a personal deity. There is the advaitic Hindu experience of *sunyata* as Brahman. And there is the Mahayana Buddhist experience of *sunyata* as the world-process, *pratitya samutpada*. Here the ultimate is experienced as wholly immanent within the immediately experienced. But the kind of theory I am now suggesting would not claim that this is the *only* authentic mode of experience of the ultimate. Rather, there is a range of different but, for all we know, equally valid modes.

So what I am suggesting in relation to questions of trans-historical fact is that it would be a mark of wisdom and maturity frankly to acknowledge our ignorance. In the case of the presently unanswered questions, we should recognise that there is a range of possibilities, and should not try to insist that everyone – neither all Christians nor (still less) all human beings – must affirm the position which appeals most to ourselves. Rather, we should realise that it is not necessary for salvation/liberation to know whether, for example, the universe had a beginning and will have an end (as western thought has generally supposed), or whether on the contrary it goes in a beginningless and endless series of cycles (as eastern thought has generally supposed). Further, we should take very seriously the Buddha's insight that to regard such questions as soteriologically significant can only hinder the salvific process. And concerning the unanswerable questions – unanswerable because posed in human terms about realities which transcend our human conceptualities – it would again be a mark of wisdom and maturity to accept our ignorance. We do not know, for example, the nature of the ultimate eschatological state – whether it is a state of what we now call ourselves, whether it is in what we now know as space or in what we now know as time, and so on. The questions that we pose about it may be so utterly wide of the mark that any answers to them are worse than useless. If a caterpillar could ask, concerning its own future post-chrysalis state, how many legs it will then have, how fast it will be able to walk, and what kind of leaves it will be able to eat, the Buddha would say, 'Number of legs, speed of walking, eating of leaves, Vaccha, do not apply. Freed from denotation by caterpillar consciousness is the butterfly.'

The suggestion, then, that we derive from the Buddha's words is that we should sit very lightly to our inherited Christian dogmas concerning creation, fall, eschatology and method of salvation. In this last item I would emphasise the word 'method'. The fact of salvation/liberation, in the concrete sense of the progressive transformation of human existence from self-centredness to Reality-centredness, or (in Christian terms) to God-centredness, is not in question. It is an observable fact – observable indirectly in its fruits in human life. But the dogma that this is made possible only by the death of Christ is a distinctively Christian theory; and it is to this and to all such theories that we should sit lightly, realising that each has been developed in the context of one particular tradition and has its use only in that context. The reality of salvation/liberation is limit- lessly more important than particular theories about it; and to try to insist that all Christians, or all human beings, must accept the tradi- tional Christian theory, or family of theories, would be – and has, I think, in fact been – soteriologically counterproductive.

Parallel considerations apply, of course, to the dogmas of the other great world faiths, though I do not have space to develop that here. But the outcome, so far as interfaith dialogue is concerned, is that the kinds of doctrinal differences that we have been considering should be matters of keen speculative interest rather than matters of ultimate concern in which our religious existence is felt to be at stake.

Finally, let us turn to the most fundamental differences of belief between the great traditions, namely, their different conceptions of the ultimate reality to which the religions constitute our human responses. In speaking of the ultimate focus of religious thought and experience, I propose to use the term 'the Real'. Is the Real, then, personal or nonpersonal? If personal, is it the Adonai of Judaism, or the Holy Trinity of Christianity, or the Allah of Islam, or the Shiva or the Vishnu of theistic Hinduism? If nonpersonal, is it the Brahman of advaitic Hinduism, or the Tao of Chinese religion, or the Dharmakaya or Sunyata or Nirvana of Buddhism? The hypothesis that I should like to consider is that the nature of the Real in itself, independently of human awareness of it, is the ultimate unanswerable question. Our human concepts, drawn as they are from our earthly experi- ence, do not apply to the Real in itself, but only to the Real as humanly thought, experienced and responded to within the differ- ent traditions. 'Thou art formless', says the Hindu *Yogava'sistha*, 'Thine only form is our knowledge of Thee'.[10] In Buddhist terms we could say: The Real is *sunyata*, empty, formless, but takes different forms within human experience. And in theistic terms: God in God's eternal self-existent nature is unknowable, but in relation to human consciousness, God becomes the range of divine personae worshipped within the different theistic traditions. Such manifestations are formed at the interface between the Real and the various streams of human life. They consist both in the personae of the Real – Adonai, the Holy Trinity, Allah, Vishnu and so on – and its impersonae, Brahman, the Dharmakaya, the Tao and the rest. And our concepts – such as personality, consciousness, goodness, love, justice, power, unity, plurality, substantiality – apply literally, in either the univocal or the analogical mode, to these manifestations. But in speaking literally in these ways about a manifestation of the Real we are at the same times speaking mythologically about the Real in itself. Thus, that the Real is love is literally true of its manifestation as the heavenly Father of the New Testament or as the Krishna of the Bhagavad Gita, and mythologically true of the Real in itself; and that the Real is being-consciousness-bliss (*satchitananda*) is literally true of its ex-perienced manifestation as Brahman and mythologically true of the Real in itself. By 'mythologically true' I mean: tending to evoke in the human hearer an appropriate dispositional response. For in so far as the personae or impersonae of the Real are authentic manifestations of it, they are in soteriological alignment with the Real, so that a right response to one of its manifestations constitutes a right response – not the only right response but *a* right response – to the Real. Thus in responding to the heavenly Father as love by loving our neighbour, or in responding to the Dharma by seeking to attain unselfcentred existence, we are responding rightly to the Real.

If this is so, the different conceptions of the Real, in terms of which the different forms of religious experience and response have devel-oped, are not literally true or false descriptions of the Real but are mythologically true in so far as they are soteriologically effective. And there is no evident reason why a variety of such mythological conceptions of the Real should not prove to be equally soteriologically effective and hence equally mythologically true. To what extent this is in fact the case cannot be decided *a priori*, but only by observing the fruits of salvation/liberation in human life, individual and communal, within the contexts of the different traditions. Such a comparative assessment is extremely difficult, in fact at present im-possible except as a very rough impression. I would only venture the view that we have at this point no adequate reason to think that any of the great world traditions is soteriologically more effective than any other.

To conclude, then, I have suggested that the doctrinal differences between the great world faiths consist in different responses, prompted by different cultural patterns, to a range of unanswered and unanswerable questions. These questions are either good ques-tions to which we do not at present know the answer, but in relation to which a variety of hypotheses and guesses are permissible, or questions to which there can be no non-misleading answer because the terms in which they are posed are not applicable to the realities to which they refer. Although dogmas concerning these realities are therefore not appropriate, myth-making is appropriate, and religious myths are true in so far as the dispositional response which they tend to evoke makes for the transformation of human existence from self-centredness to Reality-centredness.

Notes

1. Majjhima Nikāya, II.431, trans. I. B. Horner (London: Luzac, 1957) p. 101.
2. Ibid., II. 427, E. T. p. 98.
3. Ibid., 486, E. T. p. 165.
4. Ibid., 487, E. T. p. 165.
5. Sanyutta Nikāya, IV. 374, E. T. p. 266.
6. Majjhima Nikāya,II. 487, E. T. p. 166.
7. 1 Corinthians 2:9.
8. Edward Conze, *Buddhism, Its Essence and Development* (1951; New York: Harper Torchbooks, 1975) p. 39.
9. Masao Abe, 'A Dynamic Unity in Religious Pluralism: a Proposal from the Buddhist Point of View', in *The Experience of Religious Diversity*, ed. J. Hick and H. Askari (Aldershot: Gower, 1985).
10. *Yogava'sistha*, I:28.

7

Religion as 'Skilful Means'

The concept of *upaya* (or *upayakausalya*), 'skilful means', has functioned on various levels within the Buddhist tradition, with considerable differences also in its degrees of prominence. It is a major concern in the Lotus Sutra, the Prajnaparamita literature and the *Teaching of Vimalakirti*, but absent or almost absent from many other scriptures. However, I am not going to concern myself with the history of the concept. I should be totally incompetent to do so; and fortunately Michael Pye had done this authoritatively in *Skilful Means: A Concept of Mahayana Buddhism*,[1] of which I shall be making use.

There is a narrower and a broader use of the notion of *upaya*. In its narrower meaning it presupposes that a teacher knows some truth which is to be communicated to others so that they may come to see it for themselves, and the skilful means are the devices which the teacher uses to do this. Thus in the Pali scriptures the Buddha is constantly using similes and parables and often asking skilfully leading questions. Further, he is not usually declaring general truths, valid for all times and circumstances, but is speaking to a particular individual or group and is taking account of his hearers' karmic state and adapting his words to the stage of understanding at which he perceives them to be.

I think it is evident that skilful means, in this narrower sense, are used by religious teachers in all traditions. Jesus, for example, used parables and similes and asked leading questions,[2] as also did many others. Indeed, skilful means are used in all pedagogy. Any teacher of philosophy is accustomed to introduce material in a planned order, knowing that novices in the subject are often not able properly to grasp the sophisticated concepts and distinctions which more advanced students can understand and use. Further, he sometimes utters partial truths, which are also partial falsehoods, because they represent the next stage of understanding of the person he is addressing. In short, there is nothing unusual or remarkable in this narrower sense of *upaya*.

II

In its more comprehensive sense, however, the concept expresses a profound insight, excitingly illuminating or deeply disturbing according to one's presuppositions, into the nature of Buddhism, and perhaps also into the nature of religion generally. It first appears in this broader sense in the Buddha's parable of the raft in the *Majjhima Nikaya* (Book i, 134–5). A man coming to a great stretch of water sees that the side he is on is dangerous but the other side safe, and so he desires to cross over. There is no bridge or boat, so he takes branches and grass and constructs a raft and paddles successfully over to the other side. Since the raft has been so useful he is tempted to lift it on to his shoulders and carry it with him. What he should do, however, according to the Buddha, is to go on, leaving the raft behind. Likewise the *dharma*, he says, is 'for carrying over, not for retaining . . . You, monks, by understanding the Parable of the Raft, should get rid even of (right) mental objects, all the more of wrong ones.'[3] This parable is thus a skilful means in the narrower sense about skilful means in the broader sense. The contemporary western philosophical reader is at once reminded of Wittgenstein's statement towards the end of the *Tractatus Logico-Philosophicus* (6.54) that 'My propositions are elucidatory in this way: he who understands me finally recognises them as senseless, when he has climbed out through them, on them, over them. (He must so to speak throw away the ladder, after he has climbed up on it).'

This thought that the *dharma* itself is a skilful means is taken up as a major concern in the Mahayana. Michael Pye says, 'The Mahayanists saw the whole Buddhist religion as a vehicle for "crossing over" and for "bringing over", which are inseparable. In short, Buddhism is skilful means' (p. 159). This explains, Pye thinks, how it is that the Buddhist movement has been able to move into different cultures and take correspondingly different forms. For the Indian Buddhism preserved in Sri Lanka and, with variations, in other Theravada lands, and likewise Chinese, Tibetan, Korean and Japanese Buddhism, are all distinctively different in ways that reflect the characters of these different civilisations. And we may be seeing today the development, particularly in the United States, of a western form of Buddhism which again has its own distinctive emphases. For all of the successive forms that the *dharma* takes are adapted to the needs of different peoples and periods.

But this thought immediately provokes questions. How far is it to be taken? It is one thing to say that the Theravada is appropriate for some people (particularly, presumably, those in Theravada lands who have been formed by it) and Zen for others, Pure Land for others again, and Tantric Buddhism for yet others; and likewise that among the various forms of Buddhist philosophy some people will find this more illuminating, others that. But it is another and more radical thing to say that the Four Noble Truths, containing the basic concepts of *dukkha* and *nirvana*, and also the further concepts of *pratitya samutpada, anicca* and *anatta*, and again the concept, so stressed in the Mahayana, of *sunyata*, are not absolute but provisional, and relative to the human mind, or rather to some human minds, being skilful means for drawing them on from one state to another. Again, is the doctrine that all doctrines are skilful means to be applied to itself? And would not this lead to a logical paradox analogous to the statement 'This statement is false'?

It seems, then, that there must be a limit to the view that Buddhism is a skilful means. For the idea of means implies the idea of an end. Buddhism, then, is a skilful means to what end? The Buddhist answer will be awakening, enlightenment, liberation, *satori, nirvana*. But is this answer perhaps itself a skilful means? If so, we are left with nothing but means which are not means to anything, and the whole system collapses into incoherence. To avoid this it seems that we must say that the doctrine of the end to which Buddhism is a means is not itself another skilful means but is intended (to coin a not very elegant term) non-upayically.

We are led, then, to draw a distinction between the upayic and the non-upayic elements of Buddhism. In fact the distinction is not one of the totally upayic and the totally non-upayic, but of degrees of upayity. But on this continuum there are nevertheless important differences to be noted; and in locating them we can, I think, profitably use the distinction familiar within modern critical Christian thinking between, on the one hand, religious experience, and on the other the philosophical and theological theories to which it has given rise. Let us at any rate explore the possibility that we can distinguish between Buddhist experience, and the concepts and language by means of which this has been expressed, and treat the latter as much more strongly upayic than reports of the former.

III

In the stories of the Buddha's life and teaching in the Pali scriptures there seem to be two key modes of experience. There is ordinary human experience, which is pervaded by unsatisfactoriness, anguish, suffering, anxiety, not having what one wants and having what one does not want, including the unavoidable realities of sickness, pain, loss, decay and death. All this is a pervasive aspect of human experience. No honest and reflective person, however, fortunate his or her own circumstances, is likely to deny that this is indeed a feature of our human situation. The Buddha called it comprehensively *dukkha*. And so long as no additional conceptual baggage is loaded on to the term, and it is used simply as a finger pointing to an important fact, it seems to be entirely acceptable. *Dukkha* is not a metaphysical theory but refers to an experienced reality.

The other experience which lies at the origin of Buddhism is of course Gautama's nirvanic experience, achieved at Bodh Gaya and maintained through the rest of his life. It seems preferable to speak of a nirvanic experience rather than of an experience of *nirvana*, since the latter might suggest that '*nirvana*' refers to a place or entity of some kind. Those today who believe that they have experienced nirvanically do not profess to be able adequately to describe this mode of experience; and I shall certainly not try to do what they are not able to do. Nevertheless, if the word is not to be a mere sound without any conceptual content we must have some idea, even if only a relatively vague one, of what we mean by it. The Pali scriptures seem to me – though I speak subject to correction – to suggest a state of complete inner freedom,[4] equilibrium, peace, lack of angst[5] and a sense of being entirely 'at home' and unthreatened in the universe, which expresses itself both in a positive affective state[6] and in compassion for all forms of life.[7] Having encountered a few people – some of them Buddhist, others Christian, Hindu, Jewish, Muslim, Sikh – who in some degree exhibit such a state of mind or being, I have no difficulty in accepting that Gautama's nirvanic experience occurred, and occurred in unprecedented fulness. The Third Noble Truth, then, the truth of the cessation of *dukkha*, which is the truth of *nirvana*, can also be regarded as a report of experience rather than as the formulation of a theory.

Further, Gautama was aware of the way by which he had moved from his immersion in *dukkha* to the freedom of *nirvana*, a way that he spelled out for others in the fourth Noble Truth as the Eightfold

Path. This is a moral and spiritual discipline which gradually produces a cessation of self-centredness and a transcendence of the ego
point of view, thus eliminating the opposition between self and
others.[8] And like the fact of *dukkha*, the way to *nirvana* was a reality
given in Gautama's experience, a reality that he expressed in the
second Noble Truth, affirming that the *dukkha* character of ordinary
experience is a product of the ego point of view, with its self-centred
desires and aversions.

The Four Noble Truths, then, should be regarded as reports of
experience rather than as theories or speculations. But nevertheless,
we must not forget that even at this basic level there is always an
element of interpretation. All epistemic experience (experience that
purports to be experience-of) involves the use of concepts which
endow it with a meaning in terms of which we can behave appropriately in relation to that which is thus experienced. Our conceptual
system is embodied in language, and the world as described is
therefore always partially formed by the human experiencer and
language user. This legacy of the Kantian epistemological revolution, recognising the active and creative role of the mind in all
awareness of the phenomenal (that is, experienceable) world, and
the consequent 'theory-laden' and hence relative and provisional
character of all affirmations about it, has important implications for
the study of religion. It entails that all human awareness necessarily
exhibits distinctively human forms, and that an intuition of the
universe as it is in itself, rather than as it appears within human
consciousness, could not be expressed in any language but would
require silence.

As soon, then, as the Buddha decided to break his initial silence
and communicate the truth to a suffering world, thereby setting the
wheel of *dharma* in motion, he was using skilful means in the sense
that he was conveying in language something that cannot in principle be captured in language. For, as Michael Pye surely correctly
insists, 'The concept of skilful means has to do with the status of
religious language and symbols of all kinds.'[9]

There are however (as we noted above) what we may clumsily
call degrees or, perhaps better, levels of upayity. Whilst all statements, from the four Noble Truths to the most manifestly speculative positions of later Buddhist philosophy, are necessarily 'theory
laden', they can nevertheless be classified on different levels according as the concepts employed are universal human concepts – for
example, the concepts of space, time, causality, thinghood – or are

products of specialised theories, occurring within particular optional ways of seeing and understanding the world: for example, the Yogacara concept of the 'store consciousness' (*alayavijnana*) or the notion, affirmed by some but denied by other schools of Buddhist philosophy, of the essential self (*pudgala*). Using this distinction of levels we may say that the concepts of suffering, desire and greed, the cessation of desire and greed, morality and meditation, are more or less universal and that the four Noble Truths accordingly operate at a relatively low level of upayity.

Let us now turn to the notion of *pratitya samutpada* ('codependent origination'), arrived at by the Buddha during the weeks of meditation following his enlightenment at Bodh Gaya. As it appears in the Pali canon, this is a spelling-out in more detail of the second Noble Truth concerning the source of *dukkha*. The list of elements in the continuous loop varies slightly in different texts. Here it is given, not as an account of the arising of *dukkha*, but of its ceasing:

> Lo! I have won to this, the Way to enlightenment through insight. And it is this, that from name-and-form ceasing, cognition ceases and conversely; that from cognition ceasing, the sixfold field ceases; from the sixfold field ceasing, contact ceases; from contact ceasing, feeling ceases; from feeling ceasing, craving ceases; from craving ceasing, grasping ceases; from grasping ceasing, becoming ceases; from becoming ceasing, birth ceases; from birth ceasing, decay and dying, grief, lamentation, ill, sorrow and despair cease. Such is the ceasing of this entire body of Ill.[10]

This analysis seems to me to involve a considerable use of optional concepts and assumptions. The basic observation, embodied in the second Noble Truth, that *dukkha* is a product of the point of view of the self-enclosed ego, with its ruling desires and aversions, could surely be spelled out in detail in a variety of other ways, using different systems of psychological and physiological concepts and distinctions. *Pratitya samutpada*, in the sense in which it first appears in the Pali scriptures, thus strikes me as on a distinctly higher level of upayity, or theory-ladenness, than the four Noble Truths. It points – surely correctly – to the closed circle of *dukkha*; but the precise way in which this circle is divided and labelled seems to be to some extent optional. This is a cake that can be cut in different ways.

However, in the Mahayana *pratitya samutpada* took on a larger meaning which links it with the notions of *anicca* (transitoriness) and *anatta* (no soul) and, in a further extension, with the key Mahayana notion of *sunyata* (emptiness). In this larger use *pratitya samutpada* means that the entire life of the universe consists in the ceaseless change of a kind of gravitational system of mutually dependent elements in which nothing exists independently but everything is partly constituted by the influences upon it of everything else. What we call a 'thing' comes to exist and ceases to exist as an outcome of innumerable interacting forces, and consequently has no ontological status in isolation from the rest of the world and outside the universal flow of change. This applies to ourselves also. We are not permanent mental substances – this is the truth of *anatta* – but are temporary elements in the ever-changing life of the universe. Indeed, the whole world is empty of the independent substantiality that we project upon it in awareness. It is empty of the entire conceptual structure and ego-related meaning in terms of which we construct our ordinary experience. This is the truth of *sunyata*.

It appears to me that the doctrine of *anicca*, in its extended form, affirming that the universe is an endless continuum of change, without beginning or end, must be a theory rather than a report of experience. That everything we observe, including even an apparently unchanging mountain, is in fact changing, however slowly, and that human life is subject to the inevitability of old age, decay and death, represents a very widespread, indeed probably universal, perception in all ages and cultures. But that the entire universe, in the most comprehensive sense of that word, shares this evanescence and that there is accordingly no reality that transcends the flow of time, is surely a larger claim than can legitimately be made on the basis of our own experience. That everything we observe is transient can safely be affirmed; but the evidence on which this is affirmed cannot authorise the further claim that there is no eternal reality transcending the realm of temporal change.

Further, such an affirmation would conflict with another aspect of the Buddha's teaching, namely, that the transition from *dukkha* to *nirvana* is a real possibility for everyone because it is based upon the permanent ultimate nature or structure of reality. The universe has a certain objective character which grounds the possibility of *nirvana* for all conscious beings. It is this that makes the *dharma* good news and that motivated the Buddha to preach it to needy humanity.[11]

This understanding of Buddhism as involving a conception of the ultimate as the ground or source of all temporal existence, in virtue of which the *dharma* is good news for all men and women, is an understanding of it as a religion of liberation or (in Christian language) salvation. But there is also another understanding of Buddhism as a psychological technique with no metaphysical implications. On this interpretation Buddhism is essentially the practice of meditation as producing an inherently valuable state in which the anxieties created by the ego point of view melt away and are replaced by a serene state of consciousness. This understanding of Buddhism has been eloquently expressed in the west by Don Cupitt in such books as *Taking Leave of God* (London: SCM Press, 1980) and *The World To Come* (London: SCM Press, 1982). It seems to appeal particularly to westerners who have been repelled by the anthropomorphism of much Christian thought about God and by the mythology that goes with it.

This latter form of Buddhism is not so much a gospel for the world as a special option for a fortunate few. For it is not held that the structure of the universe is such that the limitlessly desirable nirvanic state is possible for everyone. In a purely theoretical sense its attainment is of course possible for everyone; but in the actual conditions of human life it is available only to a minority. Just as it is true, but is an ironic truth, that everyone in an impoverished third world country is free to become a millionaire, so it is true, but only in an ironic sense, that the attainment of *nirvana* is a present possibility for the millions around the world who are struggling simply to survive under the pressure of desperate poverty, many as refugees close to starvation, or under soul-destroying oppression and exploitation. The Buddha himself recognised that *nirvana* is not a practical possibility for most people in their present life.[12] Most people still have to progress towards it through a long continuing succession of lives. However, in the purely psychological form of Buddhism this picture of a vast karmic progress through many rebirths until awakening/enlightenment is at last attained is regarded as an imaginary projection with no foundation in reality. The present life is the only one there is, and only those who attain *nirvana* in this life ever attain it.

We have to accept that there are different forms of Buddhism, or even in a sense different Buddhisms, with an important division between that which includes a metaphysic – that is, a picture of the nature or structure of the universe – which constitutes good news for the whole human race, and that which does not. There are also, in this sense, different Christianities; and in the work of Don Cupitt a non-metaphysical Buddhism and a non-metaphysical Christianity come together in a mutually reinforcing way. Epistemologically, the debate is between the realist and non-realist interpretations of religious language. Is the Buddhist language that is apparently about the structure of the universe to be understood in a non-realist way (that is, not as referring to anything beyond ourselves, but rather as giving symbolic expression to our own mental states); or in a naïve realist way (in which it is assumed to apply literally to that to which it seems to refer); or in a critical realist mode (as referring to realities beyond ourselves, but realities that are always apprehended in terms of human concepts)? I take it that naïve religious realism is not a live option for most of us today and that the issue is between non-realism and critical realism.

Within a non-metaphysical version of Buddhism as a meditational practice which deconstructs the *angst*-laden ego, offering however no comprehensive insight such as would constitute the *dharma* good news for all humankind, the notion of *upaya* covers all Buddhist teachings beyond 'the doctrine of Sorrow, of its origin, of its cessation, and the Path',[13] seeing them as skilful means to lead people to the practice of meditation. From this point of view the whole notion of the limitless outgoing compassion at the heart of the universe manifested in awakened beings who seek the enlightenment of others, is an attractive piece of wishful thinking. And it must be granted of course that this may indeed be mere wishful thinking. But this sceptical view does not seem to me to fit well either the teachings of Gautama as reflected – admittedly at some remove of time – in the Pali scriptures, or in most of the later developments of Buddhist teaching. It will therefore be worth while to go on to ask what part the idea of *upaya* plays in a Buddhism whose language is understood in a critical realist mode as referring – though always through inadequate human thought-forms and language – to the ultimate structure of reality. Let me outline a possible such view.

IV

Within the Mahayana tradition a distinction is drawn between, on the one hand, the indescribable ultimate reality in itself, variously referred to as the Buddha nature or the Dharmakaya or (in the *Ratnagotravibhaga*[14]) as 'the perfectly pure Absolute Entity' (*dharmadhatu*), and on the other hand the manifestations of this to human consciousness, varying according to our varying human receptivities: 'The Absolute Body (*dharmakaya*) is to be known in two aspects. One is the Absolute Entity which is perfectly immaculate, the other is its natural outflow, the teaching of the profound truth and of the diverse guidance.'[15] I take it that this is also the distinction used by Shinran when he cites this passage of T'an-luan:

> Among Buddhas and bodhisattvas there are two aspects of dharmakaya: dharmakaya-as-suchness and dharmakaya-as-compassion. Dharmakaya-as-compassion arises out of dharmakaya-as-suchness, and dharmakaya-as-suchness emerges into [human consciousness through] dharmakaya-as-compassion. These two aspects of dharmakaya differ but are not separate; they are one but not identical.[16]

In his Introduction to Shinran's text Yoshifumi Ueda says that 'the ultimate formless and nameless dharmakaya-as-suchness (nirvana) manifests itself in the world as Amida Buddha, dharmakaya-as-compassion, emerging in this samsaric ocean to make itself comprehensible to men'.[17]

Given this distinction between the ultimate inconceivable reality, the *dharmakaya*, and its manifestations to human consciousness, we can say that the negative Buddhist language about the *dharmakaya* as formless or ineffable is far less upayic than the positive, specific, detailed language about its manifestations. The first, very limited, range of discourse is upayic only in the minimal sense in which all human thought and language is inescapably so, that is, it inevitably reflects some aspect of the 'shape' of the human mind as embodied in the kinds of concepts of which it is capable. But the second range of discourse is upayic in the more substantial sense that it involves a (conscious or unconscious) selection from a range of possible concepts. Thus the Theravada thinks in terms of *nibbana* but not of the Trikaya. Large sections of the Mahayana, but not of the Theravada, use the concept of *sunyata*. Jodo and Shin, but not Zen, think in terms of the manifestation of the ultimate Buddha nature in the Pure Land. Tantric Buddhism thinks in terms of yet other manifestations of the Buddha nature. And all these different modes in which the ultimate Reality is manifested to Buddhist understanding are modes of *upaya*. They are ways in which particular Buddhist faith communities, formed by their own powerful traditions, conceive and experience the Ultimate in relation to themselves.

In this use of the term *upaya* it is assumed that the ways in which the ultimate *dharmakaya* affects our human consciousness differ according to the varyingly distorting effects of *avidya*. We are thus presupposing the basic epistemological principle that was formulated by St Thomas Aquinas (in *Summa Theologica*, II/III, Q. 1, art. 2) as *cognita sunt in cognoscente secundum modum cognoscentis* ('things known are in the knower according to the mode of the knower'). It was above all Immanuel Kant who brought into the stream of modern western thought the realisation that the human mind is active in all awareness, shaping the phenomenal (that is, experienced) world in the process of cognising it. His insight has been massively confirmed by more recent work in cognitive psychology and has been given a new cultural dimension in the sociology of knowledge; and we can now apply it in the epistemology of religion in the hypothesis that the Ultimate is manifested to us in a range of ways formed by the culturally variable structures of the human mind. We can say this is Buddhist terms by speaking of the *dharmakaya* as manifested to us in a range of ways formed by the versatile operations of *upaya*.

This interpretation presupposes, first, the experience of the Buddha and, in varying degrees, of many others who have followed his Way, and secondly, the faith-conviction that this experience is not simply the psychological state of a relatively few but is at the same time the manifestation, or presence, within human life of the eternally Real, so that on the basis of this experience affirmations can be made about the ultimate nature or structure of reality. The notion of *upaya* is, then, the notion that the cosmic significance of the nirvanic experience can be conceptualised in a variety of ways, all of which communicate the importance and availability of the experience, but none of which constitutes the one and only correct way of conceptualising it. These schemes of thought are provisional and instrumental, and are to be discarded like the raft in the Buddha's parable once they have fulfilled their function. Further, there are a number of different conceptual rafts, each of which may serve the same purpose, perhaps equally well, for different people, or even for the same person at different times.

V

I now want to suggest that this pattern of a liberative and transform-

ing experience accepted by faith as manifesting the presence to or
within human life of the ultimate transcendent Reality, and conceptualised in the history of the tradition in a range of ways, occurs not
only in Buddhism but in all the great salvific religions. I only have
space here to spell this out a little in the case of Christianity, and then
to indicate in the sketchiest way how it may also apply yet more
widely.

What, then, would this notion of *upaya* sound like if translated
into Christian terms? It would mean that there is a basic Christian
experience and a range of theological conceptualitities in terms of
which this can be understood; and it would imply that these theologies are all provisional and instrumental, as alternative ways of
setting the experience in an intelligible context.

As in the case of Buddhism, we should begin by assembling some
indications of the nature of the core experience. It is variously called
– in terms which already embody theological commitments – the
experience of salvation (presupposing the Fall–Redemption scheme),
or of being indwelt by the Holy Spirit (presupposing a Trinitarian
scheme), or of being in Christ or Christ in the believer (presupposing
a distinction between the historical Jesus and the transcendent Christ),
or again in such more consciously contrived terms as Paul Tillich's
notion of participation in the New Being. Leaving these labels aside
and looking at the experience itself as it is reflected in the New
Testament documents, we see in the very early Christians a conscious re-commitment to God as made real to them by Jesus, an
excited and exhilarating sense of participating as 'insiders' in God's
final act of inaugurating the Kingdom, and a joyful liberation from
the fear of both demonic and human powers. We see also a freedom
from self-concern, based on trust in God, within a close-knit faith
community in which 'all that believed were together, and had all
things in common' (Acts 2: 44). These early Christians were indeed
new people, born again into a new spirit, no longer living for themselves but for the lord Jesus who, they believed, was soon to come
again to rule in the new Jerusalem.

Can we prescind from the special historical circumstances of the
first Christians – particularly their belief that the end of the Age was
about to come and Jesus to return in glory – in order to identify a
core of Christian experience which has continued through the ages?
I suggest that when we look at those whom we regard as Christian
saints (who are not by any means always those who have been
officially declared saints by the church) we see above all the central-

ity of the divine in human lives, relegating the little human ego to a subordinate role. To the extent that they are filled with the divine Spirit they are freed from natural self-centredness, with its manifold anxieties, so that they are no longer ultimately oppressed by the *dukkha* aspects of life, for 'neither death, nor life, nor angels, nor principalities, nor powers, nor things present, nor things to come, nor height, nor depth, nor any other creature, shall be able to separate us from the love of God, which is in Christ Jesus our Lord' (Romans 8: 38–9). Fundamental to this cosmic confidence is the radical ego-transcendence that St Paul expressed when he wrote, 'I live, and yet not I, but Christ liveth in me' (Galatians 2: 20); and he lists the fruits of this new spirit as 'love, joy, peace, longsuffering, gentleness, goodness, faith, meekness, temperance' (Galatians 5: 22–3).

The experience of a new life is believed by Christians to rest upon the ultimate nature of reality. The basic religious faith, in its Christian form, is that the love and power of God revealed in Christ are not figments of our human imaginations.[10] Thus far the basic formal inner structure of Christianity parallels that of Buddhism.

The parallel continues with the development of the Christian interpretative theories that we call theological doctrines. The transformed outlook, with its new mode of experience, was explained by soteriological theories, beginning with the idea that we have been made at-one, or at peace, with God by being ransomed on the cross from the power of the devil; and moving in the medieval period to the idea of being pardoned and reinstated by God because Christ's death was accepted as a 'satisfaction' to appease the offended divine majesty; and again at the Reformation by the idea that on the cross Jesus was bearing as our substitute the just punishment for human sin. These are all Christian doctrines of the atonement, explaining how Christ has enabled God to forgive sinful men and women and accept them into the heavenly kingdom. Many Christian theologians today regard these theories as highly implausible, picturing God as they do as a finite deity bargaining with the devil, or on the model of a medieval feudal baron concerned for his own dignity and status, or again as a stern cosmic moralist who is incapable of genuine forgiveness. However, these ideas, which today seem so strange and unattractive, have in the past enabled Christians to put their experience of salvation into a (to them) intelligible context and so to accept God's acceptance of them. They have thus functioned in different past states of society as skilful means. They are upayic formulae designed to render intelligible the fact of salvation – the way of being in the world that flows from seeing God through the eyes of Jesus.

The various other elements of Christian doctrine – the idea of the Fall presupposed by the traditional atonement theories, the idea of the Trinity and of the deity of Jesus as the second Person of the Trinity incarnate, the pictures of heaven, hell and purgatory, the doctrine of the church as the Body of Christ and of the sacraments as channels of divine grace – are on this view likewise upayic. They are not absolute and eternal truths but optional conceptualities which have proved useful to those whose formation they have influenced, but not generally to others.

This is not of course the way in which Christian doctrine has been officially understood within the churches. The view I have outlined represents rather a development of the approach initiated in the nineteenth century by the great Protestant theologian Friedrich Schleiermacher. And it remains a complication that there is no such thing as *the* (universally agreed) Christian understanding of God, Christ, redemption, humanity, the church and its priesthood, of the nature of theology, or of the things to come. Christian interpretations of all these major themes vary from one historical epoch to another, and in a given epoch from one region to another, and within a given region, from one group to another, and within a given group often even from one individual to another. Amidst all these variations it is worth remembering that the Christian dialogue with the other world faiths has so far been largely based within the western or Latin development of Christianity embodied in the Roman and Reformed churches. But in the rather different eastern or Greek development, embodied in the Orthodox churches, there are some interestingly differently approaches. This is true, for example, of the understanding of salvation. Whereas in western Christianity salvation has generally been understood by means of a transactional model, according to which the death of Christ cancelled a debt or penalty of some kind, in eastern Christianity it has been predominantly understood by means of a transformational model, according to which men and women are gradually changed under the influence of divine grace on their path towards 'deification' – not that they literally become God but that they are transformed into what Irenaeus called the finite likeness of God. This way of thinking is sufficiently analogous to that of Buddhism for it to be natural to ask whether the awakened human being and the deified human being are not the same person described in different conceptual languages?

VI

If we have thus far been at all on the right lines we have seen that Buddhism and Christianity are both skilful means to a radically new or transformed state of being – a state which is intrinsically desirable and which is believed both to depend upon and to manifest the ultimately real. In each case descriptions of the core experience are upayic in the minimal sense that all our concepts and language are perforce distinctively *human* concepts and language. But the further more specific ideas used in conceptualising this experience arise from the different characteristics of the various cultural streams of human life. Within some cultures people find it more natural to think in monistic, in others in dualistic, and in yet others in pluralistic ways; in some to conceive the ultimate in personal, in others in non-personal terms; some cultures prefer imaginative richness, others an austere sparseness in the formation of myths; some opt for intellectual complexity, others for simplicity, in the formation of doctrine; and so on.[19]

Phenomenologically, the Buddhist experience of awakened life and the Christian experience of the new life in Christ are different; for different concepts are required to describe them, and these are integral to different comprehensive conceptual systems. But at the same time the two types of core experience have very important features in common. They both hinge upon a radical shift from self centredness to a new orientation centred in the Ultimate, even though the latter is conceptualised and therefore experienced in characteristically different ways. Further, the fruit of the transformed state, in basic moral and spiritual attitudes and outlooks, is very similar. The awakened person is filled with a compassion (*karuna*) and the saved person with a love (*agape*) which seem in practice to be indistinguishable. The Buddhist and the Christian thus appear to be responding to a cosmic reality which affects them in essentially the same way – although this effect may also be expressed within different cultural contexts in different concrete ways.[20]

The possibility, then, that so obviously presents itself is that these two great religious traditions constitute different – indeed very different – human responses to the Ultimate or Real which, in itself beyond the scope of human concepts, is manifested to humankind in ways to which our concepts importantly contribute. In Buddhist terms the Ultimate is *sunyata*, or the Dharmakaya, the reality that is empty in respect of all that we can think or say, for it is beyond everything that human thought projects in the act of cognition. In parallel Christian terms, the Ultimate is the transpersonal Godhead that is manifested within Christian experience as the heavenly Father. The Ultimate is thus the 'God above the God of theism';[21] or the 'real God' who is an 'utterly unknowable X', in distinction from the 'available God', who is 'essentially a mental or imaginative construction';[22] or again 'the noumenal Focus of religion which . . . lies beyond the phenomenal Foci of religious experience and practice';[23] or again the noumenal 'Real *an sich*' in distinction from its experienced personae and impersonae.[24]

Within Christian history this distinction, as explicitly drawn, has until recently been largely confined to the more mystical side of the tradition. But nevertheless it has been implicitly recognised by virtually all the great theologians. For whilst they have developed an elaborate positive language about God as Father, Son and Spirit (debating whether the Spirit proceeds from the Father and the Son or only from the Father), and about the divine attributes of omnipotence, omniscience, goodness, justice, mercy and so on, they have also stressed that God in God's ultimate being is ineffable, beyond the range of our human thought. This recognition of the sheer transcendence and mystery of God runs through the history of Christian thought. For example, Gregory of Nyssa wrote:

> The simplicity of the True Faith assumes God to be . . . incapable of being grasped by any human term, or any idea, or any other device of our apprehension, remaining beyond the reach not only of the human but of the angelic and all supramundane intelligence, unthinkable, unutterable above all expression in words, having but one name and can represent His proper nature, the single name being 'Above Every Name'.[25]

And St Augustine declared that 'God transcends even the mind',[26] whilst St Thomas Aquinas said that 'by its immensity the divine substance surpasses every form that our intellect reaches'.[27] Clearly such statements presuppose a distinction between on the one hand, God in God's ultimate reality, beyond the reach of human conceptuality, and on the other hand God as humanly known and described, a distinction between God *a se* and God *pro nobis*.

Analogous distinctions occur in the other great world traditions. Hindu thought distinguishes between *nirguna* Brahman, Brahman without attributes because beyond the scope of human thought, and *saguna* Brahman, Brahman with attributes, humanly experienced as Ishwara, the personal God who is known under different aspects by different names. Jewish and Muslim mystical thought distinguish between, on the one hand, *En Soph*, the Infinite, or *al Haqq*, the Real, and on the other hand the self-revealing God of their scriptures. In Taoism the *Tao Te Ching* begins by declaring: 'The Tao that can be expressed is not the eternal Tao.' And we have already noted the distinction in Mahayana Buddhism between Dharmkaya-as-suchness and Dharmkaya-as-compassion.

In the light of this widely recognised distinction the possibility emerges that the great world traditions constitute different ways of conceiving, and therefore of experiencing, and therefore of responding in life to the Ultimate. They are thus different forms (each including many sub-forms) of *upaya*, skilful means to draw men and women from a consuming natural self concern, with all its attendant sins and woes, to a radically different orientation in which they have become 'transparent' to the universal presence of the Ultimate.

Notes

1. Michael Pye, *Skilful Means: A Concept of Mahayana Buddhism* (London. Duckworth; and Dallas. Southwest Book Services, 1978)
2. See Arvind Sharma, ' "Skill in Means" in Early Buddhism and Christianity', *Buddhist–Christian Studies*, vol. 10 (1990) pp. 23–33.
3. *The Middle Length Sayings*, vol 1, trans. I. B. Horner (London: Pali Text Society, 1954–9) pp. 173–4.
4. 'My heart is utterly set free' (*Theragatha*, x).
5. 'When such conditions are fulfilled, then there will be joy, and happiness, and peace, and in continual mindfulness and self mastery, one will dwell at ease' (*Digha Nikāya*, I, 196).
6. 'He who doth crush the great "I am" conceit – this, even this, is happiness supreme' (*Udana*, II, 1).
7. 'because of his pitifulness towards all beings' (*Digha Nikāya*, II, 38). *Dialogues of the Buddha*, 4th edn, vol. II, trans. T. W. and C. A. F. Rhys Davids (London: Pali Text Society, 1959) p. 31.
8. 'Thinking on there being no self, he wins to the state wherein the conceit "I am" has been uprooted, to the cool [*nirvana*], even in this life' (*Anguttara Nikāya*, IV, 353).
9. Michael Pye, 'Skilful Means and the Interpretation of Christianity', *Buddhist–Christian Studies*, vol. 10 (1990) p. 19.
10. *Digha Nikāya*, II, 34–5 (Pali Text Society translation, p. 27).
11. *Majjhima Nikāya*, I, 169.
12. *Digha Nikāya*, II, 36. Cf. 'Here, in this world, it is quite rare to obtain the

pure gem . . . the sight of the Buddha should be known as not easily achieved in this luckless world by those whose mind is afflicted by various passions' (*Ratnagotravibhaga*, Karika 51, Takasaki p. 372).

13. *Digha Nikāya*, II, 41. *Dialogues of the Buddha*, 4th edn, trans. T. W. and C. A. F. Rhys Davids, Part II, (London: Pali Text Society, 1959) p. 34.

14. Jikido Takasaki, *A Study of the Ratnagotravibhaga* (Rome: Is. MED, 1966) p. 284.

15. Ibid.

16. Shinran, *Notes on 'Essentials of Faith Alone'*, *A Translation of Shinran's Yuishinsho-mon'i* (Kyoto: Hongwanji International Center, 1979) p. 5.

17. Ibid., p. 6.

18. Accordingly the non-realist interpretations offered in the nineteenth century by Ludwig Feuerbach and today by such writers as Don Cupitt and D. Z. Phillips, retaining the entire corpus of Christian language whilst understanding it as non-referential, are deeply subversive.

19. The anthropologists, ethnologists and sociologists have only begun to trace the ways in which these variations in basic ways of thinking have come about. But Max Weber, in the early twentieth century, laid the foundations for this research. See, for example, his *Sociology of Religion* (1922; Boston, Mass.: Beacon Press, 1964).

20. For example, in the centuries before the rise of modern democracy, when power was concentrated in the hands of emperors and kings, Christian love had to be expressed in personal rather than political ways; and a like consideration applies to Buddhist societies.

21. Paul Tillich, *The Courage to Be* (New Haven, Conn.: Yale University Press, 1952) p. 189.

22. Gordon Kaufman, *God the Problem* (Cambridge, Mass.: Harvard University Press, 1972) pp. 85–6. Cf. *The Theological Imagination* (Philadelphia, Pa: Westminster Press, 1981).

23. Ninian Smart, 'Our Experience of the Ultimate', *Religious Studies*, vol. 20, no. 1 (1984) p. 24. Cf. *Beyond Ideology* (San Francisco, Cal.: Harper & Row, 1981), ch. 6.

24. John Hick, 'Towards a Philosophy of Religious Pluralism', *Neue Zeitschrift für systematische Theologie and Religionsphilosophie*, vol. XXII, part 2, no. 2 (1980). Cf. *An Interpretation of Religion* (London: Macmillan; New Haven: Yale University Press, 1989).

25. Gregory of Nyssa, *Against Eunomius*, I, 42, *The Nicene and Post-Nicene Fathers*, series 2, vol. V, trans. P. Schaff and H. Wace (Grand Rapids, Mich.: Eerdmans, 1954) p. 99.

26. St Augustine, *De Vera Religione*, 36: 67.

27. St Thomas Aquinas, *Summa contra Gentiles*, Bk. I, ch. 14, para. 3.

Part IV
Religious Pluralism

8

A Personal Note

I became a Christian by conversion whilst a first year law student. The converting power was the New Testament picture of Jesus Christ. During a period of several days of intense inner turmoil the Christ-centred world of meaning, previously dead to me, became overwhelmingly alive as both awesomely demanding and irresistibly attractive, and I entered into it with great joy and excitement. And as is so often the case in youthful conversions, the Christian friends who encouraged and supported me were more or less fundamentalist in their beliefs, so that the set of ideas which I received as part of my initial Christian package was Calvinist orthodoxy of an extremely conservative kind.

A little over a year later I left these circles to serve – this was during the Second World War – in the Friends' Ambulance Unit in Britain, the Middle East, Italy and Greece. When I returned, to study philosophy as a preliminary to training for the Presbyterian ministry, I was still theologically very conservative but was beginning to be aware of a lack of intellectual integrity in fundamentalist circles, in that any potentially unsettling questions were regularly suppressed rather than faced. My philosophical training at Edinburgh, and then at Oxford, made it impossible to be satisfied with an ethos in which clear thinking and the honest facing of problems were viewed as lack of faith, and I moved out of the evangelical student movement. I remained, however, for nearly 20 more years fully convinced of the truth of the basic doctrines of Trinity, Incarnation and Atonement more or less in the form in which I had first learned them. I remember being shocked by theologians who questioned these traditional formulations in just the way that some conservative Christians are shocked by my own questioning of them today.

During this period I had virtually no contact with other religious traditions – neither Judaism and Islam, nor the faiths of Indian and Chinese origin. In spite of having spent many months in Muslim Egypt, Syria and Lebanon, and a short time in Palestine (as it then was), I had no appreciation whatever of Islam or Judaism as religions. Nor, except for one short course, was I introduced during my theological training to the history or the theology of religions; and during my subsequent pastorate in rural Northumberland such matters were far beyond the horizon alike of my congregation and of myself. Even as a teacher at Cornell University, Princeton Theological Seminary and Cambridge University it did not occur to me that the subject which I taught, namely the philosophy of religion, should properly be just that and not simply the philosophy of the Judeo-Christian tradition. Further, I long shared the common ecclesiastical assumption that the whole human race ought to be converted to Christianity. I remember being indignant at Reinhold Niebuhr's statement that the mission to the Jews was a mistake – though I can now see that he was entirely right.

However, in 1967 I moved from my Lectureship in the Faculty of Divinity at Cambridge to the H. G. Wood Chair of Theology at Birmingham University. Birmingham, in the middle of England, is an industrial city and was one of the main centres of immigration during the 1950s and 1960s from the Caribbean islands and the Indian sub-continent. There was thus a sizeable presence of several non-Christian traditions, consisting in the new Muslim, Sikh and Hindu communities as well as a small but long-established Jewish community. Immigration was a hotly debated issue, and the neo-Nazi National Front was active in the area, generating hatred and promoting violence against black and brown immigrants and against Jews. It was a challenging time and place, and I became deeply involved in a variety of 'community relations' organisations, being chair of the activist AFFOR (All Faiths for One Race) based in the largely black area of Handsworth, and chair likewise of the Birmingham Inter-Faiths Council; of the Religious and Cultural Panel of the Birmingham Community Relations Committee; and of the co-ordinating committee of the Statutory Conference convened under the 1944 Education Act to create a new agreed syllabus for religious education within the city's schools – this latter operation lasting two years and producing a new multi-faith curriculum to replace the older exclusively Christian one. This was a busy and sometimes exciting period. The first director of AFFOR was physically assaulted by National Front thugs; the Jewish investigative journalist with whom I collaborated in a published exposure of the records of the National Front leaders was knifed; and others of us received threats. In all this I found myself in active comradeship with Muslims and

Jews, Hindus and Sikhs, Marxists and humanists, practising what has come to be called liberation theology.

In the course of this activity I was frequently in Jewish synagogues, Muslim mosques, Sikh gurudwaras and Hindu temples, as well as Christian churches. In these places of worship I soon realised something that is obvious enough once noticed, yet momentous in its implications. This is that although the language and the liturgical actions and the cultural ethos differ greatly in each case, yet from a religious point of view basically the same thing is going on; namely, human beings are coming together within the framework of an ancient and highly developed tradition to open their hearts and minds to God, whom they believe to make a total claim upon the living of their lives, demanding of them, in the words of one of the prophets, 'to do justice, and to love kindness, and to walk humbly with your God' (Micah 6: 8). God is known in the synagogues as Adonai, the God of Abraham, Isaac and Jacob; in mosques as *Allah rahman rahīm*, God most beneficent, ever merciful; in the Sikh gurudwaras as God, who is Father, Lover, Master and the Great Giver, referred to as *wah guru*; and in Hindu temples as Vishnu, Krishna, Rama, Shiva – who are all manifestations of the ultimate reality of Brahman; and in the Christian Church as Father, Son and Holy Spirit. But all five communities agree that there is ultimately only one God. It therefore seems evident that this one God is somehow being encountered in different ways within these different traditions.

Thus it was not so much new thoughts as new experiences that drew me, as a philosopher, into the issues of religious pluralism, and as a Christian into inter-faith dialogue. (Subsequent visits to Hindu India, the Sikh Punjab, Buddhist Sri Lanka and multi-faith Japan were prompted by the initial impact of the Birmingham experience.) Encounters with remarkable individuals of several faiths, people whom I cannot but deeply respect, and in some cases even regard as saints, have reinforced the realisation that our very different religious traditions constitute alternative human contexts of response to the one ultimate transcendent divine Reality.

As an implicit belief this same perception is today widespread among those Christians who have any real contact with their Muslim, Sikh, Hindu, Jewish and now also, increasingly, Buddhist neighbours – though often without realising that this new insight has important implications for their Christian belief-system as a whole.

In Birmingham in the 1970s Christians (though, alas, only a small minority of them) were actively combating the neo-Nazi movements and were helping the immigrants to establish themselves, to create their own places of worship, to bring up their children in their own faiths, to gain access to the media, and so on – all on the unstated assumption that these other faiths are independently valid and authentic religions, to be respected as such. There was no attempt by this group of Christians to convert the newcomers, and apparently no sense that this would have been a religiously appropriate thing to do. In other words, they were acting upon an implicit theology which sees these other religions as valid responses to the same ultimate Reality that we Christians know as the Heavenly Father. And yet in church on Sunday they continued to join in services, to sing hymns and hear sermons expressing the traditional Christian conviction that God is fully and finally self-revealed only in Jesus Christ, and that 'no man comes to the Father, but by me' (John 14: 6) so that 'there is salvation in no one else [than Christ], for there is no other name under heaven given among men by which we must be saved' (Acts 4: 12).

There are, then, a large number of Christians today who continue to use this traditional language whilst nevertheless acting in relation to their Muslim, Jewish, Hindu, Sikh, Buddhist neighbours in terms of a very different implicit theology. And one of the tasks of theologians who have entered into the wider vision is to make this different theology explicit so that it can gradually modify the developing Christian tradition as a whole.

This is being attempted today in an increasing variety of ways; and indeed, there will probably never be a single Christian replacement for the old exclusivist position. Outside the large continuing fundamentalist wing, Christian theology is likely in the future to take a variety of forms.

The major debate is between 'inclusivist' and 'pluralist' alternatives to the old but now widely abandoned exclusivism. Probably the majority of theologians who write about inter-faith matters today accept some version of inclusivism. Here salvation/redemption/liberation is seen as available, not only to Christians, but in principle to all human beings; but with the understanding that wherever it occurs it is the work of Christ. Thus Pope John Paul II wrote in his first Encyclical, *Redemptor Hominis*, in 1979, that 'man – every man without exception – has been redeemed by Christ' and with 'each man without any exception whatever Christ is in a way united, even when man is unaware of it' (para. 14). In a famous formula, Karl Rahner assigned to those who are saved by Christ without knowing it the status of 'anonymous Christians'; and various other formulations have also been used. Such positions are 'inclusivist' in that non-Christians are included within the sphere of Christ's atoning work. They therefore do not need – for the more liberal versions of inclusivism – to be converted to Christianity, at any rate in this life, but can be saved by Christ within their existing religious traditions.

The attraction (to those who hold it) of this inclusivist position is that it negates the old missionary compulsion and yet is still Christocentric and still leaves Christianity in an uniquely central and normative position. For the Christian inclusivist can continue to hold that Jesus was in a literal sense God the Son incarnate, adding (a) that the same divine Son or Logos who became incarnate as Jesus has also been at work in other ways within other religions as 'the unknown Christ of Hinduism' and so on; and (b) that the redeeming work which required his incarnation as Jesus of Nazareth was for the benefit of all people, within all religions and even outside all religions. Muslims, Hindus, Sikhs, Buddhists and Jews are accordingly redeemed by Christ as Muslims, Hindus, Sikhs, Buddhists and Jews. But Christians are those who know this, whilst the people of other religions do not; and Christians consciously centre their lives upon the Redeemer, whilst others, outside that personal relationship, are unknowingly benefiting from his saving work. Thus Christianity can continue to regard itself as uniquely superior to all other religions.

Some of us however – and a growing number – have rejected this inclusivism as an unsatisfactory compromise. We have moved to a pluralism which sees the other great world faiths as authentic and valid contexts of salvation/liberation, not secretly dependent upon the cross of Christ. Each tradition has its channel of revelation or illumination, expressed in its sacred scriptures and responded to in distinctive forms of worship or meditation and in its own unique history of individual and communal life. Muslims, Hindus and the rest are not anonymous Christians, nor are Christians anonymous Muslims, Hindus and so on. Each constitutes a uniquely different (though overlapping) awareness of the ultimate transcendent Reality as perceived through the 'lens' of a particular religious tradition.

Clearly, such a pluralist conception requires a rethinking of the traditional formulations of incarnation, trinity and atonement. For if

Jesus was literally God (the Son) incarnate, this being the one and only time when God became directly present on earth, it follows that Christianity is the only religion to have been founded by God in person; and this singles it out as having a uniquely central, normative, final status among the religions of the world, constituting it a more effective context of salvation than any other. Thus the superiority of Christianity becomes an *a priori* dogma, excluding any true religious pluralism. The dogma implies that Christianity has a unique salvific superiority – which, when spelled out concretely, must mean that it has produced more or better saints per million of population, and has had better social, political and economic effects than any other religion. But when this ceases to be an *a priori* dogma, and becomes an empirical claim to be judged by historical evidence, I do not think that it can be substantiated. The great world religions appear to me to constitute, in their different ways, more or less equally effective – and, alas, at the same time more or less equally ineffective – contexts of human transformation from self-centredness to a new orientation centred in the divine Reality. Each is, historically, a unique mixture of good and evil; but none stands out on balance as morally and spiritually superior to the others.

It therefore appears to me that the Christian pluralist should see the idea of divine incarnation as a metaphorical rather than a literal idea. To a startling extent Jesus embodied the divine love in his own life. In this metaphorical sense he 'incarnated' *agape* – as indeed, in their varying degrees, do all who are transformed in response to the Ultimate. Such a Christology does not require a traditional form of trinitarian theology, or a satisfaction or penal-substitutionary concept of redemption. These Christian themes can now be identified as metaphorical, or mythological. As such they can have great value; but they must not be understood literally and then used as premises from which to draw literal conclusions. For it is these literal conclusions that have conferred the sense of unique superiority upon Christendom which has distorted the relationship of Christians to much of the rest of the human race, particularly in anti-Semitism and in western imperialism.

From a pluralist point of view, then, I do not, in inter-faith dialogue, have politely to conceal an assumption of the religious superiority of my own tradition. I am not set in judgement over the other great world faiths, but can explore, often with great fascination and profit, other ways in which other human beings know the one ultimate divine Reality. Because our traditions represent different limited ways of conceiving, experiencing and responding to that Reality, I sometimes come to see through others' eyes what are to me exciting new glimpses of the Transcendent as reflected in the meaning and possibilities of our human existence. I rejoice in the moving beauty of the Jewish way of life, with its ancient symbols through which God's presence has been felt during so many centuries; I rejoice in the impressive voice of the Qur'an, in the Muslim awareness of God as awesome and yet always gracious and merciful, and in the ordered structure of life which it makes possible; I rejoice in the marvellous openness and mystical fervour of Guru Nanak and the communal dedication of the Sikh tradition which he founded; I rejoice in the consciously mythological way of thinking symbolised in Hindu temples, in their ecstatic moments, in the orderly shape of human life within the Hindu world of meaning; and I rejoice in the transcendence of ego that occurs in Buddhist awakening to *nirvana* and the outgoing compassion that it releases. But I have myself been formed by the Christian vision of God as revealed in the life and teaching of Jesus as reflected in the Gospels, and continue to be most at home in this, despite family disputes with more conservative fellow Christians. And yet looking out towards my friends of other faiths I recognise, with Jalaluldin Rumi, that 'The lamps are different, but the Light is the same: it comes from Beyond.'[1]

Note

1. Jalaluldin Rumi, 'The One True Light', in *Rumi: Poet and Mystic*, trans. R. A. Nicholson (London and Boston, Mass.: Unwin Mandala Books, 1978) p. 166.

9

Jews, Christians, Muslims: Do We All Worship the Same God?

I

As Jews, Christians and Muslims we all believe – do we not? – that it is true in some important sense that we all worship the same, because the only, God.

Certainly, our scriptures encourage us to think this, at least in that each later holy book assumes that the God of whom it speaks is that previously made known in earlier revelations. Thus we read in the Qur'an that a Muslim is to say to Jews and Christians, as people of the Book, 'We believe what has been sent down to us, and we believe what has been sent down to you. Our God and your God is one, and to Him we submit' (28: 46, Ahmed Ali translation, Princeton, N.J.: Princeton University Press, 1984). We also read: 'We have sent revelations to you as We sent revelations to Noah and the prophets [who came] after him; and We sent revelations to Abraham and Ishmael and Isaac and Jacob and their offspring, and to Jesus and Job . . . and to Moses God spoke directly' (4: 163–4). Clearly, if it was the Allah of the Qur'an who inspired the Hebrew prophets and spoke directly to Moses, and who was later inspiring Jesus, then to worship the God of these earlier revelations is to worship the Allah of the Qur'an.

Again, the New Testament is full of references to the Torah and assumes throughout that the God whose coming kingdom Jesus proclaimed is the God of Abraham, Isaac and Jacob. Jesus himself was a devout Jew, and during his lifetime some of his fellow Jews speculated that he was one of their ancient prophets returned to life: ' "Who do men say that I am?" And they told him, "John the Baptist; and others say, Elijah; and others one of the prophets" ' (Mark 8: 27). Again, in preaching Jesus as the messiah, the early Church presented

146

him as the fulfilment of the expectations of the Jewish scriptures. Thus according to Acts, Peter, preaching in Jerusalem shortly after Jesus' death, declared that 'The God of Abraham and of Isaac and of Jacob, the God of our fathers, glorified his servant Jesus, whom you delivered up and denied in the presence of Pilate' (Acts 3: 13–14). Clearly then, according to the New Testament, the God whom Jesus called his heavenly Father was also the God of whom the Torah had previously spoken.

The Torah itself does not, of course, speak of Jahweh as being also the God of the later New Testament and the still later Qur'an. But it is a very natural Jewish view, in the light of Jesus' manifest Jewishness, and of Islam's continuation of a strict monotheism within the Semitic tradition, that Christians and Muslims are, at least in intention, worshipping the same God whom the Jews have always worshipped.

Let us, then, adopt as our initial position, which we are however prepared to modify or complicate if and as required, that we all – Jews, Christians and Muslims – worship the same God.

II

Having said that, however, we must immediately begin the complicating process. For within the conception of God found in each of our three traditions there are both a universal aspect, relating God to the whole world and the entire human race, and a more particular aspect relating God in a special way to a particular historical group or individual. The universal aspect is common to Judaism, Christianity and Islam, whilst the particular aspect is distinctively different in each case. The term 'ethical monotheism' points to the former. Each tradition speaks of God as the sole creator of heaven and earth, indeed, by implication as the creator of everything other than God; and clearly there can only be one such being. Thus the Jewish and Christian scriptures begin by affirming that 'In the beginning God created the heavens and the earth' (Genesis 1: 1) and the Qur'an likewise declares that 'Your Lord is God, who created the heavens and the earth in six spans' (10: 3). This one and only God, the supreme being, the Lord of all, is also understood within each tradition to have a moral nature encompassing both the more demanding attributes of justice, righteous wrath, absolute claim, and the more tender and giving qualities of grace, love, mercy, forgiveness. Thus according to the Hebrew scriptures Jahweh 'judges the world with righteousness' (Psalm 9: 8) and yet is 'merciful and gracious, slow to anger and abounding in steadfast love' (Psalm 103: 8). And according to the New Testament 'the wrath of God is revealed from heaven against all ungodliness and wickedness' (Romans 1: 8), and yet at the same time 'God is love' (1 John 4: 8) and 'If we confess our sins, he is faithful and just, and will forgive our sins and cleanse us from all unrighteousness' (1 John 1: 9). And according to the Qur'an, 'The Lord is quick in retribution, but He is also oft forgiving, most merciful' (7: 167). Thus in their universal aspect, as forms of ethical monotheism, these three intertwined traditions proclaim God as creator of the universe, self-revealed to humanity as our just judge who is at the same time loving, gracious and merciful. Thus far it can indeed readily be said that we are all worshipping the same God.

But when we move to the historically particular aspects the picture becomes more complicated, and it ceases to be evident that we are all speaking about the same God. For the particular forms in which the universal deity is experienced within the events of human history are so different as to create a presumption of three Gods.

Thus the God of Judaism, in his particular aspect as the Jahweh of the Hebrew Bible, is distinctively the God of the Jews, standing in a unique relationship to his chosen people, who are linked to him in a special covenant. The prophet Amos relays the word of the Lord, 'You only have I known of all the families of the earth' (Amos 3: 2). The Jahweh of the Torah is also, to be sure, aware of other nations. But he generally subordinates them, within his concern, to the children of Israel. Thus he encourages the Israelites to slaughter the original inhabitants of Caanan in order to make it their own, and later uses the Assyrians to chastise his people when they had turned away from him, and later again he has them taken into exile in Babylon. For the special covenant relationship with God is not only a great honour and blessing but also a great trial and responsibility – the divine word given to Amos continues, 'therefore I will punish you for all your iniquities'. But Israel is still at the centre of Jahweh's attention. He is integral to the history of the Jews, as they in turn are integral to the biography of Jahweh. He cannot be extracted from this context of Jewish history. He could not, for example, have switched his sphere of operation from Palestine to China without so changing his character as to become, in effect, a different deity. He is thus a particular divine personality with a certain distinctive provenance: he is deeply involved in the affairs of the ancient Near East, but has no real relationship to the rest of the human race living in China, India, Russia, Europe, Africa, Australia and the Americas. The universal deity of ethical monotheism thus seems in the Hebrew scriptures to have taken on a particular, limited, local form as the Jahweh of Israel.

Again, the God of Christianity in his particular aspect as the God of the New Testament, and as further defined by the Ecumenical Councils, is a triune Being related to humanity through one particular individual who is God the Son incarnate. Modern New Testament scholarship has made it extremely doubtful whether this belief in divine incarnation can be attributed to Jesus himself. But we are concerned here with Christianity as a vast long–lived historical reality; and by the early fourth century (at the Council of Nicea, 325 CE) the church had established Jesus' identity as the second Person of a divine Trinity living a human life. And clearly the Trinity, consisting of God the Father, God the Son and God the Holy Spirit, is not identical with Jahweh as described in the Jewish scriptures and tradition. One obvious difference is that between a pure monotheism and a modified trinitarian form of monotheism; and another is that between a divine concern centred upon the children of Israel and one that embraces all humanity, and even stigmatises the Israelites as those among whom God became incarnate but who wilfully rejected him.

And yet again, the Allah of Islam, in his particular aspect as interacting with the Muslim community in seventh-century CE Arabia, is different from the Jahweh of Israel and from the Holy Trinity of Christianity. The Qur'anic revelations often occurred in response to specific issues arising in the life of the prophet or of the early Muslim community. Like Jahweh, Allah gives commandments to a particular community, aids them in battle and uses them as his chosen servants. He is as strongly linked to the prophet Muhammad and the Muslim community in Mecca and Medina as is the Christian God to the 'Christ event' in first-century Palestine or Jahweh to the events of biblical history. Thus the God of Islam, as a concrete divine figure who speaks in the Qur'an, is distinct from the God of Christianity, in that Allah is not a Trinity and did not become incarnate in Jesus of Nazareth; and different also, though to a lesser degree, from Jahweh in that the Qur'anic Allah's focus of interest is in Arabia rather than Palestine, and that the Jews have a secondary rather than a central place in his concern.

Thus when we think of God, not in God's universal aspect as the creator of the universe and the gracious Lord of all humankind, but as a concrete divine personality intervening in human history and interacting with particular individuals and groups, we find that the scriptures of our three faiths depict three distinct divine personalities. One of these is the God of a group of Semitic tribes whom he adopts as his specially chosen or treasured people; another is a complex Trinity, one aspect of whom becomes incarnate on earth and founds a new religion; whilst another enters into a special relationship with a prophet in Arabia through whom he creates the community of those who submit their lives to Allah. Thus the personal profiles and stories of Jahweh, the Holy Trinity and Allah, although overlapping, are sufficiently different for it to be difficult to say that those who worship them are all worshipping identically the same God.

But whilst the three biblical deities are concretely described in unique terms, yet each description also includes a universal element. Thus in the Hebrew scriptures we read that 'thou art the God, thou alone, of all the kingdoms of the earth' (2 Kings 19: 15); and rabbinic Judaism concluded that 'the righteous of all nations have a share in the world to come' (Talmud: *Sanhedrin*, 13). Within Christianity it is possible to hold that the divine Logos who or which became incarnate as Jesus of Nazareth is also at work in other ways within the other religions of the world. And in Islam there is the Qur'anic concept of the Jews and Christians as people of the Book, and also the idea that all sincere monotheists are Muslims in the basic sense of those who submit themselves to God. And so it is possible in each case to see lying behind these concrete historical divine personalities the infinite depth of the Godhead transcending the particular relationship to humanity recorded in each scripture and indeed, according to the deeper thinkers of each tradition, transcending altogether the range of our finite human understanding.

At the same time, however, the historical particularity of each tradition provides a basis for the assumption of its unique superiority among the religions of the world. The Jewish concept of the chosen people, in so far as it is taken seriously, must make Jews feel that they have a specially important role within God's providence. This role is a burden and responsibility as well as a privilege; but on both counts it singles them out as living in a unique relationship with God. The Christian belief in Jesus as God the Son incarnate entails that Christianity was, uniquely, founded by God in person. It would seem to follow that Christianity must have a privileged status among the religions of the world and, indeed, that it must be the religion that God intends for the whole human race. And the Muslim claim that Muhammad was the seal of the prophets, and the Qur'an the final revelation completing and perfecting the earlier ones, gives to Islam the sense of superseding Judaism and Christianity and being God's appointed religion for all humanity.

To some extent these claims to unique superiority can be modified or de-emphasised by the more ecumenically minded within each tradition. Thus a Jew can say that every people is in its own different way chosen by God and has its own special vocation within the divine plan. A Christian can say that whilst God is self-revealed to Christians by becoming personally incarnate, God is also self-revealed in other lesser ways within other religious traditions. And a Muslim can speak of the eternal heavenly Book of which the Arabic Qur'an is a human reflection, other sacred scriptures being different reflections created for the benefit of other communities. We must note, however, that each of these ways of ameliorating the overt absolutism of one's own tradition conceals a residual covert absolutism. We are all God's chosen peoples; but still Israel is chosen for the central and most important role. God is known within all the great traditions; but still only in Christ has God become directly and personally present on earth. We all live in response to genuine divine revelations, but still only the Muslim *Umma* is living in response to God's final and definitive revelation. Thus these modifications are more of the nature of concessions to ecumenical politeness than unreserved acceptances of the others' equal status before God.

III

With these various reminders and discriminations in hand, let us return to our original question: Do we all worship the same God?

As we have seen, the difficulty in answering this question arises from the historical particularities of the three traditions rather than from their common ethical monotheism. Let us first try out some fairly simple ways of holding that, despite these different particularities, we do all worship the same God.

One obvious possibility is to say that we worship the same God but call that God by different names. (Thus Joseph Campbell once said, 'There you have the three great Western religions, Judaism, Christianity, and Islam – and because the three of them have three different names for the same biblical God, they can't get on together'.[1]) But the difficulty facing this suggestion is that it is not only the names but also the descriptions which go with them that are different. We cannot claim that the three scriptures describe recognisably the same concrete divine Being but refer to that Being by different names – as I might be called John by some, Professor Hick by some others, and the Reverend John Hick by yet others; for the story of my life is a single story which includes the three contexts in which I am called by these three different names. But the Qur'anic Allah is not the subject of the same story of divine–human interaction as the Christian Trinity; nor does the Trinity, with its second Person becoming incarnate, figure in the Torah and Talmud. Thus with the different names there go – as we have already noted – significantly different descriptive stories.

Could we perhaps, however, as a second possibility, combine the three stories into a single more complex narrative of divine activity on earth? Could we say that the one God was first self-manifested within Jewish history for some two thousand years; and then became incarnate as Jesus of Nazareth, thereby revealing a previously hidden trinitarian nature; and then some six centuries later reverted to the original unitarian nature as the Allah of the Qur'an, now denying that he had ever become incarnate? This is, surely, not an option that can be seriously contemplated from within any of our three traditions.

But, as a third attempt, we should note that it is sometimes possible to refer successfully to one and the same entity by means of quite different descriptions, and even to do so without being aware that these descriptions have the same referent. A well-known example is that of the evening star and the morning star, which are described and identified differently, one as appearing at dusk and the other at dawn, so that they were long assumed to be two different stars, known to the ancient Greeks as Hesperus and Phosphorus respectively. We now know them both to be the planet that we call Venus. Could Jahweh and the heavenly Father and Allah likewise be the same being, mistakenly thought to be three? Again, to adapt another well-known example, the same person, namely Sir Walter Scott, is truly described as the author of *Waverley*, as the greatest Scottish novelist and as the sheriff-depute of Selkirkshire in 1800. Could not the same God, then, be differently described by Jews,

Christians and Muslims as a result of their encountering that God in different historical situations? The difficulty here is that varying descriptions of the same entity must be mutually compatible.[2] It must be possible for them to apply to the same being – as for the author of *Waverley* to have been also the greatest Scottish novelist and the sheriff-depute of Selkirkshire in 1800. But this is not analogously the case with our different descriptions of God. The Qur'anic account explicitly contradicts the Christian account of God as a Trinity, one member of whom became incarnate as Jesus of Nazareth. Again, the understanding of God in the Torah implicitly, and the continuing rabbinic understanding of God explicitly, conflicts with the Christian trinitarian and incarnational concept. The divergence between the Torah's and the Qur'an's descriptions of God is much less extensive and might permit a theory that the same God had moved his focus of interest and sphere of operation from Palestine to Arabia, and from the Jews to the Arabs, in the seventh century CE. However, any such theory would be firmly, and surely rightly, rejected by post-biblical Judaism as imperialistically supercessionist.

And so it does not seem sufficient simply to say that the same identical God is being named and described differently. The differences between these describable divine personalities go too deep for that to be plausible. Nor, as a final attempt at a simple and easy solution, can any of us accept a polytheism, even a limited triadic polytheism, according to which there exist a Jewish God, a Christian God and a Muslim God. For we are united in believing that there is but one God who is the creator and ultimate ruler of all things. We all affirm *La-ilaha-ill'allah* – there is no God but God.

The next possibility, then, is for us each to revert to a traditionally confessional position from which we claim that our description of God is the true description and the others mistaken in so far as they differ from it. On this absolutist basis a Jew will hold that Christianity is profoundly in error in claiming that God (that is, God the Son) became incarnate and summoned both Jews and Gentiles to accept him as their divine Lord and Saviour; and that Islam is in error, though perhaps less profoundly so, in claiming that God spoke to Muhammad in a way that entails a switch of the focus of divine concern from the Jews to the Arabs, from Palestine to Arabia, from Jerusalem to Mecca. On this same absolutist basis a Christian will hold that both Jews and Muslims are profoundly in error in turning their backs on God's redeeming presence on earth in Jesus Christ. And a Muslim, again on this absolutist basis, will hold that Chris-

tians are profoundly in error in their belief that Jesus was God's
only-begotten Son; and that the Jews are also in error, though less
profoundly so, in failing to acknowledge God's final revelation in
the Qur'an. These confessional claims are not only possible, but
represent the attitude – whether or not explicitly articulated – of the
large majority within each of our three traditions. And indeed, if we
each take what our scriptures and tradition say in a straightforward
and literal way, this kind of absolutism seems unavoidable. Our own
tradition, whichever it is, must be right and the others wrong on any
central matters on which they differ; and our own tradition must
accordingly be superior to the others is virtue of its greater access to
the truth and its more direct relationship to God. This implication of
our traditional belief-systems should be frankly acknowledged rather
than merely tactfully overlooked if we are ever to move beyond the
static situation of rival absolutisms. For it is discomfort with these
absolute claims that forces us to ask important further questions.

In speaking of this discomfort I can only report my own experience. When as a Christian I look at my Jewish and Muslim colleagues – who have become Jewish and Muslim friends – I have to
say that they do not seem to me as they ought to seem if the traditional absolutism of my own tradition is valid. For if it is valid it
follows that they have a lesser access to vital truth and live in a less
direct relationship with God than I do. But I do not find that I can
honestly believe this to be the case.

However, I realise on further reflection that this 'not seeming as
they ought to seem' does not necessarily follow from the Christian
absolutist premise; for it could well be that they are exceptionally
good products of their traditions and I an exceptionally bad product
of mine, so that the manifest integrity of their faith, and their evident
dedication to God's service, is only impressive relatively to my own
deficient standpoint. But then when I look more widely at the many
Jews, Christians and Muslims whom I know, I still do not find that
the generality of Christians are more truly religious, or more honest
and truthful, or more loving and compassionate, or more thoughtful
for others, than are the generality of Muslims or Jews. And I ask
myself, is this what I should expect if Christ is the unique saviour
of humankind and Christianity, as the stream of life in which his
influence is most powerfully felt, is religiously superior to other
traditions?

I therefore look next at the long histories of our three faith-
communities, at their scriptures and literatures, their saints and

sinners, the societies and cultures that they have inspired; and again I do not find that one stands out as manifestly superior, morally and spiritually, to the others. Each is a complex historical mixture of good and evil, each with its strong points and its weak points, its shining peaks, its grey doldrums and its dark caves. But if I try to quantify these immensely varied goods and evils, spread as they are across the centuries, so as to produce three numerical conclusions, I find that the complexities and incommensurabilities make this impossible in practice. Further, each of these traditions has, so far as we can tell, been more or less equally fruitful in saintliness, producing extraordinary men and women whose spirit and lives make God more real to the rest of us.

These are of course empirical (in the sense of observational) judgements. *A priori*, each tradition has presumed a superior access to truth and a uniquely close relationship to God, resulting in a morally superior culture and history and in the production of more and/or better saints. Otherwise what would be the concrete value of a final divine revelation; what human difference would it make? However, empirically these *a priori* claims cannot be at all easily sustained, and indeed in my view cannot be sustained at all. In saying this I am, of course, making a statement in an area of virtually infinite complexity, in which no one can know all the facts and concerning which endless discussion will always be possible. But rather than needing to prove that my own global impression is correct, I suggest that the onus of proof falls upon anyone who wishes to maintain that some one tradition (namely their own) is observably morally and spiritually superior to the others.

But perhaps someone will respond that these comparative questions are out of order. Perhaps our three traditions are simply different and incommensurable. Perhaps there are no inter-traditional criteria, but by Christian criteria Christianity is superior, by Jewish criteria Judaism, and by Muslim criteria Islam. This is at first glance an attractive idea. However, it does not seem so attractive if we distinguish between, on the one hand, basic moral principles, such as valuing and caring for others as much as for oneself, and on the other hand, specific community norms, such as not eating pork; or observing the eucharist; or fasting during Ramadan. On this latter level it will, of course, follow that those who do not observe our particular code of practice must be judged to be falling short. But on the level of basic moral principles I suggest that there is sufficient convergence of ethical insight for common assessments to be possible. Each of our three traditions calls us to treat others as we would wish to be treated ourselves. Jesus taught, 'As ye would that men should do to you, do ye also to them likewise' (Luke 6: 31); the Talmud teaches, 'What is hateful to yourself do not do to your fellow man. That is the whole of the Torah' (*Babylonian Talmud*, Shabbath 31a); and Muhammad taught that 'No man is a true believer unless he desires for his brother that which he desires for himself' (*Hadith*: *Muslim*, chapter on iman, 71–2; *Ibn Madja*, Introduction, 9; *Al-Darimi*, chapter on riqaq; *Hambal* 3, 1976). Again, each tradition calls us to be just, honest and truthful, and to care for those – primarily recognised in earlier societies as the widows and orphans – who cannot care for themselves. It accordingly seems to me possible, from a Christian point of view, to make some comparative judgements that could be assented to by Muslims and Jews. Thus I would put to the historical credit of Judaism, for example, its being the birthplace of ethical monotheism in the West, and its production of an enormous wealth of significant individuals who have contributed notably to virtually every aspect of western civilisation; and to its discredit, for example, the contemporary misuse of power, now that it has power, in relation to the Palestinians. I would put to the historical credit of Christianity, for example, its civilising of pagan Europe and its being the birthplace of modern science; and to its discredit, for example, its motivating and validating of vicious anti-Semitism, and of the destructive colonial exploitation of what today we call the third world. And I would put to the historical credit of Islam, for example, its positive and constructive influence in millions of lives and its great cultural contribution to a considerable segment of the world; and to its discredit, for example, the continued practice of hideously inhumane forms of punishment in some Islamic countries.

Of course, not all Christians would concur with these judgements concerning the debit side of their own tradition; nor would all Muslims and Jews concur concerning the debit sides of theirs. But I fancy, nevertheless, that many thoughtful Christians, Muslims and Jews are in fact in broad agreement on such matters. When we think of the fruits of religion in promoting human welfare, seen in terms of the universal human values of justice, peace and happiness, I suspect that we all operate on essentially the same fundamental moral insights. This, at any rate, is the thesis that I am proposing.

Essentially the same seems to me to be true when we consider what are often called spiritual criteria, meaning the criteria by which we may recognise saintliness. Is it the case that by Christian criteria

Christian saints are superior, by Jewish criteria Jewish saints, and by Muslim criteria Muslim saints? I do not think so. I am not of course thinking, in the Christian case, of the tests for canonisation used by the Roman Church. By these criteria it is true by definition that all saints are Christians. Nor am I thinking of saints as a separate species of humanity; saintliness is a matter of degree. I am thinking of those all-too-rare individuals who are manifestly much more advanced than the rest of us in the transformation from natural self-centredness to a new orientation centred in the transcendent reality that we in our three traditions call God. I know a small number of people in whom I can see very clearly the fruits of this transformation, and I know by report a larger number of others. These are spread over the Christian, Jewish, Muslim, Hindu, Buddhist and Sikh communities. And it is my strong intuitive conviction that if they were brought together each would feel a deep affinity with the others, despite the fact that they adhere to different religions, think in terms of different theological and philosophical systems, and engage in different religious practices; and despite the fact that some are contemplatives and others political activists. Again, I cannot prove this; and yet I think it likely that many of us share the same intuition.

IV

If you have been sympathetic to what I have thus far been saying you will experience a discomfort analogous to my own with the assumption that one's tradition must be morally and spiritually superior to all others. However, this discomfort will exist alongside a continuous awareness that this is the tradition into which I was born and which has formed and nourished me, so that I am inextricably a part of it and it a part of me; and I cannot imagine myself being transplanted into any other tradition. But, further, what we have also recognised in our interactions and discussions is that not only do I, as a Christian, feel this intrinsicality to the Christian tradition, but I know that others as Jews and as Muslims feel a like intrinsic relation to their own tradition; and each in turn knows this of the rest of us. Where, then, do we go from here; and where do we arrive in response to our original question whether we all worship the same God?

Here I can only offer a suggestion, draw a picture, spell out a possibility, and wait to see if you also find that it makes good sense.

If then we hold, with the universal aspect of our three faiths, that there is only one God, who is the source of all other existence and the ultimate Lord of the universe, and if we also hold that the particular God-figures of our three traditions are, as concrete historical realities, significantly different, does it not follow that these three divine personalities cannot each be simply identical with the one universal God? They may be authentic manifestations, 'faces', forms, expressions, of that one God, or ways in which the one God appears to human beings from different points of view or within different human contexts, but they cannot all be purely and simply identical with the one God. And so we have either to revert to the residual absolutism of our own faith or draw a distinction of some kind between the one universal God and our three particular manifestations of that God. Such a distinction seems to me unavoidable once we take serious account of religious realities beyond the borders of our own tradition.

The simplest and most satisfactory way to draw this distinction is, I suggest, between, on the one hand, God *a se*, in God's eternal self-existent being, 'before' and independently of creation, and on the other hand, God in relation to God's creation and thus as thought of and encountered by human beings. This is the familiar distinction, classically drawn by Immanuel Kant, between something as it is in itself, a *Ding an sich*, and that same thing as humanly perceived, with all that the human mind contributes in the process of perception. In using this basic distinction we do not of course need to adopt Kant's own particular account of the way in which the mind organises the impacts of the environment through an innate system of categories, bringing it to consciousness as the three-dimensional world of objects of which we are aware. We are concerned only with his more basic thesis that awareness of our environment is not a purely passive registering of it in consciousness but an active process of selecting, ordering and interpreting. We know from many sources that the world as we are aware of it represents our distinctively human selective simplification of a virtually infinitely richer and more complex reality that would utterly bewilder and overwhelm us if we were immediately conscious of it. Our perceptual machinery is attuned only to a minute proportion of the total range of information flowing through and around us: for example, to electromagnetic waves between 16 and 32 millionths of an inch out of a spectrum extending from cosmic rays as short as 10 thousand millionths of an inch to radio waves as long as 18 miles. And after this physical filtering has taken place there is a constructive activity of the mind whereby we order the world by means of a system of concepts which endow it with forms of meaning in terms of which we can behave appropriately within it. For example, when I see a fork on the table I see what is there as a fork, an instrument to aid eating, this seeing-as having as its dispositional aspect my being in a state of readiness to behave in ways appropriate (as it seems to me) to that thing's being a fork. But a Stone Age person transported here in a time machine would not see what is there as a fork, for he or she would not have the concept of a fork with which to experience in this way. A large part of the field of meaning in terms of which we experience our everyday environment is thus culturally formed. In other words, we ourselves partially construct the meaningful world which we inhabit. All this is, I think, so widely agreed today, as a result not only of the philosophical analyses of Kant and others, but also of an accumulation of work in cognitive psychology and the sociology of knowledge, that we can safely proceed to ask if it offers any useful hints for the epistemology of religion.

Can we apply the distinction between a reality as it is in itself and that reality as humanly perceived in terms both of the universal 'shape' of the human mind and of its culture-specific conceptual systems, to our awareness of God? It seems to me that we can; and that this will enable us to understand the relationship between our three traditions. (It can also, in an extended form, enable us to understand the relationship between religions more generally; but that is not our immediate concern here.) We shall then say that we are aware of God, not *an sich* – that would be equivalent to perceiving the world as it is unperceived, – but as God is thought of and experienced through the conceptual 'lens' of our own tradition. For each tradition functions as a kind of mental 'lens' – consisting of concepts, stories (both historical and mythical), religious practices, artistic styles, forms of life – through which we perceive the divine. And because there is a plurality of such 'lenses' there is a plurality of ways in which God is concretely thought and experienced.

This suggests that each concrete historical divine personality – Jahweh, the heavenly Father, the Qur'anic Allah – is a joint product of the universal divine presence and a particular historically formed mode of constructive religious imagination. That there is an element of human imaginative projection in religion has surely been undeniable since the work of Feuerbach in the nineteenth century, reinforced by the more recent discoveries of the ethnologists, anthropologists and historians of religion in correlating concepts of God with cultural circumstances, which rest in turn upon a complex of geographical, climatic, economic and political factors. For example, ancient settled agricultural societies tended to worship female deities, whilst pastoral herd-keeping societies tended to worship male deities. The sociobiologist Edward O. Wilson says,

> The God of monotheistic religions is always male; this strong patriarchal tendency has several cultural sources. Pastoral societies are highly mobile, tightly organized, and often militant, all features that tip the balance toward male authority. It is also significant that herding, the main economic basis, is primarily the responsibility of men.[3]

A range of other instances were assembled by the great pioneer in this field, Max Weber.[4] The principle that he and others have uncovered means that, for example, the female divine personalities worshipped by the pre-Aryan inhabitants of Harappa in India and the male divine personalities worshipped by the pre-Islamic nomadic tribes of Arabia owed their gender to the basic economic and cultural patterns of these different human communities. Of course from a naturalistic, or reductionist, point of view they were all created solely by the human imagination. But even from a religious point of view we have to accept that they were *partially* so created. And it seems evident to me that this general principle applies also to the 'high' religions of Judaism, Christianity and Islam. Each different awareness of the divine includes an element of creative human imagination guided by concrete historical circumstances.

This means in turn that the biblical Jahweh was formed at the interface between the transcendent universal God and the particular mentality and circumstances of the people of Israel; later taking on a more universal character, whilst however retaining continuity with the tribal past, in the Judaism of the rabbis. With the birth of Christianity and its splitting away from Judaism, this divine personality can be said to have divided into two, one form developing into the Adonai of rabbinic Judaism and the other into the heavenly Father – later elaborated into the Holy Trinity – of Christianity, with both universal characteristics and a particular historical linkage to Jesus of Nazareth and the Christian church. Later again the divine presence that had formed in interaction with the Jewish people took yet another 'name and form' as the Allah of the Qur'an, again with both a particular historical linkage to the prophet Muhammad and the life of seventh-century CE Arabia, and universal characteristics which became increasingly prominent as Islam developed into a world faith.

This model of one ultimate divine Reality, God in Godself, and a plurality of human communal awareness of that divine Reality, does justice, as it seems to me, to the two perceptions on which we want to insist. One is the sufficiency and beauty and life-giving and life-transforming power of our own tradition at its best, with its unique remembered history, way of life, manner of prayer, cherished literature, its saints and scholars, its architecture, music and other artistic creations, such that we rightly cling to it and seek to live within it and to contribute to its ongoing life. The other perception that most, perhaps all, of us want to insist upon is our acceptance of the equal right, and indeed necessity, for our colleagues to view their own tradition in precisely the same way. Further, this recognition is not merely a matter of politeness, concealing a belief that God as thought and encountered by another faith-community is less authentic than God as known by us. By that route we only make a circular return to the traditional superiority-claim, discomfort with which caused us to look further.

I believe that it is an authentic religious intuition that requires us each to move beyond politeness to a deeper acceptance of the validity – and so far as we can tell the equal validity – of the other two Abrahamic traditions. To unfold the implications of this move must involve extensive new thinking. I have been pointing to one possible direction for such thinking. But I do not suggest that this is the only possible way. If there is another that seems more adequate, may we please have it set before us?

If we do adopt some such pluralistic model, will it not follow that we should each try to influence our own community towards a de-emphasising and eventual elimination of its absolute claim over against other traditions – the claim to be in a uniquely important sense God's chosen people; the claim that Christianity alone was founded by God in person, incarnate as Jesus Christ; the claim that Islam alone is a response to God's final and unsurpassable revelation? It is not appropriate, in my view, for any of us to presume to tell our colleagues of other faiths how to try to influence the development of their own tradition so that it can contribute to the hoped-for world community of the twenty-first century, a world community without which there will be world chaos and destruction. As a Christian I can make suggestions within my own community, and what I and a number of other Christian theologians have collaborated in suggesting is that we should regard the idea of divine incarnation as a metaphorical or mythic concept, so that the revelation through Jesus can be understood as being of the same kind as the revelations through Moses and Muhammad.[5]

I know, of course, that this kind of revisionary work is much easier in some circumstances than in others. Within Christianity it is easier for someone like myself who is a Protestant, rather than a Catholic, and who is working in a secular university rather than a church seminary setting; though even in such maximally favourable circumstances one must expect to be a target of fundamentalist wrath and unceasing conservative criticism, and to be excluded from any official influence within one's own church. Among Muslims revision is clearly easier for those working in the West rather than in most Muslim countries today. And among Jews there must be comparable distinctions between easier and more difficult settings. It is thus to be expected that different people will be able to proceed at different paces in publicly thinking through the implications of the insight that one's own tradition is not the one and only 'true religion'. However, the world needs this developing pluralistic outlook, not only because it is intellectually realistic but also because it can defuse the religious absolutism which has validated and intensified virtually every international conflict in every age. The modern weaponry that we saw in use in the Gulf war, and on an even more frightening scale at Hiroshima and Nagasaki, has produced a world which can no longer afford such intra-human conflicts. Hans Küng has written: 'There will be no peace among the peoples of this world without peace among the world religions.'[6] I would add that there will be no true peace among the world religions without the recognition by each that the others are different but equally valid responses to the ultimate divine Reality that we call God.

Notes

1. Joseph Campbell, *The Power of Myth* (New York and London: Doubleday, 1988) p. 21.
2. More precisely, when they exceed a certain degree of incompatibility it becomes implausible to think that they have the same referent.
3. Edward O. Wilson, *Of Human Nature* (Boston, Mass.: Harvard University Press, 1978) p. 190.
4. Max Weber, *Sociology of Religion* (1922; Boston, Mass.: Beacon Press, 1963).
5. See, for example, John Hick (ed.), *The Myth of God Incarnate* (London: SCM Press; and Philadelphia, Penn.: Westminster Press, 1977).
6. Hans Küng, *Christianity and the World Religions* (New York: Doubleday, 1986) p. 443.

10

The Real and its Personae and Impersonae

What do we mean by 'the Ultimate'? That beyond which there is nothing further. But then this could be simply the physical universe (including ourselves); there may be nothing more than this. However, the term 'the Ultimate' is useful mainly to signal the view that there *is* something more, something that transcends the physical universe, when the notion of A transcending B means not only that A is other than B but also that A is in some significant sense prior to, and/or more important or more valuable than, and/or explanatory of, B. I therefore propose to mean by the Ultimate that putative reality which transcends everything other than itself but is not transcended by anything other than itself. The Ultimate, so conceived, is related to the universe as its ground or creator, and to us human beings, as conscious parts of the universe, as the source both of our existence and of the value or meaning of that existence.

This concept *may* be uninstantiated. It may be contingently uninstantiated, like the concept of a unicorn, or necessarily uninstantiated, like that of a square circle. But on the other hand it may not be like either of these. Notions of the Ultimate may be adequate or inadequate concepts – wholly or partly instantiated – of an all-important reality which transcends the physical universe and our own psycho-physical selves. Whether such concepts are instantiatable, and if so instantiated, is of course the fundamental issue in the philosophy of religion. I have tried to address that basic question elsewhere. Acknowledging that it remains open, I propose nevertheless to discuss now a further question which arises for those who believe that there is or at least may be an ultimate reality which appropriately evokes human responses of the kind that we call religious.

The concept of the Ultimate to be outlined in this chapter differs in an important respect from those that operate within a particular living religious tradition, entering into its distinctive mode of religious experience, shaping its liturgical language or meditative practice, and being reflectively described in its philosophy or theology. Each of these can be categorised as a primary religious concept defining that (putative) reality, transcending the worshipper or meditator, upon which worship or meditation is focused. In contrast to this, the concept to be discussed here has been formed in the attempt to understand the relationship between those primary concepts. It functions within the philosophy of religion when this is not confined to the data of any one tradition but has a global scope. For it is the concept of the ground of this plurality of forms of religious experience and thought – the ultimate reality which is variously conceived, experienced and responded to within the different traditions of the world.

It is the plurality of traditions that creates the problem which, as it seems to me, requires this concept for its resolution. If we can imagine there being only one religion in the world, and all religious persons thinking and experiencing in the same way, it would then be a natural and universal conviction that the Ultimate is as conceived in that tradition. But in fact, as we know, there are a number of religious histories each with its own concept or indeed family of concepts of the Ultimate. Hence the problem of the relationship between these and between the modes of religious experience which they inform. And the hypothesis that I want to consider is that what they describe is not the Ultimate as it is in itself but as it is conceived in the variety of ways made possible by our varied human mentalities and cultures – our different modes of religious experience being in turn made possible by those concepts.

Such terms as the Real, the Ultimate, Ultimate Reality are commonly used to refer to this supposed *ne plus ultra*. None of them will suit everybody's linguistic taste. Accepting this I propose, arbitrarily, to speak of the Real, corresponding as it does to the Sanscrit *sat*, the Arabic *Al Haqq*, and the Chinese *zhen*. And I shall be distinguishing between, on the one hand, the Real *an sich* – to use an expression which avoids the neuter as well as the masculine and the feminine – and on the other hand the Real as variously thought and experienced within the different religious traditions.

The paradigm of the Real *an sich* and its varied manifestations to human consciousness has to justify itself by its power to illuminate the history of religions. This offers significant pointers to it within each of the major traditions. Thus Christian thought has sometimes distinguished between God in God's eternal self-existent being, before or independently of creation, and God in relation to and thus as known by created beings – God *a se* and God *pro nobis*; Judaism, in its mystical Kabbalistic strand, has distinguished between the infinite divine reality, *En Soph*, and the concrete God of the Bible; Islam, in its own mystical Sufi strand, has likewise distinguished between the ultimate reality, *Al Haqq* and the Qur'anic Revealer to humanity; again Hindu advaitic thought distinguishes between *nirguna* Brahman, beyond the scope of all human concepts, and *saguna* Brahman, humanly known as Ishwara, the personal deity; and Buddhist thought, in the Mahayana, distinguishes between the eternal *dharmakaya*, which is the ultimate and ineffable Buddha nature, and the *sambhoga-kaya* and *nirmana-kaya*, in which that nature takes the form of individual Buddhas, some of whom become incarnate on this earth; and again, in recent Western thought, Paul Tillich has distinguished between God and the God above the God of theism,[1] and Gordon Kaufman between the real God and the available God.[2]

These distinctions were drawn for different purposes, each internal to its own tradition, and accordingly do not precisely coincide with the distinction that I want to draw. They do, however, suggest it to anyone who has the wider problem in mind. We can approach the distinction that we need through the familiar fact that even within a single theistic community of faith different individuals commonly operate with different mental pictures of God. If, for example, it were possible to inspect the images of God in the minds of a typical congregation of worshippers in a Christian church one Sunday morning, we should undoubtedly find wide variations. These images would range from the stern judge who sends misfortunes as punishments and whose presence inspires fear, to the gracious heavenly Father whose warm love envelopes us; and would range in another dimension from God as an invisible person observing our every thought and act and prepared to intervene in answer to prayer in the smallest affairs of our lives, to God as 'high and lifted up' and 'inhabiting eternity', the maker and Lord of the universe, whose purposes are seen in the grand design of nature rather than in a detailed manipulation of events on earth. No doubt these images can be synthesised in a comprehensive theoretical definition. But the religious activities of worship, and the related forms of religious experience, involve limited images of God varying in their character and in the practical dispositions that they evoke. Nevertheless, it seems natural and indeed almost inevitable, from a Christian point of view, to say that Christians are all worshipping the same God, but each doing so through an image which focuses upon that aspect of the divine nature which is most relevant to their spiritual needs at the time. It is important to add that it is also possible for an image, at the extremes of the spectrum – for example, a Nazi image of God as the Lord of the Aryan race – to be so distorted that it cannot mediate a relationship with God as known in the central Christian tradition. But whilst our human images of the deity can thus be more adequate and less adequate, even the most adequate still require a distinction between God in the divine fulness and God as imaged in a variety of overlapping ways by different individuals and groups. And when we enlarge our field of vision to include the distinctively different but still overlapping concepts of God operating among Jews and Muslims, we shall naturally understand this wider range of differences in the same way though on a larger scale. For the three Peoples of the Book share a common biblical vision of the history of God's dealings with humanity. They manifestly intend to be worshipping the same, because the only, deity even though their mental images of that deity differ in the ways that separate the three traditions. For it is part of the distinctively Jewish self-understanding that the divine relationship to humanity is centred in God's dealings with the children of Israel; and part of the distinctively Christian self-understanding that God became incarnate as the founder of the Christian church; and part of the distinctively Muslim self-understanding that God has spoken finally and decisively in the Holy Qur'an. And so within each tradition it is believed that the other two Abrahamic faiths worship the same God through largely overlapping mental images of that God, whilst being, however, in each case mistaken at one key point. Each thus, whilst recognising a common history, maintains its own unique centrality or sense of superiority.

There is, however, another possible interpretation of the situation, and one which does better justice to the apparently equal quality of worship and religious experience and of the fruits of this in human life within the three traditions. This is that their overlapping mental images of God are all produced by the impact of the divine Reality upon these three different streams of religious consciousness; but that the exclusivist interpretation which each tradition has put upon its own self-understanding is a human and limiting contribution. From this point of view God is authentically and savingly known to

Jews in the Torah and the Rabbinic tradition; to Christians in the life
and teachings of Jesus as mediated through the New Testament and
the church; and to Muslims in the Qur'anic revelation through the
prophet Muhammad. But in so far as Jews think of themselves as
God's Chosen People in a sense which relegates all other peoples to
an inferior relationship to God; and in so far as Christians think of
Christianity as superior to all other religions because founded by
God in person, with the implication that all human beings should
become Christians; and in so far as Muslims think of the Qur'an as
God's final revelation, superseding all others, with the implication
that all human beings should become Muslims, they are each
absolutising their own human image of God in a way which denies
the universal divine love and saving activity.

One way in which we can express the situation as we have thus
far traced it is by saying that each stream of religious experience and
thought has generated its own distinctive halo of self-validating
mythology or self-enhancing metaphor – the mythologies of the
Chosen People, of the uniquely incarnate God, and of God's definitive revelation to a particular people, the Arabs, in a particular
human language. These are nevertheless true mythologies or true
metaphors in so far as they evoke an appropriate response of devotion, in Jews to the Torah, in Christians to Christ, and in Muslims to
the Qur'an. But none of these mythologies, nor the equivalent self-
validating mythologies of other traditions, has universal validity,
speaking to human beings as such; rather, each is part of the history
of a particular religio-cultural form of human life. And when we
now take a yet larger view, and include the concepts of God operating within the Hindu tradition – Vishnu and Shiva, Kali and Durga,
and the many other gods and goddesses of India – we find, at least
among reflective worshippers, a general awareness that 'the Real
(*sat*) is one, but sages name it variously'.[3] Accordingly Vaishnavites,
whose devotional life is focused on the figure of Krishna as the
saving incarnation of Vishnu, and Shaivites, with their devotional
life focused on Shiva, do not dispute as to which of these is the true
God; for they are conscious that both are authentic, though different
and distinct, manifestations of the one ultimate reality of Brahman.
The same is true within Mahayana Buddhism, in which Amida
Buddha and Mahavairocana Buddha have been worshipped as the
central Buddha by Pure Land and Esoteric Buddhists respectively
for many centuries, and yet their difference in worship has led to no
serious conflicts between them. This is because both Amida and

Mahavairocana are regarded as different manifestations of the same *dharmakaya* which is in itself empty, open and formless.[4]

Although the Indian and the Semitic deities lack a relationship to a common strand of human history, both groups function in the same way within the forms of life to which they belong. They should accordingly be interpreted on the same principle. Shiva and Krishna and Yahweh and Allah and the Heavenly Father, then, name different concrete images of the Real operating in the religious consciousness and life of different human communities. Each is thought of, experienced and responded to as the Lord, the object of our devotion, the determiner of our destiny, the Ultimate in relation to us. And from a religious point of view we must say that each is indeed an authentic, life-giving manifestation of the Real within a different strand of human life. We thereby differ from the traditional formulations of faith, not in their affirmation of a transcendent divine Reality, but in the claim made within each tradition that it alone embodies the only fully valid and efficacious form of relationship to that Reality.

This position would seem to be in competition with three others. One is atheism; the Gods are all imaginary projections of the human mind. This is the naturalistic possibility which I noted but set aside at the beginning; for I am seeking here a *religious* interpretation of the phenomena of religion. A second possibility is that of religious exclusivism: our own God – whether we be Jew or Christian, Hindu or Muslim – exists, whilst the others are figments of human imagination. This possibility, however, is rendered implausible, in my view, by the fact that the effects in human life of devotion to these different Gods are so similar – both the good effect of the overcoming of self-centredness and the growth of love or compassion, and the bad effect of providing a validation of collective greed and aggression. If in one case the good is to be attributed to the influence of a real divine being and evil to human perversion, the same should be done in each case – unless there is some clear reason to the contrary; and the only reason offered is each tradition's conviction, in its more exclusivist moods, of its own unique superiority.

The third possibility is polytheism; the Gods are all real as ontologically distinct beings. One could, of course, apply this principle to all of the hundreds of thousands of deities known in the history of religion: but let us simplify our task here by restricting it to the Gods of the great monotheistic faiths. Yahweh or Adonai, then, is a real divine Person, and the Heavenly Father (or perhaps the Holy Trinity considered as a unity) is another real divine Person, and Allah is yet another real divine Person, and God as worshipped by the Sikhs is another, and Shiva yet another . . .

In commenting upon this possibility let me distinguish it from the hypothesis that I am advancing and show why the latter seems to me preferable. There is a sense in which, for example, the Yahweh of the Hebrew scriptures and the Krishna of the *Bhagavad Gita* are two different Gods. Yahweh is known only in his relationship to the Jewish people; he is a part of their history and they are a part of his. The universe of discourse which he inhabits is that of distinctively Jewish faith, and the strand of history in which he has operated runs through the Middle East and into the Jewish diaspora. Krishna, on the other hand, belongs to a different universe of religious discourse; and the strand of history within which he has revealed himself is that of ancient India. We have here two spheres of religious consciousness which do not at any point touch one another. Yahweh exists within and indeed as the centre of the Jewish world-view, and only a Jew can know Yahweh as his or her God. Krishna, on the other hand, exists within and at the centre of the quite different Vaishnavite Hindu world-view, and only Hindus can know Krishna as their God. Thus far it looks as though there are here two autonomous language-games which should not be confused or mixed, even though they are indirectly related as distant members of the wider family of religious language-games. But nevertheless, when we take note of them both in the same field of intellectual vision a problem becomes evident. Within the Hebrew would view Yahweh (or Adonai) is believed to be the sole maker of heaven and earth,[5] and in the world-view of the *Bhagavad Gita* Krishna is believed to be the sole source of the universe.[6] If, then, we take the polytheistic view that Yahweh and Krishna both exist in some relatively straightforward sense, one (at most) can be the true creator or source of the universe, whilst the other must either be a deceiver or be deceived. Thus the worshippers of either Yahweh or Krishna must be worshipping a false god. And yet each is at the centre of an equally rich and spiritually sustaining religious life within which men and women are – and so far as we can tell are to an equal extent – brought to a self-giving love of God and to compassion towards their neighbours. The fruits of faith do not distinguish between the two Gods as respectively real and unreal, authentic and spurious. It therefore seems to me that the two viable options at this point are the naturalistic denial of both as figments of our imagination and the religious acceptance of both as authentic manifestations, or 'faces', or personae, or appearances to human consciousness, of the Real *an sich*.

Let me now adopt one of these terms and develop a little the idea of a plurality of divine personae. By a human persona I mean a public mask or social role which has developed in one's interaction with others and which has its existence within the ongoing process of a system of personal relationships. A permanently solitary consciousness – if we can imagine one – would have no persona since it would not exist in relationship to other consciousnesses. Personality is essentially interpersonal, and presupposes a common world within which social life can take place. Accordingly the various divine personae, Yahweh and Krishna and Durga and Allah and Shiva and the Heavenly Father (or the Father, Son and Holy Ghost) and so on, have been formed in the interaction between the Real and different human religio-cultural communities. They exist at the interface between the Real and the various streams of historical consciousness. Thus the Yahweh persona has come about and developed in the impact of the Real upon the distinctively Hebraic consciousness of the Jewish people through the centuries; whilst the Krishna persona has come about in the impact of the Real upon distinctively Indian consciousness within the Vaishnavite tradition. And the reason why the Real is so preponderantly thought and experienced as personal in the history of religions is presumably that as persons we need, in our relationship with the Real, a personal cosmic presence to address and to be addressed by. Accordingly the different divine personae have formed as manifestations of the Real in relation to the different streams of human life. They are the Real as known, necessarily in human terms, within this or that religious tradition.

Can this paradigm of the Real becoming manifest in different ways, which have been partly formed by our human contribution to awareness of them, be applied also to the thought and experience of the non-theistic traditions – advaitic Hinduism and most of Buddhism? I have suggested that the Real as perceived through one set of religio-cultural 'lenses' appears as a range of personal deities, who are the personae of the Real. Can we also say that the Real as perceived through another set of religio-cultural 'lenses' appears as a range of non-personal absolutes, which are the impersonae of the Real? I believe that we can; though only after two obstacles have been surmounted.

The first obstacle is the question whether what is experienced in non-theistic mysticism is indeed believed to be the Ultimate. So far as Hindu mysticism is concerned the answer is non-controversially yes; Brahman is thought of as the Ultimate Reality. But what of Buddhism? Here we must remember that there is (as in the case of the other great traditions) not simply Buddhism in the singular but Buddhisms in the plural. The full range of meditational practices and philosophical interpretations inspired by the Buddha covers territory on both sides of the border between what I shall call the naturalistic or humanist, and the supranaturalistic or religious, types of world-view. As I am using the terms, humanism or naturalism does not require a concept of the Ultimate; whereas religious, or supranaturalistic, world-views do – each religious tradition having its own distinctive variation. There is, then, a humanist form of Buddhism which consists essentially in the practice of meditation without any associated supranatural beliefs. The fruit of meditation in the purification of the mind from the corrosions of ego-anxicty, and a consequent non-judgemental acceptance of this transitory world of which we are part, is an end in itself. The trappings of zazen drawn from Japanese monastic life – the meditation hall, the discipline, the drums and chants – are accepted as helpful aids to meditation; and such traditional Buddhist ideas as innumerable rebirths, the heavens and hells, the gods and bodhisattvas, are demythologised and regarded as popular aids to the imagination. All this is within the humanistic or naturalistic assumption that we are simply fleeting moments of consciousness, here one moment and gone the next, within the continuously transforming field of energy which is the physical universe.

I fully accept that Buddhism permits this kind of humanistic development; and indeed it is this that constitutes much of its attraction to many Western minds reacting against simplistically literal understandings of theism. However, I question whether the main streams of Buddhist thought have understood themselves in this way.

In the Pali scriptures of the Thervada, *nirvana* (*nibbana*) is certainly sometimes presented in purely negative terms as simply the cessation of the grasping self and its attendant anxieties. It is the 'blowing-out' of the ego with its inevitable sorrows. But there is also in the tradition a strong element of positive and indeed supranaturalistic teaching about *nirvana*. Thus the Buddha declares, in a famous passage, 'Monks, there is a not-born, a not-become, a not-made, a not-compounded. Monks, if that unborn, not-become, not-made, not-compounded were not, there would be apparent no escape from this here that is born, become, made, compounded.[7] Again, in the *Majjhima-Nikāya nirvana* is described as 'the unborn . . . unaging . . . undecaying . . . undying . . . unsorrowing . . . stainless',[8] and in the *Samyutta-Nikāya* as 'the further shore . . . the unfading . . . the stable . . . the invisible . . . the taintless . . . the peace . . . the deathless . . . the excellent . . . the blissful . . . the security . . . the wonderful . . . the marvellous . . . the free from ill . . . the island . . . the cave of shelter . . . the stronghold . . . the refuge . . . the goal'.[9] This sounds more like supranaturalistic-religious than naturalistic-humanist language. And it is, I think, so understood by most of the leading Theravadins of today; for example, Narada Mahathera, in his commentary of *The Dhammapada*, speaks of *nirvana* as 'the permanent, immortal, supramundane state which cannot be expressed in mundane terms'.[10]

This positive use of the concept of *nirvana*, as pointing to the ultimate ineffable reality with which religion is concerned, was further developed within the Mahayana. Edward Conze summarises:

> The ultimate reality, also called Dharma by the Buddhists, or Nirvana, is defined as that which stands completely outside the sensory world of illusion and ignorance, a world inextricably interwoven with craving and greed. To get somehow to that reality is the supremely worthwhile goal of the Buddhist life. The Buddhist idea of ultimate reality is very much akin to the philosophical notion of the 'Absolute', and not easily distinguished from the notion of God among the more mystical theologians, like Dionysius Areopagita and Eckart'.[11]

And when we turn to Zen, which is the strand of Buddhism that is most readily open to a purely humanistic interpretation, we find members of the very influential Kyoto school speaking of religion as 'man's search for true reality', indeed for the 'Great Reality' (Keiji Nishitani),[12] and saying that 'nirvana is nothing but Ultimate Reality' (Masao Abe).[13] They emphasise that the characterisation of Reality as *sunyata* (Emptiness, Void, Nothingness) is a way of expressing a transcendence of all human thoughtforms. As D. T. Suzuki wrote, 'To say that reality is "empty" means that it goes beyond definability, and cannot be qualified as this or that.' Again, '*Dharmakaya* or *prajna*, being "emptiness" itself and having no tangible bodily existence, has to embody itself in a form and be *manifested* as a stalk of bamboo, as a mass of foliage, as a fish, as a man, as a Bodhisattva, as a mind, and so forth. But these manifestations themselves *are* not the

Dharmakaya or prajna, which is more than forms or ideas or modes of existence.'[14]

Thus it seems that there is deeply embedded in the Buddhist tradition the belief in an ultimate Reality, the eternal *dharmakaya* or Buddha nature, also characterised as *sunyata,* with which a right relationship, unitive or communitive, is attained in the final experience of enlightenment.

But what of the distinctive Mahayana discovery, central to Zen, that *nirvana* and *samsara* are one? What is discovered is a way of experiencing the world as it is, in its pure 'suchness'. This 'suchness', or as-it-is-ness, is also its 'emptiness' of any substantiality or permanence, and this 'emptiness' is, paradoxically, fulness of 'wondrous being'[15] in the ever-new reality of the present moment. This depth of reality is experienced by transcending the normal ego point of view, in which everything is perceived as it affects the self, and seeing things as they are for their own sake in their presentational immediacy. Like other modes of Buddhist experience this can be interpreted, or contextualised, both religiously and humanistically. For Zen-humanism the experience of the world in its full wonder and beauty is an end in itself, devoid of any implications concerning the structure of the universe beyond the evident fact that its incessant flow includes this present moment of experience. Religious Zen, on the other hand, also finds in this experience of the world a clue to the nature of reality, transcending our own individual experience, as to be rejoiced in because it offers the bliss of *nirvana* to all conscious beings. Such an affirmation of the good in the sense of the to-be-rejoiced-in character of reality as a whole – not just good for a fortunate few but eventually for all – is of the essence of religion. For if the goodness thus affirmed is secure and reliable it cannot be a mere chance moment waiting to be dissolved again in a structureless flow of change. To affirm the goodness of the universe – which William James, in my view rightly, identified as the essential message of religion[16] – is to affirm an ultimate reality transcending the flux of change and chance, a reality which is in its relation to us to be rejoiced in. And in the Buddhist tradition this eternal reality is variously known as *nirvana,* the *dharmakaya, sunyata.*

Thus it seems to me that our hypothesis, in its application to the non-theistic traditions, is able to surmount this first obstacle. In Hinduism and Buddhism there is an affirmation of the Ultimate either as the infinite consciousness of Brahman or as the ultimate character of reality which is from our point of view good.

The second obstacle arises from a general difference between the traditions of Semitic and of Indian origin. If by the mystical we mean, as I think we should mean, simply the top end of the scale of intensity within the experiential element in religion, then mysticism plays a much more central role in the eastern than in the western traditions. Hinduism centres upon human consciousness, in all its emotional, volitional, intellectual and intuitive modes, and offers a transition from the anxiety-ridden delusion of *maya* to the blissful self-consciousness of the *atman*, which is one with Brahman, the Ultimate itself. Buddhism likewise centres upon our present consciousness, suffering from the anguished fears and worries generated by the self-concerned ego. For the ego is attached by a thousand bonds of grasping desire and fearful avoidance to a world that it cannot control, so that the ever-changing stream of life, involving the ineluctable possibilities of sickness, poverty, shame, injustice, and the inevitabilities of old age, decay and death, are felt as a perpetual threat. All this is the *dukkha* from which we can be liberated only by transcending the self-centred point of view and entering into the egoless state of *nirvana*. Thus, for both the Hindu and the Buddhist traditions, right experiencing is an end in itself, whilst right believing has a subsidiary and instrumental value in pointing out the way to liberation.

For Judaism, Christianity and Islam, on the other hand, experience has generally been secondary to right belief or right behaviour. In Christianity right belief has been given a primary place, so that those who harbour 'wrong beliefs' have had to be cast out of the Church as heretics – and *extra ecclesium nulla salus!* In Judaism participation in the ritual life of the people through the centuries has generally been regarded as more important than the holding of correct beliefs; orthopraxy has had priority over orthodoxy. In Islam certain basic beliefs – above all in the uniqueness and absoluteness of God and in God's revelation through the Prophet – have been seen as essential; but beyond this the stress has been upon the activities of prayer, fasting, alms-giving, pilgrimage and the organisation of life in an Islamic pattern. Of course, there are profound mystical strands within each of these traditions of Semitic origin. But, historically, those strands have had a marginal place and have not infrequently been objects of suspicion or even hostility on the part of the orthodox.

Now mysticism, such as is central to the non-theistic strands within Hinduism and Buddhism, reports a direct, unmediated, often unitive, awareness of the Ultimate. The subject–object relationship is said to be transcended. There is no longer any epistemic distance between the human consciousness and the Ultimate itself, and accordingly no scope for a human activity of interpretation. Thus according to *advaita* Vedanta liberation involves the experience of oneness with Brahman; and according to Buddhism the attainment of *nirvana* is the experience of one's eternal Buddha nature, or (in Zen) of the ever-changing world, no longer seen in the distorting perspective of the ego, but experienced now as itself *nirvana*. But such a unitive and unmediated experience of the Ultimate does not fit the model that we have adopted for the theistic forms of religious experience, namely a reality, itself beyond the scope of human thought and experience, being mediately known in different ways from within the different religio-cultural streams of life. Thus far, then, it would seem that the model will apply to the theistic but not to the non-theistic religions.

However, recent epistemological discussions of mysticism have suggested that an interpretative element is always and unavoidably present even in the ostensibly unitive experience. For the mystic is still an embodied human mind; and this always functions in accordance with its own inherent structure, its cultural formation and individual experience. And there is considerable evidence that a person who has been spiritually trained by an *advaitic* guru, whose mind has been steeped in the Vedas and Upanishads and the writings of Shankara, and who has for years practised a form of *advaitic* yoga, will have a characteristically different experience of the Ultimate from one who has been spiritually trained by a Zen master, whose mind is steeped in Zen literature, and who has practised zazen for years in a monastery or meditation centre. The one will have a distinctively *advaitic* experience of the Ultimate as Brahman, the other a distinctively Zen experience of the Ultimate as the pure 'suchness' of everything seen as 'wondrous being', devoid of all ego-distortion. The strong correlation of the type of experience with the spiritual practice and its associated philosophy unmistakably suggests that the two minds bring their Vedantic or Zen ideas and modes of apperception with them into their mystical experiencing, determining the form that it takes.

It therefore seems to me that the second hurdle can also be surmounted. There does seem to be in the non-theistic forms of religious experience a culturally variable human contribution paralleling the culturally variable contribution to the different kinds of theistic experience.

There are, then, according to the hypothesis I am outlining, a plurality of impersonae as well as of personae of the Real. None of these is the Real *an sich*; but each of them is the Real as it affects a particular stream of religious consciousness. In Kantian terms, the noumenal Real is experienced – that is, enters into the phenomenal or experienceable realm – through one or other of two basic concepts – the concept of deity, or of the Real as personal, and the concept of the absolute, or of the Real as non-personal. (The term 'absolute' seems to be the nearest we have, although it is by no means ideal, being less congenial to Buddhist than to Hindu thinking.) However, we do not experience deity or the absolute in general. The human mind is always conscious of either in a specific way and as having a particular character. And because there are many consolidated historical forms of human mentality, reflecting the different ways of being human that have developed over the millennia, the history of religions shows a corresponding range of divine personae and of metaphysical impersonae.

What can we say about the Real *an sich*? Only that it is the ultimate reality that we postulate as the ground of the different forms of religious experience and thought in so far as they are more than human projection. To affirm the Real is to affirm that religious belief and experience in its plurality of forms is not simply delusion but constitutes our human, and therefore imperfect, partial and distorted range of ways of being affected by the universal 'presence' of the Real. But we cannot apply to the noumenal Real any of the distinctions with which we structure our phenomenal, including our religious, experience. We cannot say that it is personal or impersonal, one or many, active or passive, substance or process, good or evil, just or unjust, purposive or purposeless. No such categories can be applied, either positively or negatively, to the noumenal. Thus, whilst it is not correct to say, for example, that the Real is personal, it is also not correct to say that it is impersonal – nor that it is both personal and impersonal, or neither personal nor impersonal. All that one can say is that these concepts, which have their use in relation to human experience, do not apply, even analogically, to the Real *an sich*.

Thus the Real *an sich* cannot be the object of a religious cult. We cannot worship it or achieve union with it. We worship one or other of its personae, or we seek union with one or other of its impersonae. And in so far as a deity or an absolute is an authentic manifestation of the Real, promoting the transformation of human existence from self-centredness to Reality-centredness, the form of worship or of meditation focused upon him or her or it constitutes 'true religion'. In principle we are free to choose between the personal and non-personal manifestations of the Real; and among the personae, to choose which God or Goddess, or group of deities, to worship; and again, among the impersonae, to choose to meditate towards the realisation of Brahman or of Nirvana. In practice, a small minority do so choose; and it may be that that minority is becoming bigger. But for the large majority of us it has always been the case that the choice is in effect made by birth and upbringing.

What I have been outlining is a theory or hypothesis, a possible framework for thought concerning the religious life of humanity. What use might such an hypothesis have?

(1)   It may satisfy our intuition that each of the great world faiths has such value that it is false and harmful to regard any one of them alone as true or authentic and the others as false or inauthentic. The hypothesis spells out to some extent the insight expressed by the Muslim mystic Jalaluldin Rumi, 'The lamps are different, but the Light is the same.'[17]

(2)   At the same time, however, the hypothesis can remove any temptation to think of the different traditions as 'all the same' or 'all alike', and can free us to notice and to be fascinated by all the differences that the phenomenology of religion reveals.

(3)   The hypothesis may thus provide a framework for inter-faith dialogue, and an explicit basis for the hope that each tradition may learn from and be changed by its encounter with the others. For if each represents a different human perspective on the Real, each may be able to enlarge its own vision by trying to look through the lenses that others have developed.

Notes

1. Paul Tillich, *The Courage to Be* (New Haven, Conn.: Yale University Press, 1952) p. 190.
2. Gordon Kaufman, *God the Problem* (Cambridge, Mass.: Harvard University Press, 1972) p. 86.
3. *Rig Veda*, I, 164, 46.
4. Masao Abe, 'A Dynamic Unity in Religious Pluralism', in John Hick and Hasan Askari (eds), *The Experience of Religious Diversity* (London: Gower, 1985) pp. 178–9.
5. Genesis 1: 1.
6. *Bhagavad Gita* 9, 4.
7. Udana, 80.
8. *Majjhima-Nikāya*, I, 163. *The Middle Length Sayings*, trans. I. B. Homer (London: Pali Text Society, 1954–9) vol. I, pp. 206–7.
9. *Samyutta-Nikāya*, IV, 369–71. *The Kindred Sayings*, trans. C. A. F. Rhys Davids (London: Pali Text Society, 1950–6) Part IV, pp. 261–3.
10. Narada Mahathera, *The Dhammapada*, 2nd edn (Colombo: Vajirarama, 1972) pp. 24–5.
11. Edward Conze, *Buddhism, Its Essence and Development* (New York: Harper Torchbooks, 1975) pp. 110–11.
12. Keiji Nishitani, *Religion and Nothingness*, trans. Jan Van Bragt (Berkeley, Cal.: University of California Press, 1982) pp. 6 and 20.
13. Masao Abe, 'God, Emptiness, and the True Self', in *The Buddha Eye*, ed. Frederick Frank (New York: Crossroads, 1982) p. 65.
14. D. T. Suzuki, 'The Buddhist Conception of Reality', in ibid., pp. 103 and 97.
15. 'True Emptiness is Wondrous Being', *Mōjingengenkan*.
16. William James, *The Varieties of Religious Experience* (1902, London: Collins, 1960) beginning of Lecture XX.
17. 'The One True Light', in *Rūmi: Poet and Mystic*, trans. R. A. Nicholson (London and Boston, Mass.: Mandala Books, 1978) p. 166.

Part V
Life and Death

11

A Possible Conception of Life after Death

It has often been assumed that the notion of human survival of bodily death poses a straightforward question, 'Do we live on after bodily death?', which rightly expects a straightforward 'yes' or 'no' answer. Few have indeed thought that the true answer is easy to come by; but many have thought that the question itself is easy enough to ask. Much of the empirical evidence, in the form of 'spirit communications' through mediums, seems at first to support that assumption. A deeper analysis, however, has opened up more complex possibilities. To a great extent this deeper analysis was achieved in the classic period of parapsychological research towards the end of the nineteenth and early in the present century. The observations, analyses and theorising of some of the workers of that period were of the highest order and have indeed seldom been equalled since. Modern parapsychologists, of course, have at their command greatly superior technology, more sophisticated mathematical techniques and a more impressive line of jargon; but not often a better, or even an equal, theoretical power and intellectual penetration. In praising those classic contributions I am not referring to work on physical phenomena – spirit materialisation, direct voice mediumship, poltergeists and so on – which does often seem to have fallen far short of the rigorous standards of control, aided by such devices as infra-red photography, that we rightly require today. I am referring rather to work in the field on trance mediumship, including automatic writing, and in particular to the investigations of the small group of outstanding mediums, such as Mrs Piper, Mrs Verrall, Mrs Leonard and Mrs Willett (whom we now know to have been Mrs Coombe-Tennant). It is true that such researchers as Richard Hodgson, Mrs Sidgwick, William James and others would have been aided by tape-recorders if these had then been invented; but not, I think, to an extent that would have made any significant difference to their conclusions. Their reports are now buried in the back numbers of the

Proceedings of the Society for Psychical Research, and a subsidiary reason for my referring to them here is to draw attention to a very rich store of what is today largely neglected material.

When we read the transcripts of the trance communications, and the texts of the automatic writings of Piper and Leonard, our first impression is one of the presence of still-living personalities who have passed through bodily death. We find the 'spirits' (I shall use invisible quotations marks around the word in the rest of the paper) talking very much as though they were living people communicating from a distance by telephone or letter. Sometimes, of course, the person on the phone (speaking, that is, through the entranced medium) or writing the letters (that is, producing automatic scripts through the medium's hand), is a 'control' (again, invisible quotation marks henceforth) relaying messages from some other deceased individual who is thus communicating indirectly through both control and medium. But whether operating through a control or directly through the medium, these spirits, and also the spirit controls, seem essentially like living people who have moved to a distant part of the world, or better, if we may anticipate the likely technology of the future, who have emigrated by rocket to live on the surface – or perhaps beneath the surface – of another planet. They seem to be the same conscious individuals, with memories connecting them continuously with the time when they were here on earth. They speak the same language, and apparently operate in terms of the same system of concepts and framework of presupposition. They are, so to speak, still on the same mental wavelength as we are and still very interested in our goings-on in this world.

There is, however, one puzzling feature of most of the well-known published trance material. This is that the spirits say very little about their own world and their own lives in it. We gain no impression of their activities apart from the brief periods when they are communicating with us on earth. I know that there are exceptions to this; but the prevailing general impressions is that expressed, back in the classic period of trance communications, by Professor J. H. Hyslop when he said, in his long discussion of the Piper mediumship, that 'there is not one sentence in my record from which I could even pretend to deduce a conception of what the life beyond the grave is'.[1] It is almost as though the spirits' whole life took place in the seances, with only blank periods in between! And this is precisely what some very experienced and thoughtful early students of the phenomena concluded might well be the case. William James, for example, in his study of the Piper material, favoured the idea of the communicators 'all being dream creations of Mrs Piper, probably having no existence except when she is in a trance, but consolidated by repetition into personalities consistent enough to play their several roles'.[2] For example, Mrs Piper's spirit control Phinuit claimed to be a French doctor, Jean Phinuit Scliville, who had practised in London as well as in France and Belgium in the first half of the nineteenth century. However, that he was not what he claimed to be was established by Richard Hodgson by ordinary detective methods. Phinuit could not speak French; he displayed no special medical knowledge; and there was no record of his having attended the medical schools at which he claimed to have studied. In order to understand what he was Mrs Sidgwick drew upon the phenomenon of hypnosis. Mrs Sidgwick, who was Principal of Newnham College, Cambridge, was one of the most powerful intellects of her generation, and what looks in the bibliographies like a modest article in the *Proceedings of the SPR* called 'A Contribution to the Study of the Psychology of Mrs Piper's Trance Phenomena',[3] is in fact a book-length study (of 657 pages) which constitutes one of the most important contributions that we have to parapsychological literature.

Under hypnosis – as many have today witnessed in the performance of stage hypnotists – people may exhibit considerable powers of impersonation. If the hypnotist suggests to them that they are, say, visitors from outer space, they will play out this role, mobilising their relevant knowledge and a latent dramatic ability and inventiveness to sustain it, and will, at least on one level of their consciousness, actually believe that they are the person being impersonated. Sometimes another level of consciousness monitors all that is going on without, however, being able to intervene, whilst at other times the whole person is completely immersed in the hypnotic role and on return to normal life has no memory of what took place under hypnosis. Mrs Sidgwick suggested that Phinuit, as also Mrs Piper's other controls, were Mrs Piper herself in an auto-hypnotic state, impersonating spirits who had been suggested to her jointly by the spiritualist subculture of her time and by her circle of sitters. Phinuit accordingly existed only in this intermittent context; but in it he elaborated and solidified his own character, developing his identity from seance to seance.

Thus far, then, we have the hypothesis that the medium goes into a self-induced hypnotic state in a context which suggests to her the role of a spirit control relaying messages between the spirit world and earth. If we add the further feature, for which there is independent evidence, that genuine (that is, non-fraudulent) mediums tend to be excellent ESP subjects, we have a possible explanation of how it is that, to a much greater extent than could be accounted for purely by chance, the spirit messages are appropriate to the deceased individuals from whom they purport to come. For it could be that information in the sitters' minds about a deceased person, including character impressions, affects the medium's mind in its highly suggestible hypnotic state, and is built into the drama of spirits presenting themselves to the control, who then relays their messages to the sitters.

However, both Mrs Sidgwick and Richard Hodgson, who spent so much time investigating the Piper mediumship, thought that her controls may well sometimes have displayed information going beyond what might have been derived telepathically from her sitters. And they point out that if human personality survives bodily death there may be ESP between living persons and disembodied survivors, as well as between the living. And so one possibility is that deceased persons sometimes try to use a medium's personation of them by impressing her mind with the information which they want to have conveyed, in this indirect and hard-to-control way, to the sitters on earth. This might account for the very uneven quality of the material. However, yet another possibility to be considered is that the medium receives telepathic impressions of the deceased Mr X, without Mr X himself being consciously involved. For telepathy does not normally require the conscious intent of the sender. In this scenario it would not be correct to say that Mr X is, from his own point of view, communicating through the medium with relatives and friends on earth. The situation would be more like someone else writing letters in his name and without his knowledge. Yet a further possibility to be noted is that Mr X no longer exists as a conscious person, but that when we die there remains something like what C. D. Broad called a psychic factor,[4] consisting in a more or less coherent nexus of ideas, character traits and memories which persists for a longer or shorter period until it gradually disintegrates, and that it is this that a medium is able to tap for impressions that feed her hypnotic impersonations. This latter hypothesis could perhaps even be stretched to cover those cases – such as the famous

Chaffin will case – in which information which was not at the time known to any living person is presented through a medium.

This range of possibilities – reflecting our ignorance rather than our knowledge – shows how difficult it is, with our present evidence, to establish the straightforward survival hypothesis. That hypothesis is fully compatible with the facts, but represents by no means the only possible way of accounting for them. Many who have personally conversed through a medium with what professes to be a deceased relative or friend have been unable to doubt that this was indeed the person whom they had known on earth, still intellectually alive and with the same distinctive character, emotional pattern and personal mannerisms. But those who have not had that experience may well feel that it is possible in such a situation to be mistaken, misled by a natural desire for contact with loved ones who have died and for assurance that they have not finally perished.

Where then does the empirical research leave us? It leaves us at present in uncertainty. One recent attempt to weigh up the parapsychological evidence is that of the veteran psychologist and former President of the Society for Psychical Research, who died in 1988, Dr Robert H. Thouless, in a lengthy discussion in the Society's 1984 *Proceedings* of the question 'Do we survive bodily death'?[5] He concluded:

> There seem to be many converging lines of evidence which suggest that [death] is the passage to another life, but we cannot yet be certain that this is the case. It is a future task of parapsychology to reduce to a minimum this uncertainty and to find out all we can about the nature of this future life. This task is very far from being yet completed. (p. 50)

This would seem to be a fair, if not very startling or newsworthy, conclusion at this point in time.

But, needless to say, the fact that we cannot as of now establish life after death by empirical evidence does not mean that there is no life after death. We must not mistake absence of knowledge for knowledge of absence! We should therefore keep in mind the other possible ground for expecting such a continuation, namely that offered by the world's religious tradition. I am not going to attempt here to justify religious belief – though I have tried to do that elsewhere – for the subject is much too large to be treated within the limits of the present chapter. Accordingly what now follows is addressed primarily to those who are convinced that the religious experience of humanity does not consist purely of human projection – although it does undoubtedly involve a considerable human element, varying from culture to culture – but is at the same time a cognitive response to a divine reality transcending physical nature and human consciousness. Each of the great historical ways of experiencing and conceiving that reality has found that it must include within its understanding of the universe a belief in a larger human existence that transcends our present life. But this belief takes a number of very different forms. I propose to treat these different religious conceptions of life after death as providing our range of options, and then try to see if there are any considerations that can reasonably guide us in an attempt to choose among them.

One major difference between the traditions concerns the time scale of the formation of perfected or fully developed human creatures. Each of the great religions holds that the ultimate human state – whether it is to be attained by all or only by some – is one of union or communion with the divine reality. From our present earthly standpoint the difference between union and communion seems considerable, but in that final state it may perhaps be transcended – somewhat as in the Christian conception of the Trinity as three in one and one in three. At any rate the traditions all point in their different ways to an eschaton which lies beyond our present conceptuality.

But when we turn from that ultimate state to possible penultimate states, and thus from eschatology to pareschatology, we meet more clearly defined options. The big distinction is between the western doctrine of a single temporal life and the eastern doctrine of many such lives. The dominant Christian (and also Jewish and Muslim) view is that our temporal existence, during which moral and spiritual change and growth are possible, is limited to this present life; and after this comes a divine judgement followed by eternal heaven or hell, or heaven via a purgatorial phase which is not, however, thought of as a further period of active living and growing. Our existence, according to this view, consists of two very unequal phases – an eternal state, preceded by this brief earthly life in which we exercise a fateful freedom and responsibility.

Thus it is assumed that the function of our present life is to be the arena in which we become, through our own free responses and choices, persons to whom either eternal heaven or eternal hell is appropriate. But is this picture morally realistic? Consider the facts that (a) a large proportion of the human babies who have been born during the last hundred thousand years or so, a proportion probably approaching, and quite possibly exceeding, 50 per cent, have died at birth or in infancy, so that for them it would seem that the purpose of life has remained unfulfilled; (b) the circumstances into which people are born and in which they have to live vary so greatly in their propitiousness for moral and spiritual growth that it is hard to see how we could be fairly assessed on our performance in this one brief and chancy life; and (c) very few people can be said to be morally fitted, by the time of their death, for either eternal bliss or eternal torment. To some extent this last point is met by the fact that, in traditional Christian theology, the divine judgement is not so much ethical as theological – the saved are those who believe in Jesus Christ as their Lord and Saviour and who put their trust in the efficacy of his atoning death. However, in our pluralistically conscious age this seems arbitrary and implausible; and much Christian thought has moved decisively away from it.

Such a move may well lead Christians to consider again the alternative view of the Hindu, Buddhist, Jain and Sikh traditions, or some further variation of its central theme. The basic thought here is that one life-span is not enough for the transformation of human beings from the self-centredness of our natural state to the unity or community with the divine reality which is the ultimate aim of human existence. And I think we must admit that this is a morally realistic view. But another important insight accompanies it. This is implicit rather than explicit in most Hindu and Buddhist discussions, but can be made explicit as follows. It is the very finitude of our earthly life, its haunting brevity, that gives it shape and value by making time precious and choice urgent. If we had before us an endless temporal vista, devoid of the pressure of an approaching end, our life would lose its present character as offering a continuum of choices, small and large, through which we participate in our own gradual creating. There is thus much to be said for the view that the formation of persons through their own freedom requires the boundaries of birth and death. But if one such natural span is not sufficient for our growth to a total unitive or communitive centredness in the divine reality, then our present life would seem likely to be followed by further such finite phases, rather than by a single unbounded existence continuing without end. And so perhaps we should consider seriously the basic eastern option of a series of finite lives, the series ending only when we have attained to a final self-transcendence, when the discipline of temporal life is no longer needed.

Eastern thought has always assumed that any such further lives will be lived on this earth. The Hindu and Buddhist traditions do indeed speak of a great range of other spheres of existence, heavens and hells, in addition to this earth. But they also hold that it is only as human beings in this world that we can make substantive progress towards final liberation from the self-centred ego. I see in this belief an implicit recognition of the need for the boundary pressures of birth and death to make possible any profound development of the self. Hindus and Buddhists accordingly see it as a rare privilege to have been born into this world; for here and here alone do we have the opportunity of spiritual growth.

However, when we turn to the empirical evidence for reincarnation or rebirth we find, in my opinion, the same kind of ambiguity and uncertainty that we discovered in the empirical evidence for survival. There are innumerable claimed memories of former lives, including spontaneous memories of children, and sometimes of adults, and also memories systematically induced under hypnosis. A large collection of spontaneous memories has been made by Professor Ian Stevenson of the University of Virginia in his four volumes of *Cases of the Reincarnation Type*[6] from India, Sri Lanka, Lebanon and Turkey, and Thailand and Burma; and many further instances of apparent memories of previous lives have been garnered through hypnotic regression, some of the best known being the Bridey Murphy case[7] and the cases reported by Alexander Cannon.[8] But although the best examples in both categories are impressive, and satisfy some people, they are not objectively convincing in the sense of convincing any and every rational person who studies them. I think it must be admitted that the majority of people who dismiss this range of evidence as insufficient have never in fact made a serious detailed study of it, and are therefore expressing a prejudice rather than a responsible judgement. But nevertheless, there are some who have looked rather carefully at the detailed reports – I would include myself among them – who still do not consider that they constitute conclusive or even nearly conclusive evidence. Often the reported spontaneous childhood memories of a previous life come from societies in which reincarnation is a matter of general belief. The believer in reincarnation will say that it is in these societies that children with such memories are allowed to express them rather than being treated as over-imaginative or untruthful. The sceptic on the other hand will say that in those societies the idea is suggested to children by their surrounding culture, and sallies of the imagination can be too readily accepted as previous-life memories and encouraged by the family. Further, the interest of investigators, particularly visiting foreign investigators, may enhance the family's local importance and may in general be something for the village to encourage rather than discourage. Again, it was inevitable that Stevenson's well-recorded cases were not investigated as soon as the child had begun to speak of a previous life but after a longer or shorter lapse of time during which the story had time to develop, to become consolidated, and to attract supporting testimony that was later hard to test in any rigorous way. It is also regrettable, from an ideal point of view, that in almost all cases the investigation had to be conducted through an interpreter, with the consequent difficulty of discounting all possibility of bias or misunderstanding. Yet another difficulty, of a different kind, is suggested by the range of options which we noted concerning human survival. Could it be that those who have 'memories' of previous life are good ESP subjects, receiving genuine impressions of persons who have died derived either from those persons, still existing in a spirit world, or from a 'psychic factor' or set of mental traces left behind by them? Once again, it is impossible to banish the spectre of ambiguity. And there is also ambiguity in the hypnotic regression cases, witnessed to by the controversy which has always surrounded them.

However, these ambiguities and uncertainties are only ambiguities and uncertainties. They do not authorise us to dismiss the idea of reincarnation. Nor should we necessarily treat it as a simple all-or-nothing issue. Conceivably some people reincarnate and others not. And there is a yet further possibility which deserves to be identified and considered. This is that we do indeed go through a series of lives, each having its own beginning and end, and being a sphere for the exercise of freedom and responsibility, but that these are not all in the same world but on the contrary in different worlds. Perhaps Hindu and Buddhist teaching is right in holding that there are many spheres of existence but wrong in holding that none of them, other than this earth, is such as to provide opportunity for further moral and spiritual growth. If we are going seriously to consider the idea of other worlds why should we exclude the possibility that they may be at least as appropriate to a person-making process as is this world?

If there should be such other worlds in which continued person-making can take place, where are they? Contemporary physics and scientific cosmology are in such a state of flux that they intensify the general ambiguity. But, nevertheless, they do seem to speak today of the possibility of plural spaces within a single superspace. Thus Paul Davies, Professor of Theoretical Physics at the University of Newcastle, England, says that 'what is usually regarded as "the universe" might in fact be only a disconnected fragment of space-time. There could be many, even an infinite number of other universes, but all physically inaccessible to the other.'⁹ A plurality of spaces might include a plurality of worlds, some of them sustaining intelligent life, each such world having its own unique history, its own proper concerns and excitements, achievements and dangers, and each constituting a possible environment for moral and spiritual growth through practical challenge and response.

Let us, then, tentatively entertain the thought that having died in this world we are, either immediately or after an interval, born in another physical world in another space. This thought also, of course, carries with it the possibility that we have already lived before in another such world.

Major questions now arise. One concerns the nature of the 'we' who are to be thus re-embodied. What precisely is it that reincarnates?

We have noted the effect of temporal boundaries in giving shape, character and meaning to our present life. This insight has a further implication which can be expressed by saying that we human creatures, living between birth and death, are essentially historical beings, constituents of a certain particular segment of the human story. And as historical beings we are largely formed by the culture into which we were born. There are no such things as human beings in general, but only beings who are human in this or that particular cultural pattern and as part of this or that stage of history. Thus you and I are not incidentally but essentially twentieth-century western persons. We cannot be abstracted from our cultural and historical setting. This, at least, is true of what we may call the empirical self, created by heredity, environment, and life-experiences within a particular historical and cultural setting.

But this is not a complete account of us. In addition to this empirical or public self, formed in interaction with others within a common historico-cultural matrix, there is a basic moral and spiritual nature, or dispositional structure, for which I propose to use the traditional name 'soul'. I said that this exists in addition to our empirical self. But that may be a misleading way of putting it. For our empirical self and our basic nature are not two distinct entities. The terms refer, rather, to two continuously interacting levels on which the stream of self-consciousness which I call 'me' operates. One is the level of moral and spiritual response and choice. Here our fundamental nature is expressing itself. Such basic dispositional attitudes as a tendency to be compassionate, generous and forgiving, or to be unloving, grasping and resentful, and again, to be open or closed to the divine mystery, can express themselves through a variety of different empirical selves enmeshed in different historico-cultural contexts. They could be lived out, or incarnated, in the lives of, let us say, a male Tibetan peasant of the fifth century BCE and a female American lawyer of the twentieth century CE. In these extremely different circumstances the same basic dispositional structure would result in very different empirical lives. Further, we must not think of the soul, as our most basic nature, as fixed and unchanging. On the contrary, like the empirical self, it is changing in some degree all the time as we respond to life's tasks and experiences. The main distinction, for our present purpose, is that whereas our empirical self can only be described in terms of a particular historico-cultural context, our basic nature or soul can be described independently of the concrete ways in which its basic traits express themselves in particular sets of circumstances.

You will appreciate that I am not here propounding a dogma but constructing a thought-model to stimulate reflection. This thought-model suggests that what is going on in human life is the growth of a multitude of souls – individual moral and spiritual natures – towards union or communion with the divine life. And it may be that in this long process souls are embodied a number of times as a series of different empirical selves. What reincarnates on this view – which is fairly close to both Hindu and Buddhist teaching – is not the empirical self but the basic moral and spiritual dispositional structure, the soul. At bodily death the empirical self, with its culture-bound personality and time-bound memories, begins gradually to fade away, our consciousness becoming centred in the moral/spiritual attitudes which constitute the soul; and that soul, or dispositional structure, is then able to be embodied again to engage once more in the creative process.

A further question that arises for this hypothesis concerns its relation to time. Do all these supposed worlds exist within the same time frame, so that our life in world two is subsequent in the same time-sequence to our life in world one? If we are relating the plurality-of-worlds conception to the physicists' talk of a plurality of spaces, we must be prepared also to follow them in what they say about time. They seem to have abandoned the Newtonian notion of a single absolute time within which each event occurs either before or after or simultaneously with each other event. Time is conceived of as relative to the observer, and spaces that are not spatially related to one another will accordingly not be related within a single time-frame. It would thus not be appropriate to say that life two comes *after* life one; and neither would it be appropriate to say that it occurs before it or simultaneously with it! On the other hand, the idea of re-embodiment in many worlds does seem to require a causal relationship such that the basic character of my deeper self in world two depends upon the basic character that I had when I died in world one. The distinction that we have already drawn between the basic moral/spiritual character, or soul, and the psycho-physical self, is relevant at this point. For the causation involved between worlds one and two will not be physical but more like the kind of mental resonance that occurs in ESP. It will involve the transmission of information, but information whose content is a basic character, or system of moral/spiritual traits. This body of information is called in some Hindu systems the *linga sharira*, sometimes translated as 'spiritual body', and in some Buddhist systems is called a karmic system, and is regarded in each as constituting the continuant from life to life. However, whereas Hinduism and Buddhism hold that the karmic system or *linga sharira* influences the development of a new empirical self within the evolution of life on this earth, I am suggesting the possibility that it may influence the formation of a new individual within the process of life in another world which is part of another space.

Understood from a religious point of view such a series of lives constitutes a long creative process leading to unity with or community within the divine life. The formation of new empirical selves will go on as long as they are needed as vehicles for the development of the deeper self or soul. Then, eventually, temporal life will be subsumed into eternal life, *samsara* into *nirvana*, history into the Kingdom of Heaven.

Let me return in conclusion to the parapsychological evidence for survival. I suggested that this evidence remains inconclusive. But, nevertheless, it may be of interest to relate it to a plurality-of-worlds hypothesis such as I have very sketchily outlined.

If after death our basic nature is embodied again as another empirical self, it is, of course, theoretically possible that this happens immediately. The Theravada tradition within Buddhism teaches precisely that. On the other hand the Hindu tradition, and much of the Mahayana tradition, speak of an intermediate period between embodied lives, and if we want to keep open the possibility of incorporating the spiritual evidence we shall opt for this scenario.

Let us entertain the hypothesis, then, that after bodily death consciousness continues, in a now disembodied state, as a centre both of moral and spiritual freedom and of memories and personality traits formed in relation to this world. In this next phase, as it is described in the classic Buddhist *Bardo Thödol*, there is no new sensory input and the environment of which we are aware is a mind-dependent projection of our own memories, desires, fears and beliefs. Such a dream-like phase would seem to correspond with what in western Spiritualist literature has been called illusion- and/or Summer-land. The *Bardo Thödol* describes the experiences that a devout medieval Tibetan Buddhist may be expected to have in this state. But a modern western and largely secular mind might well project the kind of banal continuation of the present life that we find in, for example, the Raymond communications through Mrs Leonard, recorded by Lodge – this being one of the notable exceptions to the generalisation that the spirits tell us practically nothing about their own world.

But this *bardo* (meaning 'between two') phase only lasts for a certain time, during which the memories and characteristics of the empirical self gradually fade and the deeper nature, now at the centre of consciousness, moves on to a new phase which is evidently beyond the possibility of communication with persons in this world. In the Spiritualist scenario this next phase is roughly equivalent to the *deva* worlds of Buddhist and Hindu cosmology. I have, however, been suggesting the possibility that the phase after the *bardo* period may be (as the *Bardo Thödol* itself teaches) a new embodiment; and that this may be in another world which is part of another sub-space within this unimaginably vast and complex universe. In Christian terms, of course, such a re-embodiment is what is pointed to by the idea of the resurrection of the dead, and the novelty, from the Christian point of view, of this idea is that it includes a series of resurrections instead of only one.

I need hardly say that this thought-model is highly speculative. It is offered as an attempt – a feeble attempt whose only merit might be to provoke others to make their own attempts – to discriminate among the options offered by the great religious traditions and by such ambiguous empirical evidence as we have.[10]

Notes

1. J. H. Hyslop, 'A Further Record of Observations of Certain Trance Phenomena', *Proceedings of the Society for Psychical Research*, vol. 16, no. 41 (1901) p. 291 (hereafter *Proc. SPR*).
2. William James, 'Report on Mrs Piper's Hodgson–Control', *Proc. SPR*, vol. 23, no. 58 (1909) p. 3.
3. Eleanor M. Sidgwick, 'A Contribution to the Study of the Psychology of Mrs Piper's Trance Phenomena', *Proc. SPR*, vol. 28, no. 71 (1915).
4. C. D. Broad, *The Mind and its Place in Nature* (New York: Harcourt, Brace, 1925).
5. Robert H. Thouless, *Proc. SPR*, vol. 57, no. 213 (1984).
6. Ian Stevenson, *Cases of the Reincarnation Type*, 4 vols (Charlottesville, Va: University of Virginia Press, 1975–83).
7. M. Bernstein, *The Search for Bridey Murphy* (New York: Doubleday, 1956).
8. A. Cannon, *The Power Within* (New York: Dutton, 1953).
9. Paul Davies, *Other Worlds: Space, Superspace and the Quantum Universe* (London: J. M. Dent, 1980).
10. For a further development of these and related ideas see my *Death and Eternal Life* (London: Macmillan, and New York: Harper & Row, 1976, rev. edn 1987).

Index